‘Rarely, one encounters a book so startlingly original and insightful; it not only captivates one’s attention, but thereafter shapes the development of one’s thought. Such is my experience after reading Hannah Intezar’s book on vegan identities, which situates the journeys of individuals into and out of veganism within the extraordinarily illuminating theoretical framework of Bakhtinian dialogism. A model of clear and vivid exposition, the book is replete with arrestingly novel ideas and perceptions; compellingly readable, thought-provoking, and wholly fresh.’

John Ackroyd, *Assistant Professor in Philosophy and Intellectual History, University of Bradford, UK*

MAPPING THE HOLISTIC JOURNEY OF FORMER VEGANS

This book explores Veganism through the holistic journeys and lived experiences of former vegans, with a particular focus on the impact this has on their *Selfhood* and identity. It delves into the complexities underpinning definitions of Veganism and vegan identities.

Based on original qualitative research charting the experiences of ten former vegans, the text offers a theoretical lens for understanding evolving self-perception, identity, and experience, exploring what leads to initiating a transition in and out of Veganism and how former vegans reconcile with losing their vegan identity. Applying a Bakhtinian model of *Selfhood*, this book explores the tensions between *'Voices'* representing values within social discourse, such as Veganism, and how individuals co-construct their identity and self-perception through said *Voices.* Chapters explore the *Polyphony* within Veganism and offer an insight into the embodied experience of former vegans. Each analysis chapter has been divided into three distinct *Threshold-moments* of beginning, middle, and end.

Mapping the Holistic Journey of Former Vegans: The Polyphony within Veganism is intended for scholars and postgraduate students interested in Veganism, *Selfhood* and identity, and behaviour change and anyone looking to understand the context of Veganism in practice.

Hannah Intezar is an Assistant Professor at the University of Bradford, UK. Her research interests are interdisciplinary, encompassing Psychology, Philosophy, Sociology, and Literature. She, therefore, has and continues to collaborate with academics from politics, philosophy, and psychology. Hannah has a particular interest in qualitative dialogical epistemology and visual methods within the Social Sciences.

MAPPING THE HOLISTIC JOURNEY OF FORMER VEGANS

The Polyphony within Veganism

Hannah Intezar

Routledge
Taylor & Francis Group
LONDON AND NEW YORK

Designed cover image: Stephen Dwyer / Alamy Stock Photo

First published 2025
by Routledge
4 Park Square, Milton Park, Abingdon, Oxon OX14 4RN

and by Routledge
605 Third Avenue, New York, NY 10158

Routledge is an imprint of the Taylor & Francis Group, an informa business

British Library Cataloguing-in-Publication Data
A catalogue record for this book is available from the British Library

ISBN: 9781032470863 (hbk)
ISBN: 9781032470795 (pbk)
ISBN: 9781003384526 (ebk)

DOI: 10.4324/9781003384526

Typeset in Galliard
by codeMantra

For my parents, Talat and Intezar

CONTENTS

FOREWORD

I am delighted to write this foreword for Hannah's book. In some ways, this book is a Trojan horse. Inside it, you will discover not only a book about *Veganism* but also a new way of seeing *Ideology* and ideologically. This is the original take on the great theorist of language – Mikhail M. Bakhtin – which Hannah draws attention to. So, this book has both a perspective on *Veganism* and from there a reverse perspective on *Ideology* and *Dialogue*. Such double-ness and interknitting of the double helix of *Aesthetic* form and content is entirely in the spirit of Bakhtin. Hannah will carefully outline this in the chapters to come. For now, there are three summary comments that are worth making in this appetiser for this book.

First of all, the ambition to write *Polyphony* into Veganism considered as an *Ideology*. Any *Ideology* in practice gravitates towards a monological *Aesthetic*. Such an *Aesthetic* is characterised by a singular truth; by an authenticity performance, by Scientism or an assumption that the world is fully transparent and can, as a consequence, have its mechanisms discovered to improve a particular vision of humankind and by the pleasure in unity or in *Monism*. It is a *Centripetal* force that imposes order on the chaotic human world but as an *Aesthetic* has a tremendous appeal of living in purified meaning or living *istina*. This at least is the purified version of *Ideology* that begets fundamentalist practice. Of course, in the lived world of experience, *Ideology* has the potential to be more complex. *Pragmatism*, *Humanism*, learning, compromise prevail and are championed in liberal democracies. Nonetheless, the monological *Aesthetic* has a grip on purified meaning.

Thus, the ambition to write *Polyphony* into this context is brilliantly conceived and executed. Away from the high principles of *Ideology*, what are the *Voices* at play in living the *Ideology*. Not for all or for everyone, but for the participants in this study. Do not be fooled, however, by the 'small sample size' and principles of generalisability. The point here is that the monological *Aesthetic* has a dialogical counterpart. That is the key touchstone of this book around which the rest revolves. In other words, this book presents a gestalt shift towards *Veganism* as containing a *Dialogical Aesthetic*. In contrast to the monological *Aesthetic*, this is characterised by *Syncrisis* and *Anacrisis*, by knowledge that is not given but bound to be questioned by *Others* and those *Others* are sometimes internalised *Others*; sometimes outside *Others* and sometimes on the boundary. Where knowledge as principle is stretched and elaborated on the torture rack of hypocrisy, contradiction, and performance that reflexively structures awareness of the vegan life. This is an *Aesthetic* form that compels us as the novel does; as an *Unfinalisable* searching for meaning rather than as an imposition of meaning. With it comes uncertainty, anxiety, ambivalence, and well-intentioned groping in the dark. The tug and pull of the monological and *Dialogical Aesthetic* as a *Centripetal-Centrifugal* creative tension allows for the truth of *Veganism* to be accentuated by the intonation of *Voice*.

To get us to this point, Hannah brings a *Centripetal-Centrifugal* tension of her own. She imposes the order and discipline of a methodology, a *Dialogical* methodology. She innovates with existing dialogical methods to carefully expose the varying dimensions of *Ideology* as it structures discourse and vice versa. Yet, she also writes *Polyphonically* of the *Voices* – the quotations in particular – of her participants and her key academic sources of the dialogue. By this, I mean that there is an opening up and reflective conversation with the *Voices* and the *Voices* are put in dialogue with one another, in a way that cannot be pre-determined in advance, irrespective of the method. This is the *Centrifugal*, *Centripetal* force in academic prose I refer to as the bureaucratic-charismatic tension elsewhere. It's a tension that is crucial to embrace in qualitative analysis because it allows recognition that academics are 'giving voice' in response to but with a different purpose than, participants. In this arena of Veganism and *Ideology*, that contains so much righteous feeling, such an opening up is an invitation to all to dialogue, listen, and respond. It acts as a palliative to the monological *Aesthetics* but without crushing it; by asking it to participate as a significant *Voice* in her own artistic-academic vision.

The flip side of *Aesthetics* is ethics. *Aesthetics* without ethics is what Milan Kundera refers to as the 'unbearable lightness of being.' Ethics without *Aesthetics* on the other hand becomes unbearably heavy, insistent, and authoritarian. This monograph offers ethical insights but through a subtle interrogation of what it means to live ethically within the *Architectonics* of an *Answerable* life in an *Aesthetic*, ideological form. So, the ethics will not help questions of the variety of 'is it ethical to eat animals or animal products'. Such ethical questions already have well-rehearsed efforts at a resolution through *Utilitarianism*, *Pragmatism*, empathy, *Speciesism*. Invariably, such efforts at *Finalised* resolutions end up *Unfinalised*, with temporary *Loopholes* and with irritation at '*Others*' from both sides, who do not work out conclusions to what the *Other* sees as the logical view; precisely because they are viewed as an ideological view.

This frustration with the *Other* could beget a turn to large powerful interests that create a false delusion of reality; that mystify and obscure facts and power that corrupts ethics. Such grand theorising, however, is nimbly avoided by Hannah. Her focus is on the *prosaics* of imagination in ethics. What goes right or wrong in the ethics of a good life. How is that experienced? It is a more humble intellectual exercise but one strangely missing in the academic enterprise and one that actually fundamentally underpins and is the first step (*Postupok*) in addressing more finalisable ethical questions.

Overall, this book will take you on an exciting intellectual adventure that bursts the banks of *Veganism*, exposes *Ideology* as a *Dialogical Aesthetic* and invites the reader into profoundly ethical questions in a deeply *Aesthetic* form. Enjoy!

Dr. Paul Sullivan
Reader in Psychology

PREFACE

Inspired by socio-cultural paradigms on sustainable consumption, individual accountability, and Veganuary, for anthropological reasons, curiosity led me to practise Veganism for 12 months. Due to a plethora of reasons, unfortunately, I only lasted nine. A wealth of psychological research has illustrated how one's eating behavioural habits are intrinsically linked with emotional cognition, and that altering these habits, such as practising and leaving Veganism, can potentially lead to disordered eating patterns and emotional distress; it was no different for me. Although my motivations behind abstaining from consuming animal products were not ethical or moral, it did nonetheless spark my curiosity around the experiences of former vegans. Therefore, I would like to clarify that this book is about the experience of those who are no longer vegan, and is not attempting to, or wishes to, represent the Vegan movement in its entirety. Rather, it is a snapshot of embodied and lived experiences.

First, it presents an exploration of the phenomenological experiences of such individuals with, and within Veganism. As the dietary lifestyle is kaleidoscopic, with distinct health, environmental, and moral ethea, which can be convoluted through blurred boundaries, particularly in online spaces. Indeed, I know that there may be a pocket of readers who may contest my use of the term 'dietary lifestyle' in relation with Veganism. Essentially, this monograph is not a commentary on the phenomenology of Veganism as a movement. Rather it aims to carve out a space for the passionate and multi-layered *Voices*, and narratives of the participants who took part in this study, as they 'moved through' their vegan journey. Following our conversation, I have received several follow-up emails from some participants, not only wanting to know about the status of the project and when they may be able to read it in print, but also to give me updates about themselves and their 'post-vegan' experiences. Second, for a broad range of academics and students, appropriating Mikhail Bakhtin's (1895–1975) works on *Polyphony* and the *Dialogism*, it presents an alternative lens for not only foregrounding underrepresented *Voices*, but also tools for analysing the plurality and *Unfinalisability* of *Selfhood* and identities.

Finally, this book has been consciously designed for a wider audience beyond academia. Therefore, for some unavoidable complex terminology, a glossary has also been provided at the end of the monograph, where key Bakhtinian concepts have been summarised. However, for those who, like me, find toing and froing between the glossary and their page-to-page reading an encumbrance, the main text contains *'Sideward Glances,'* in the form of 'pop-outs.' The purpose of these *'Sideward Glances'* is to act as a reminder or a guide for understanding any complex terms referred to on a given page. I hope you, as the reader, find the content engaging and feel that you too are a part of the dialogue presented in this monograph.

ACKNOWLEDGEMENTS

I confess that I have not been gifted with the talent of emotive writing and feel wholly inadequate as I try to transfer my gratitude onto the page, nonetheless, I will try.

The decision to write this project into monographic form began as a meandering river in the recess of my mind, which unexpectedly became turbulent rapids once Routledge decided to accept my proposal, leaving me somewhat blindsided. During the writing of this project, however, I have been immensely fortunate for having the opportunity to cultivate my thoughts and ideas with expert-peers and friends. As a last-minute request, Paul Sullivan, a Bakhtin scholar, kindly agreed to write a foreword for this monograph, for which I am grateful. Now that my venture has come to a conclusion, I am also thankful for Paul taking on the role of the critical-*Other* (always constructive, of course), and prompting me to challenge and develop my own intellectual understandings of *Dialogism* and the Bakhtinian concepts. Especially at moments when I simply wished to 'get the job done.' I would also like to extend my gratitude to John Ackroyd, who became a personal in-house philosopher of sorts. John, thank you for your continual, unwavering support, and confidence in my ability, throughout the writing process. I am truly grateful for your feedback on chapters from this book, as well as your reflections on the intellectual synergy between Bakhtin, Kant, and Hegel, which have been thought-provoking.

I would also like to thank others whose expertise and guidance has been important at different stages of this project. Professor Peter Mitchell for his invaluable advice during a, potentially, precarious stage; without it, I may not have had the resolve to see this project may not have come to fruition. Similarly, thank you to Jo Pei-Tan at Manchester Metropolitan University for being a source of motivation during the initial stages of this project. Also, Professor

Wendy Stainton-Rogers, for taking the time to listen to my thoughts on this book, continually reminding me of the reader, reading a shaky first chapter and declaring, '*You have something to say.*' I will take that.

Finally, I would like to express my gratitude to the participants who agreed to come forward and share their stories, without which this monograph would not have been possible. Your passion, while relaying your experience, and desire for having your *Voice(s)* heard were great motivation.

1

INTRODUCTION

During the writing process of this project, I was advised by senior peers that every good book starts with a 'hook.' Taking their advice on board, here is my hook. During an applicant open day, towards the end of the session, I was approached by an inquisitive applicant, who had emigrated from Iceland to the UK with their parents, asking, 'what do you research?' Conversationally, I proceeded to explain that I was working on a project about the social psychology of Veganism and identity. *Former* vegans and identity, to be specific, and that, potentially, this could be perceived as an unfavourable area of study. What I chose to omit were the words of a reviewer still occupying my subconscious and wavering my resolve about committing to the project: *'I can't see the book having very wide appeal or utility.'* The applicant explained that, inspired by Veganuary, the desire to be sustainable, and ethical motivations, their entire family has 'gone vegan' while they were in Iceland. However, after experiencing physical and psychological obstacles, they continued to explain that, as a family, they felt rather disillusioned. Their unreserved parting remark, *'I'd like to read your book,'* not only silenced internal echoes of doubt but also questioned what the word 'Veganism' signifies. Considering the applicants experience, it is a word and concept that is becoming increasingly embedded within the public consciousness. What does, however, Veganism entail, and what does it mean? In recent scholarship, in both mainstream media and academic discourse(s), the term is becoming synonymous with the global drives towards sustainability (Saari, Herstatt, and Tiwari, 2021). It is not surprising then, that there have not only been calls for Veganism to be perceived as de facto mandatory for matter of sustainable food polices, that are essential in an eco-socialist society (Vettese, 2018), but also for the promotion of animal rights (Taylor and Taylor, 2020). Veganism

DOI: 10.4324/9781003384526-1

also encapsulates a myriad of broad social and political positions such as Speciesism (Horta and Albersmeier, 2020), environmental ethics, and health (Abbey, 2016; Polish, 2016). To complicate, matters further these classifications have now splintered further into subdivisions; driven by collective and individualistic incentives concerning an 'all encompassing antiexploitation ethic' (Deckha, 2018, 285; also see Guha-Majumdar, Niesen and Kymlicja, 2022). As Giraud (2021) and Costa, Gill, Morda et al. (2019) have correctly phrased it, Veganism is 'More than a diet,' especially when it becomes a core identity signifier (McIntyre, 2022; Costa, Gill, Morda et al., 2019). Scholarship within identity Veganism and aspirational Veganism is explored further in proceeding sections. The multiple positionings of Veganism considered above are not exhaustive. Nonetheless, understandably, for consistency and clarity in academic and non-academic debate, this is exactly what contemporary scholarship has attempted to do (Dutkiewicz and Dickstein, 2021; Gheihman, 2021; Beck and Ladwig, 2020), by championing distinctive conclusive definitions, which are explored below.

If you have read the preface, you will already be familiar with the overarching aspirational drives of this book. Appropriating Mikhail Bakhtin's (1895–1975) philosophy on *Dialogue* and the *Dialogical Self*, it presents an alternative lens for not only visualising the multitudinous of social-ideological movements such as Veganism, which are simultaneously monoglossic and heteroglossic, but also suggesting an onto-epistemological framework for analysing the impact the definitional plurality has on individual identity. Moreover, we explore what it actually means to *be* vegan. Through original interview material, it not only argues how a Dialogical approach discloses how kaleidoscopic socio-ideologies manifest in individual embodiment (the experience of *Being* vegan), self-perception, and identity, but also the co-determinate reciprocal nature between the practitioner and the practice. I, therefore, also critically reflect on pockets of Western scholarship that have ventured to define Veganism as a totalitarian practice, or *a priori* (a truth or knowledge independent of individual experience), and what this means for the lived experience(s) of vegan practitioners. As argued below, when discussing veganism's complex relationship with *intra*-human inequalities within social praxis, the social psychology of how individuals mediate sentiments of blame and personal responsibility is underemphasised with regard to vegan ideologies. Particularly where a given *Ideology*, or the practitioner of an ideological positioning may potentially fall-short. As Senijder and Hedwig (2004), for example, note that successful ideologies 'provide a "natural" and "inevitable" explanation of society or part of it, an adequate form of accounting for "errors" [or what Bakhtin refers to as "loopholes"] is essential' (Senijder and Hedwig, 2004: 600). Without the presence of such 'loopholes,' the *Ideology* practitioner does not retain the possibility for altering the final meaning of their practice or values, as they are closed ended. As traced throughout this chapter, the distinct contemporary definitions underpinning *Veganism* are heterogeneous; however, on a practical platform, they are also ***simultaneously*** monolithic, hence, eroding the loophole safety-valve.

By the conclusion of this chapter my aim is not to advocate for a particular definition, contemporary or historical, through disputing one against the other. Nor is it to posit a 'new' neat and minimal definition of '*Veganism*,' it is the contrary. Rather, drawing on Bakhtin's notion of the *Unfinalisability* of 'living' discourse, I hope to convey the futility of presenting Veganism as a singular practice or *Ideology*, and that vegan ideologies are infinitude. Although, currently, 'Veganism' encapsulates an extensive array of interdisciplinary concerns (Giraud, 2021; Wright, 2015), for us to truly understand the current Western discourses of Veganism, it is important to trace its origins.

Sideward Glance

At this point, I would like to outline some key Bakhtin terminology I refer to in the introductory paragraph (such as monolithic, heteroglossic, and *loophole*), as they will continue to make an appearance throughout this monograph. In a nutshell, monolithic and heteroglossic can be interpreted as two extreme bookends on a horizontal axis, which represents the number of *'Voices'* one can hear within a text or a conversation. At the one end of the axis, in a monolithic text or conversation, there is only *one voice* and with a single *opinion and value*. On the other end, however, a heteroglossic text or conversation would hold *multiple Voices*, with *different opinions and values*. Due to its multiplicity, heteroglossic texts and conversation contain what Bakhtin (1984) refers to as words with 'loopholes,' where the speaker retains the possibility for altering the final meaning of their words. In contrast to monolithic, here, one is not bound or committed to a single value or opinion.

Situating Veganism

The Vegan Society's *manifesto*, first published by Donald Watson in 1944, introduced the term 'vegan,' it also ushered an intellectual shift that decentred human superiority and advocated for the recognition of animals as sentient. Therefore, becoming what Bakhtin (1992: 106) refers to as an 'ideal form,' or a symbolic form of what it means to *be* vegan. Although it is lengthy, it is worth outlining the manifesto's dictates, and I do not use the word 'dictate' lightly. For example, as one reads the definition below, it may be worth keeping the concepts of monolithic and heteroglossic in the forefront on one's mind.

When considered in detail the language of the manifesto is unclouded in initiating what Dutkiewicz and Dickstein (2021: 58, *emphasis added*) define as a '*practice* movement,' requiring *collective action* and underscoring the moral imperatives of Veganism or *Being* vegan: 'should be,' 'seeks to abolish,' 'striving to achieve,' and '*no* honourable *alternative*.' Later, the co-founder, Leslie Cross, however, defined the term as 'the *doctrine* that man should live without exploiting animals' (Cross, 1949, *emphasis added*). Here, I would like to reiterate that the message the manifesto questions is not being questioned. Rather it is the rhetorical manner in which it is presented, and how such rhetoric can be internalised and perceived by an individual. The manifesto continues by outlining that *Being* vegan is,

> To advocate that man's food should be derived from fruit, nuts, vegetables, grains and other wholesome non-animal products and that it should exclude flesh, fish, fowl, eggs, honey, and animals' milk, butter and cheese...
>
> The Vegan Society seeks to abolish man's dependence on animals, with its inevitable *cruelty and slaughter*, and to create instead a more reasonable and humane order of society. Whilst honouring the efforts of all who are striving to achieve the emancipation of man and of animals, the Vegan Society suggests that results must remain limited so long as the exploitation in food and clothing production is ignored.
>
> The Vegan Society is eager that it should be realised how closely the meat and dairy produce industries are related. The *atrocities* of dairy farming are, in some ways, greater than those of the meat industry but they are more obscured by ignorance. Moreover, the Vegan Society asserts that the use of milk in any form after the period of weaning is biologically *wrong* and that, except when taken directly from the mother, it becomes *polluted and unsafe*. The Society, therefore, sees no honourable alternative but to challenge the traditions of orthodoxy by advocating a completely revised dietary based on reason and humane principles and guided by science to meet physiological requirements.

In 1979 Veganism became cemented as denoting a *philosophy* and a way of living, its ideologically driven principal commandment being the *exclusion of all forms of exploitation* of, and cruelty to, animals for food, clothing, or any other purpose. This was then later adapted by The Vegan Society in 1988 to conceptualise their advocation for the end of animal exploitation and commodification due to human driven Capitalism:

> a *philosophy* and way of living which seeks to exclude – as far as is possible and practicable – all forms of exploitation of, and cruelty to, animals for food, clothing or any other purpose; and by extension, promotes the development and use of animal-free alternatives for the benefit of *humans*, animals and the environment.
>
> (The Vegan Society, 2014: 6, *emphasis added*)

There are two noteworthy points that emerge from the historical definitions (*a la* Watson) and ideological positions (The Vegan Society, 2014) of being 'vegan' and 'Veganism.' First, the seemingly interchangeable use of the terms, 'doctrine' and 'philosophy,' which, arguably, can be interpreted as contradictory. While the former denotes the practice of fundamental principles guided by the doctrine's 'truth,' the latter questions the existence of a universal 'ideal' or 'logic.' The purpose of philosophical thinking is to explore and investigate, and during one of our many conversations, a philosophically inclined colleague reminded me of a memorable quote by Isaiah Berlin on the ethos of philosophy. It is, 'Not to know where to look for the answer is the surest symptom of a philosophical problem' (Jahanbegloo, 2007: 128), essentially lending itself to dialogical encounters. Therefore, arguably, becoming the epicentre of Veganism's interesting position of being simultaneously monolithic and heteroglossic. This is, to a certain degree, the root of where divergence in the *understanding* of Veganism began. For example, while the original 'ideal form' (Bakhtin, 1992) advocates for a doctrine-based-ism, the latter leads to a broader philosophy-based-ism.

The popularity of interpreting Veganism as a philosophy-based-ism was later reinforced by the twentieth-century intellectual turn towards animal ethics, driven by 'animal philosophers,' most notable Singer (1970; 1998), who took a number of positions, such as respect, speciesism, right, and suffering, towards the topic. Singer argued that,

> A diet heavy on animal products, catered for by intensive animal production, is a disaster for animals, the environment, and the health of those who eat it. The scale of the disaster will be multiplied many times over if the trend for other countries to copy Western diets and methods of production continues. It is already happening in the more successful economies of East Asia, and it seems bound to spread further as the sphere of prosperity widens.
>
> (Singer, 1998: 78)

Most contemporary justifications for extending ethical consideration to animals (Francione, 2020) broadly stem from a Singer's Utilitarianist (Singer, 2011, 2009) or animal rights perspective. The noteworthy point here is that The Vegan Society's current definition, and Singer's definition, not only includes the facet of *human* and *environmental* benefit, but also continues to use the word 'philosophy,' hence, interprets Veganism as a philosophy-based-ism. Unsurprisingly, then, The World Health Organisation defines Veganism as a dietary lifestyle where one abstains from meat, eggs, poultry, dairy, and all other animal products, and the reasons for this are environmental, ethical, and *health* (WHO, 2015, *emphasis added*). Here, I am interpreting 'health' as a reference to *human* health, which many, both academic and non-academic, maintain is an oversimplification, and underrepresents the animal rights aspects encapsulated within the original 'ideal form' of Veganism.

For many, the present tripartite approach that heavily focuses on human health and the environment, that Gheihman (2021) has determined as 'lifestyle veganism,' has derailed Veganism from its radical intent concerning animal ethics and discrimination (Wright, 2018). Similarly, although their definitions differentiate, others (Dickstein, Dutkiewicz, Majumdar et al., 2022; Dutkiewicz and Dickstein, 2021) explicitly distinguish their definitions of Veganism from popular understandings, maintaining that liberal and 'deontological' approaches (Clay, Sextion, Garnett et al., 2020) tend to inaccurately fuse Veganism with aspects that detach it from its 'ideal form.' For example, identity (Buttny and Kinefuchi, 2020, Greenebaum, 2017; Cherry, 2015), ethical behaviour (Kennedy, Baumann and Johnston, 2018), political agendas (Jallinoja, Vinnari, and Niva, 2018; Ko, 2017; Wrenn, 2017), and consumerism (Phua, Jin, and Kim, 2020). In the next few sections, we will discuss each component of the aforementioned tripartite of Veganism a little further (animal ethics, health, and environmental), and outline what each stance entails. This is essential not only for a broader understanding of what Veganism represents but will, hopefully, also help readers glimpse into the interviewees' mind-space as they discuss their motivations for becoming vegan.

Sideward Glance

Before moving forward, I think a short explanation of 'ontological' and 'deontological' Veganism may be effective. In essence, an 'ontological' approach to Veganism (Plumwood, 2003) champions a *universal* adoption of Veganism. Hence, advocating a universal law, with universal moral standards around animal ethics (the universal abstinence of animal products and challenging Speciesism). Deontological Veganism, by contrast, encapsulates motivational drives such as challenging social inequalities and exposing general structural exploitation.

Animal Ethics Veganism

For those who chose to become vegan due to animal ethics, Veganism does not only pertain a change in dietary habits but also other broader lifestyle changes, such as the avoidance of *all animal products* (Greenebaum, 2012). Their motivations are Speciesism driven, or more accurately, the eradication of Speciesism, hence, are driven by changes in the way they perceive animals and human-animal relationship. At this point, I would also like to address vegan scholarship pertaining to wider vegan motivational difficulties, in the content of moral psychology and moral Veganism. Pickett (2021), and earlier, Gjerris (2015), respectively propose that a societal 'false consciousness' and 'willed blindness' has manifested unreflective criticism towards Veganism (especially animal ethics Veganism). Simply phrased, if one acknowledges that one has a moral obligation of care towards animals, why does one continue to consume them? This is what Loughnan, Haslam, and Bastian (2010) refers to as the 'Meat Paradox.' Research in experimental psychology has proposed the individual development of cognitive dissonance strategies in order to overcome any moral conflicts among those who profess to care about animals yet continue to consume them (Ioannidou, Lesk, Stewart- Knox et al., 2023).

Perhaps it is not surprising then, that within animal ethics literature, those positing the mainstream, rationalist approach towards animal ethics and meat consumption, such as Luke (1992) and Singer (2015), have come under heavy criticism. The rational approach, for example, offers a Bakhtinian 'loophole,' in the sense that one can hold a moral value, however, also have the freedom not to act upon it. Therefore, one of the main objections with the rationalist approach is that it does not address the question of motivational drives. For example, some people may be convinced by the rationalist argument for becoming vegan or vegetarian, however, it does not explain why the same cohort of individuals may 'fail to put their beliefs into action' (Pickett, 2021: 15). Those positing 'ontological veganism,' for instance, exclusively refer to Veganism as a collective *action* that 'strengthens the resolve to dismantle' oppressive structures and act as a form of 'propaganda by *deed*' (Plumwood, 2003: 01). In this sense, it is not simply enough to *think* or *hold* a view, one must also act; Mark Twain's, 'Action speaks louder than words but not nearly as often,' springs to mind here. Veganism is also a strategy of action practised by individuals and groups, that do not centralise the *Self*, but rather is outwards and boycotts systems of exploitation. It is a *physical* and *symbolic* act (Hamilton, 2019). For the participants in this study, motivational drives, or lack thereof, were not an issue, hence, whether they became confined within the 'meat paradox,' as it is currently understood, was not under debate.

Health Veganism

The facet of health Veganism, within the tractional vegan-tripartite, is becoming increasingly complex. For example, on the one hand, for global health, scholarship argues for a transition towards 'plant-based diets.' Given the scientific consensus about the destructive impact of fast farming has led to concerns for global health (Moreno, 2022; World Health Organization, 2021), resulting in food poverty for some and an abundance of food resources for others, this is not entirely surprising. On the other hand, health Veganism also refers to individual health; as Wright (2015) notes, in popular social media discourse, 'Veganism' has become a mode of empowerment, promoting and supporting individual health, and 'even sexy' (Wright, 2015: 42). The holistic benefits of reducing meat consumption are not disputable, however, more recent scholarship has begun to explore the long-term health impacts of an animal product-free diet (Bali and Naik, 2023). I feel compelled to highlight that the health advantages and disadvantages of being vegan are not under scrutiny; rather, it is the individual experiences with health discourses surrounding Veganism, and the health benefits, both physical and mental, it supposedly promises.

Environmental Veganism

The final component of the original vegan-tripartite is environmentalism. For the past few decades, research has promoted the connection between an animal product-free diet and how it results in environmental benefits and the sustainability of the planet (Krattenmacher, Casal, Dutkiewicz et al., 2023; Scarborough, Clark, Cobiac et al., 2023; Willett, Rockstrom, Brent et al., 2019). Historically, environmental concerns have been marginalised within Veganism itself (Saunders, 2008), and have gained popularity after the recent turn towards sustainability (Cooper, 2017). For environmentalists, Veganism is the crux of their environmentalism discourse, and being vegan is a mode of instilling personal accountability for preservation of the environment (Schösler, Boer, and Boersema, 2012). Notably, this is also linked with the discourses of rapid agriculture, mass animal farming, and industrialisation in general (Dorgbetor, Ondrasek, Kutnjak et al., 2022; Klein, 2014).

Defining Veganism Through a Dialogical Lens

The section above has outlined the original vegan tripartite. Towards the end, however, I hope you began to ponder whether it is possible to wrap up motivational drives and definitions of Veganism within a neat little bow, or in Bakhtinian terms, monolithic language. Indeed, there is heated debate within Vegan Studies, and mainstream rhetoric, around what *being* vegan, and what Veganism means and represents, thus, circling us back to the question posed at the opening of this chapter.

> Such is the fleeting language of a day, of an epoch, a social group, a genre, a school and so forth. It is possible to give a concrete and detailed analysis of any utterance, once having exposed it as a *contradiction-ridden, tension-filled* unity of two embattled tendencies in the life of language.
>
> (Bakhtin, 1981, 272, *emphasis added*)

The quote above is from a seminal Bakhtinian essay, first published in *The Dialogic Imagination* (Bakhtin, 1981). It is key in foregrounding the pivotal role of language as the substrata of Bakhtinian philosophy concerning identity, culture, and society. Language is, therefore, also the crux of Bakhtin's mediations on the multiplicity of meaning-making and socio-ideological cultural movements such as Veganism. The quote also highlights another essential facet that appears throughout the Bakhtinian canon, that of *tension*. Each cultural-ideological movement is constructed through *socially shared rhetoric*, and such rhetoric is burdened with an immutable *tension and friction* resulting in a heteroglotic understanding of a phenomenon. To stem the 'problematic' heteroglotic understanding of 'Veganism,' as mentioned above, Dutkiewicz and Dickstein (2021) have proposed a strictly practice-based definition:

> "Veganism" cannot merely mean whatever a speaker wishes it to mean for the sake of communicating some point or other. The term can mean something stable and clear, and we feel that clarity can be achieved without too much difficulty.
>
> (Dutkiewicz and Dickstein, 2021: 01)

For Dutkiewicz and Dickstein (2021), the concern is not the diversity within practitioner motivation, but rather when the practitioner's 'overall normative positions' are imposed into Veganism, therefore, modifying Veganism through attributing characteristics to it, and '*delimiting* its meaning' (Dutkiewicz and Dickstein, 2021: 10). This, they argue, is a ramification of treating Veganism as a 'belief-ism.' When considered as an ideology-based-ism, there is the risk of Veganism becoming so broad and multi-representative as an umbrella term, that it can fall victim of actually meaning nothing at all. Indeed, during my research into writing this chapter, the proverbial phrase opening Pandora's box came to mind, therefore, I certainly appreciate Dutkiewicz and Dickstein's (2021) argument. To what extent, however, is it possible to pin down a singular unitary definition? From a Bakhtinian perspective, defining Veganism, or an 'ideal form' of Veganism through detaching practitioner from the ideological position is a Sisyphean endeavour.

For Bakhtin, a living discourse is heterologic and dialogic, consequently, it is also *Unfinalisable*. Although there are truths-in-themselves, or *a priori*, as Bakhtin would phrase it, there are no values-in-themselves. This is because *value* is inseparable from *pravda*, meaning truth as lived in culture. *Pravda* refers to the conditional mode of '*someone's* truth,' or 'true to someone' (Falla, Wheeler, and Unbegaun, 1995, *emphasis added*). Additionally, *istina* refers to genuine truth, the mindful recognition or perception of what exists *objectively*. Bakhtin, however, uses *istina* to refer to what is *a priori* or theoretically true, therefore, denying the independent or objective existence of *istina*. In this sense, *istina* does not attain *dana* (becomes an *objective* truth) and is always posited *zadana* (exists as a *subject* truth) within the mindful judgement, or *act* of the subject (Bakhtin, 1990 also see, Intezar, Ackroyd and Sullivan, in Press). Consequently, since a single act, or judgement, of a truth essentially constitutes a truth (for someone), making the truth *pravda*, it follows that *istina* is necessarily posited in *pravda*. Bakhtin (1990) maintains that abstract knowledge, such as the philosophy, or doctrine, of Veganism, has an 'autonomous truth [*istina*],' of which validity is 'sufficient unto itself, absolute, and eternal.' In other words, the truth of the philosophy of Veganism is a *priori*, which is based on experience, a truth that required no *objective* evidence (Bakhtin, 1990: 49, 10). However, as a *priori* truth is ideal and extratemporal, it does not exist within itself, hence, it requires to be cognised by a *subject* for it to exist. Subsequently, although a *priori* (x) is valid independently of the 'I think, or act,' it is brought into *existence* by the *subject* through their *formation* of the 'I think, or act.' Intrinsically, Bakhtin (1990) continues, the 'I think, or act' embodies the truth as *istina* (because x has a *priori* validity) for the subject as *pravda* (because of a particular act). Only a true judgement or volition, which determines the act (*postupok*) carried out by a *subject*, in the case of this monograph the vegan practitioner practising Veganism, can give it (Veganism) *value* (Bakhtin, 1993). Vegan ideologies (I am using the plural here as there are several strains of ideologically driven Veganism), their principles, values (*pravda*), and truth(s), therefore, are not self-identical, self-equivalent, or self-sufficient within themselves. They consist, or *should* consist of, the *unique* positions, or experience, of every vegan practitioner. Encapsulating, therefore, the truth (*pravda*) of each practitioner's actual concrete volition, which has given value and meaning to 'Veganism.' In this sense, Dutkiewicz and Dickstein's (2021: 15) proposition of moving 'veganism from the realm of ideology to practice,' for clear and 'neutral definition' is understandable but, perhaps, not plausible. The word is always pre-saturated with the heterogeneity of meanings and values that previous cultures have deposited in it (Bakhtin, 1981).

Sideward Glance

There is an argument that Veganism is a relatively recent cultural phenomenon, hence, can it be truly considered under a Dialogical lens. I would agree that, from a Western perspective, the concept of Veganism is 'new,' however, I would also maintain that the concept's, ethe, and values which encapsulate it have existed in the Eastern tradition for over 2000 years.

Respectfully, a contemporary understanding of Veganism will always be charged with past iterations. A word (*logos*) such as Veganism, therefore, has no ontological reality, and cannot be perceived as a 'single concrete language,' or reduced to a universal 'ideal form' (Bakhtin, 1992: 106). It can only be understood in the various collective cultural interpretations that express it and the *ought* (violation) and act, of the individual vegan practitioner. In this sense, there is no standard volition (*ought*), therefore, there is no normative way to act (*postupok*), for those practising Veganism. As outlined below, recent re-framing of Veganism within celebrity culture (Phua, Jin, and Kim, 2020) and social media influencers (Schouten, Janssen, and Verspaget, 2020) is an example of the *Unfinalisability* of ideologies and doctrines such as Veganism.

I appreciate that what I have outlined in the section above is theoretically dense and can be difficult to follow. Hence, I would like to take a short interlude and offer some further clarification and contextualisation, especially as Bakhtin's concept of a *priori* somewhat deviates from that of the natural sciences. If you are not interested in diving into the technicalities of philosophical traditions and their relationship with theoretical psychology, please feel free to move on to the next paragraph. From a Kantian tradition (1978), *priori* truths are not based on individual experiences, rather, they are *self-evident objects* of reasoning, which exist *external* to the cognition and perspective of the *subject* (that would be you and I). The subject then places meaning onto the self-evident and self-sufficient object, which is universally recognised. Kant refers to these are *priori* laws: 'all empirical laws are only special determinations of the pure laws of understanding, under which, and according to the norm of which, they first become possible' (Kant, 1978: 148). For example, all triangles are polygons. Bakhtin (1990) does not disagree with this, he does, however, suggest a deviation away from empirical law when we attempt to understand *a priori* when in the context of the human sciences, such as psychology, by adding the component of time and space. He proposes that we should consider the individual *experience* of a given *priori* within a given time and space, and not the existence of a *priori* itself. In other words, he agrees that there is an *Ideal* 'autonomous truth' *a priori* which is, 'sufficient unto itself, absolute, and eternal,' but they do not truly come into temporal existence until we *perceive* them, *experience* them, give them meaning, and doing so, bring them into reality (Bakhtin, 1990: 49).

Hence, a vital aspect that a Bakhtinian approach foregrounds, which is often undervalued in current academic research concerning the definition and practice of Veganism, is the *reciprocal dependence* between the meaning-making of concepts and the individual practitioner. Rather than taking a top-down, or ideology-based approach for defining and practising Veganism, as some scholarship suggests (Gheihman, 2021; Beck and Ladwig, 2020), arguably, Dutkiewicz and Dickstein's (2021) practice-based, or bottom-up approach carves out the space for further debate focusing on the practitioners' experience. A Bakhtinian dialogical epistemology advocates for such a bottom-up approach. Bakhtin (1990), for example, denies the *priori* nature of social cultural truths (*pravda*) and acts (*ought*). He places their reality within individual lived experiences. In doing so, situating the individual back into the mean-making process of rhetoric.

From 'Veganism' to 'Plant-Based'

The purpose of this section is to showcase the marked distinction between the original animal rights discourse of Veganism, concerned with the oppressive inequalities in human-animal relationships (Ko, 2019; Wright, 2019), and the current dominant discourse of Veganism, that is often perceived as being superficial and commodifying (Doyle, 2016). To a certain degree, scientific research has begun to utilise the terms 'vegan' and 'plant-based' interchangeably. Such scholarships, however, undervalue definitional complexities. The Vegan Society (2021, 2019), for example, have issued statements emphasising the distinctions between the values and moral philosophy each term encapsulated, respectively. The former continues to centralise animal ethics, while the latter depoliticises said form of animal ethics Veganism. As Lundahl (2020) suggests, the two terms note the 'emerging boundary between Veganism as a moral and political lifestyle, on the one hand, and the plant-based diet, on the other' (Lundahl, 2020: 257). Collins (2015), describes how vegan intersectionality, or the multiple understandings of Veganism has led the 'definitional dilemmas.' A dialogical approach foregrounds that intersectionalities within definition(s) of 'Veganism' is not a 'dilemma,' but rather inevitable. It is, perhaps, not surprising then that with the rise of social media influencers Veganism has shifted into mainstream, which as I outline below, has manifested in further evolving the unavoidable definitional development. As Gheihman (2021) phrases it, 'veganism' is now 'mainstreamed.' In order to truly comprehend the complexity of Veganism, and thus, of *Being* vegan, I think it is important to unpack this definitional shift.

It is difficult to determine exactly when the emblematic shift from ethical to popular began. Nonetheless, literature has highlighted the concerns and potential pitfalls of celebrity involvement in matters of food and ethics (Johnston and Goodman, 2015; Lewis, 2010; Littler, 2008). The Vegan Society (2019) has also updated their definition to address this (notably, the use of 'philosophy' still remains):

> *philosophy* and way of living which seeks to exclude—as far as is possible and practicable—all forms of exploitation of, and cruelty to, animals for food, clothing or any other purpose According to this perspective, individuals who eat vegan food, but still engage in other forms of animal use or exploitation are called 'plant based' or 'dietary vegans.'

For many, the mainstream re-framing of 'Veganism' through the introduction of campaigns such as Veganuary, coupled with the rise of celebrity culture (Phua, Jin, and Kim, 2020; Doyle, 2016), and social media influencers

(Schouten, Janssen, and Verspaget, 2020) has emanated the fashionability of 'Veganism and *Being* vegan.' If recent motivations for becoming vegan are not situated within animal rights, environmental ethics, and moral concerns, then what are they? Arguably, there are three specific identifiable themes in current scholarship concerning mainstream Veganism: its 'destigmatization,' its capitalisation, and its association with social media. Buttny and Kinefuchi (2020), for example, argue that the mainstream version of Veganism has been re-phrased as a 'plant-based diet,' in order to decouple it from its political and spiciest roots, which are perceived negatively by omnivores (Monin and Monin, 2012; Cole and Morgan, 2011).

Acknowledging Capitalist motivations, Giraud (2021) develops this further by introducing the phase 'plant-based capitalism' (Giraud, 2021: 130). Giraud's (2021) work also engages with 'long-term' vegans, specifically their opinion on the popular 'destigmatized' understanding of Veganism, which foregrounds the intra-vegan disquiet between advocates for the original 'ideal form' of Veganism and it's contemporary re-framing. While participants in Giraud's (2021) project were not opposed to the term 'plant-based' itself, they did, however, take objection with the fact that it not only shifted focus away from veganism's animal rights roots, but also limited it to food consumption. This, in turn, has rendered the original form vulnerable to capitalist marketing strategies, which in Bakhtinian (Bakhtin, 1986, 1984, 1981, 1968) terms, have become the dominant *Voice* of Veganism. If considered in the light of our discussion in the previous section, around the reciprocal and dialectic nature of ideologies, this is not entirely surprising.

Doyle (2016), for example, tracks the impact of the educational Veganism campaign championed by celebrities such as Alicia Silverstone and Ellen DeGeneres. She notes that, even though the campaign promoted Veganism as a diet and lifestyle that foregrounds an ethics of care for animals, *humans*, and *environment*, for marketability, the message was re-worked through the commodity logic of celebrity culture ideas and gendered lifestyle practices, where the individual choice is to be healthy, happy, and kind to oneself. Similarly, Phua, Jin, and Kim's (2020) empirical work implies a significant connection between vegan celebrity endorsers' motivation and consumers' eating habits on health consciousness. An important motivation to adopt and continue Veganism derives from social media, particularly influencers who endorse the vegan lifestyle, as they function as 'experts' with whom followers can identify and build a connection (Feng et al., 2020). To repose the question asked at the beginning of this section, if recent motivations for becoming vegan are not situated within animal rights, environmental ethics, and moral concerns, then what are they? The mainstream motivations now, it would seem, are predominantly ego-centric and identity based, rather than altruistic and ontological based.

Veganism and Identity

Although some research has opposed the frequent association of Veganism with individual empowerment, individual gain, and identity politics, there is a wealth of academic investigation and analysis exploring the identity-based Veganism. For the sake of coherency and reader accessibility, this section categorises vegan identity-based research into three specific camps: Self-Identity Theory, Collective Identity, and Social Identity Theory. Although, recent research on the area of vegan identity politics has proposed the synthesis of the latter two and interprets Collective identity as a sub-theory of Social Identity Theory (Davis, Love, and Fares, 2019). The theoretically permeability of identity theories and categories is discussed further in Chapter 2.

In the context of self-identity and self-empowerment, Heganism has emerged as a concept for delineating gender identity, which attempts to de-construct hegemonic masculinity, and re-construct it with the removal of the stigmas attached to male Veganism (Randall, 2018; Greenebaum and Dexter, 2017). Moreover, there is a plethora of research delineating how vegan practices of altering one's consumption practices dovetail with identity construction, both individualistic and collective (Cherry, 2015, 2006; Greenebaum, 2017, 2012a, 2012b; Romo and Donovan-Kicken, 2012). In terms of collective identity, Rosenfeld's (2018) and Rosenfeld and Burrow's (2018; 2017) work highlights how in-group memberships are formed between non-meat-eaters, and meat-eaters can be perceived as an outgroup (Yeh, 2014). In individualistic terms, Kirsten-Effi, Seib-Pfeifer, Lüth et al. (2020) underscore the importance of dietary habits in one's identity formation and self-concept. This is the case for all, omnivores, vegetarians, and vegan identity formation. Interestingly, Kirsten, Effi Seib-Pfeifer, Lüth et al.'s (2020) study highlighted a difference between vegetarian and vegan identity formation. They found that vegans reported more extreme scores not only in terms of in-group and out-group politics, but also feeling as though their dietary in-group was judged more negatively by others. Echoing Buttny and Kinefuchi (2020), they also posit that, statistically, vegans are more likely to adhere to their diet more strictly. Indeed, the recent revival of ethical philosophical debates (Milburn, 2022, 2021; Hunt, 2022, 2019; Alvaro, 2019) concerning the practicalities (George, 2000, 1994, 1990) of raising vegan children, indicates the extent to which Veganism can and does server as a core identity marker. Earlier, I mentioned that the general qualm with associations between Veganism and identity politics is that it can result in veganism's departure farther away from its ideal form of animal ethics, and towards a broader critique of social structural organisations (Giraud, 2021). Hence, taking on a neoliberal form, which foregrounds self-improvement and empowerment. Similarly, the issues for Dutkiewicz and Dickstein (2021), in terms of identity, self-identity and Veganism, arise when Veganism is identified as an ideological stance and becomes entangled with modes of vegan identity politics (also see Shotwell, 2016). Dutkiewicz and Dickstein (2021) present an interesting argument pertaining to Veganism and identity politics:

> And if we accept (if only conventionally speaking) modernity's elevation of belief and principles over action and ritual in the determination of personal identity, then it should strike us as odd that a person's abstention from consuming a specific category of commodities would serve as their core identity marker.
>
> (Dutkiewicz and Dickstein, 2021: 10)

I am in agreement with Dutkiewicz and Dickstein's (2021) argument to a certain degree. However, taking a Modernist approach to 'Identity,' Giddens (1991) presents it as concrete and subject to totality. That 'Identity' denotes an unchanging 'is' (i.e., one is simply in a state of *Being*). This monograph, however, takes *Dialogical* approach to 'Identity,' or perhaps the more apt word here would be 'identities,' where one's identity is transcendental and in a continual flux of *Unfinalisability*. In other words, it is constantly changing or *Becoming*. This is discussed in detail in Chapter 2.

The purpose of this chapter was not for us to question the external challenges experienced by vegans, nor the derogatory discourses relating to the lifestyle (Sanford and Lorimer, 2022; Vestergren and Uysal, 2022; Cole and Morgan, 2011). The discussion does, however, advocate for the necessitates of psychological studies that capture and build upon Veganism from the perspective of social formation and self-concepts. Specifically, the multiplicity within such lived experiences of those practising Veganism.

Chapter Summary

Our endeavour, thus far, has been to trace existing scholarship concerning the evolving definition(s) of Veganism, and situate the complex debates within the Bakhtinian notion of unfinalisability. The discussion above has certainty not offered a solution, of course that was never the aim. What it has done, hopefully, is unconcealed a cacophony, or in Bakhtinian terms *Polyphony*, of *Voices*. *Voices* that encase multiple doctrines, practices, and interpretations. In doing so, suggesting an alternative framework, which accents the complex and reciprocal nature between the mean-making of Veganism, and the vegan practitioner. Insofar as that the former can only be conceived in relation to the latter's social reality.

The aims of this book are two-folds. First, one of the focal discussion points in this chapter has been considering Dutkiewicz and Dickstein's (2021) singular practice-based definition and its plausibility when viewed through a Bakhtinian (1981) lens. We will return to this in Chapter 6. The discussion thus far has been theoretical. Through empirical interviews, an overarching aim of proceeding chapters is to showcase the *multiplicity* of experiences of vegan practitioners, and the impact *Becoming*, *Being*, and then leaving Veganism has on their identity and self-perception. Second, it explores the *Unfinalisability* or the *Polyphonic* nature of ideological concepts such as Veganism, specifically in relation to what implications this has for those practising Veganism, and vice versa. In the words of Plato and the Bakhtinian form of a *priori*, 'the world of values is at the same time the key to the world of Forms.'

Chapter 2 sketches out a *Dialogical* onto-epistemology and proposes an alternative approach to understanding identity in social psychology. It begins by discussing the key theoretical framework, the *Dialogical Self* (1981; also see; Olivera, 2013; Sullivan, 2007). From here, it delves deeper into explaining multiple discursive tools of enquiry within the Bakhtinian canon, such as *Threshold-moments* and *Speech Genres*. The purpose is to propose a dialogical onto-epistemology, which offers an analytical and theoretical framework for analysing the *Unfinalisability* of identity structures. Chapter 3, the first of three analysis chapters, that exemplifies dialogical onto-epistemology by putting it into practice, by drawing on vegan identities as a case study. For example, it focuses on practitioners' first *Threshold-moment*, which comprises of encapsulating their journeys of discovering and *Becoming* vegan. This is essential as it builds on the multi-voiced vegan scholarship discussed in this chapter, particularly the blurring understanding of Veganism, thus, in turn, generating a complex matrix of vegan identity. Chapter 4 continues by mapping participants' second *Threshold-moment* that discloses their experiences while *Being* Veganism. The discussion not only argues for identity formation in terms of *Being* vegan, but also in relation to the none-vegan-other. Chapter 5 traces the interviewees final *Threshold-moment;* the build-up towards, and experience(s) *after Being* Vegan. Drawing on the interviewee's experiences, Chapter 6 mediates on the current dominant ideological discourses, where Veganism has become synonymous with sustainability, whether it be environmental sustainability (Taylor and Taylor, 2020) or animal ethics sustainability (Vettese, 2018). Using two specific interviews as case studies, it critically questions academic and non-academic ethea that has the tendency of promoting a monolithic approach to vegan ideology.

Before we begin in earnest, it is important to clarify a few points. This project is not a commentary on the phenomenology of Veganism as a cultural movement and dietary lifestyle per se. Rather it is an exploration of what Hegel terms actuality (*Aktualität*), and what psychology may refer to as lived experiences within a given cultural reality. It is an insight into the dialogues involved in *Being* and *Becoming*, and the tensions between the self and identity in a post-modern multi-levelled socio-ideological society.

Moreover, as I briefly mentioned earlier, it is only in recent years that Veganism has become a cultural phenomenon in the West, and it is this Western form(s) of vegan discourses that are the focus. The details of the history of

Veganism throughout the world are not necessary for understating the arguments posited in proceeding chapters, as discourses surrounding Veganism in Western societies can be considered as a distinct phenomenon for study. As is the case for Western concepts of *Selfhood* and identity (Mosig, 2006). One pivotal distinction, for instance, is that in Western cultures, in most instance, individuals are not life-long vegan practitioners, following traditional and religious ideologies (see Barstow, 2019; Tuttle, 2019; Narayanan, 2018; Camosy, 2017), but rather are those who have been motivated to change their eating habits for a plethora of reasons (Ghaffari, Rodrigo, Ekinci et al., 2021). Although there is historical research available on vegetarianism that supports this differentiation (Beardsworth and Keil, 1992), empirical research specifically in this area for Veganism is limited. Nonetheless, as the Western discourses for both lifestyles involve a conscious decision to make personal change, it is not illogical to suggest that a similar notion can be appropriable for Veganism. Therefore, each time we refer to culture, or cultural understandings, it is in reference to Western understandings.

References

Abbey, R. (2016). Exploring Judith Shklar's liberalism of fear for Animal ethics. *Politics and Animals*, 2(1), 25–36.

Alvaro, C. (2019). Veganism and children: a response to Marcus William Hunt. *Journal of Agricultural and Environmental Ethics*, 32(4), 647–661. https://doi.org/10.1007/s10806-019-09797-w

Bakhtin, M. (1993). *Toward a philosophy of the act*. Austin: University of Texas Press.

Bakhtin, M. (1990). *Art and answerability: early philosophical essays*. Austin: University of Texas Press.

Bakhtin, M. (1986). *Speech genres and other late essays*. Austin: University of Texas Press.Bakhtin, M. (1984). *Problems of Dostoevsky's poetics*. Minneapolis: University of Minnesota Press.

Bakhtin, M. (1981). *The dialogic imagination: four essays*. Austin: University of Texas Press.

Barstow, G. (2019). *The fault of meat: Tibetan Buddhist writings on vegetarianism*. U.S.: Wisdom Publications.

Beck, V., & Ladwid, R. (2020). Ethical consumerism: veganism. *WIREs Climate Change*, 12(1), 1–12. https://doi.org/10.1002/wcc.689

Beardsworth, A., & Keil, T. (1992). The vegetarian option: varieties, conversions, motives and careers. *The Sociological Review*, 40(2), 253e293. https://dx.doi.org/10.1111/j.1467-954X.1992.tb00889.x.

Buttny, R., & Kinefuchi, E. (2020). Vegans' problem stories: negotiating vegan identity in dealing with omnivores. *Discourse & Society*, 31(6), 565–583. https://doi.org/10.1177/0957926520939689

Camosy, C. (2017). "Why all Christians should go vegan." *The Washington Post*, January 5. https://www.washingtonpost.com/posteverything/wp/2017/01/05/why-all-christians-should-go-vegan/

Cherry, E. (2015). I was a teenage vegan: motivation and maintenance of lifestyle movements. *Sociological Inquiry*, 85(1), 55–74. https://doi.org/10.1111/soin.12061

Cherry, E. (2006). Veganism as a cultural movement: a relational approach. *Social Movement Studies*, 5(2), 155–170. https://doi.org/10.1080/14742830600807543
Clay, N., Sextion, A. E., Garnett, T. et al. (2020). Palatable disruptions: the politics of plant milk. *Agriculture and Human Values*, 37, 945–962. https://doi.org/10.1007/s10460-020-10022-y
Collins, P. H. (2015). Intersectionality's definitional dilemmas. *Annual Review of Sociology*, 41, 1–20. https://doi.org/10.1146/annurev-soc-073014-112142
Cooper, L. (2017). A new veganism: how climate change has created more vegans, between using and abusing our planet: how climate change affects our fields of research, Granite Symposium, University of Aberdeen, 20 November 2017. [Online] Available at: https://prezi.com/view/H36SBJiihgo92Ngh7aZr/ [Accessed March 2024].
Costa, I., Gill, P. R., & Morda, R. (2019). More than a diet: a qualitative investigation of young vegan Women's relationship to food. *Appetite*, 143, 1–8. https://doi.org/10.1016/j.appet.2019.104418
Davis, L. J., Love, T. P., & Fares, P. (2019). Collective social identity: synthesizing identity theory and social identity theory using digital data. *Social Psychology Quarterly*, 82(3), 254–273. https://doi.org/10.1177/0190272519851025
Deckha, M. (2018). Postcolonial. In L. Gruen (Ed.), *Critical terms for animal studies* (pp. 280–293). Chicago, IL: The University of Chicago Press.
Dickstein, J., Dutkiewicz, L., Majumdar, G. M. et al. (2022). Veganism as left praxis. *Capitalism, Nature, Socialism*, 33(3), 56–75. https://doi.org/10.1080/10455752.2020.1837895
Dorgbetor, I. K., Ondrasek, G., Kutnjak, H. et al. (2022). What if the world went vegan? A review of the impact on natural resources, climate change, and economics. *Agriculture*, 12, 1518. https://doi.org/10.3390/agriculture12101518
Doyle, J. (2016). Celebrity vegans and the lifestyling of ethical consumption. *Environmental Communication*, 10(6), 777–790. https://doi.org/10.1080/17524032.2016.1205643
Dutkiewicz, J., & Dickstein, J. (2021). The ism in veganism: the case for a minimal practice-based definition. *Food Ethics*, 6(2), 1–18. https://doi.org/10.1007/s41055-020-00081-6
Falla, P., Wheeler, M., & Unbegaun, B. (1995). *The Oxford Russian Dictionary*. Oxford: Oxford University Press.
Feng, Y., Chen, H., & Kong, Q. (2020). An expert with whom I can identify: the role of narratives in influencers marketing. *International Journal of Advertising*, 40(1), 972–993. https://doi.org/10.1080/02650487.2020.1824751
Francione, G. L. (2020). *Why veganism matters: the moral value of animals*. Columbia: University Press.
George, K. P. (2000). *Animal, vegetable, or woman?* New York: State University of New York Press.
George, K. P. (1994). Should feminists be vegetarians? *Signs*, 19(2), 405–434. https://doi.org/10.1086/494889
George, K. P. (1990). So animal a human…, or the moral relevance of being an omnivore. *Journal of Agricultural and Environmental Ethics*, 3(2), 172–186. https://doi.org/10.1007/BF02014612
Ghaffari, M., Rodrigo, P. G. K., Ekinci, Y. et al. (2022). Consumers' motivations for adopting a vegan diet: a mixed-methods approach. *International Journal of Consumer Studies*, 46(4), 1193–1208.
Gheihman, N. (2021). Veganism as a lifestyle movement. *Sociology Compass*, 15(5), 1–14. https://doi.org/10.1111/soc4.12877

Giraud, E. H. (2021). *Veganism: politics, practice, and theory*. London: Bloomsbury Academic.

Gjerris, M. (2015). Willed blindness: a discussion on our moral shortcomings in relation to animals. *Journal of Agriculture & Environmental Ethics*, 28, 517–532. https://doi.org/10.1007/s10806-014-9499-6

Greenebaum, J. B. (2018). Vegan of color: managing visible and invisible stigmas. *Food, Culture & Society*, 21(5), 680–697. https://doi.org/10.1080/15528014.2018.1512285

Greenebaum, J. B. (2017). Questioning the concept of vegan privilege: a commentary. *Humanity & Society*, 41(3), 355–372. https://doi.org/10.1177/0160597616640308

Greenebaum, J. B. (2012a). "Face-Saving" strategies of vegetarians and vegans. *Humanity & Society*, 36(4), 309–325. https://doi.org/10.1177/0160597612458898

Greenebaum, J. (2012b). Veganism, identity and the quest for authenticity. *Food, Culture & Society*, 15(1), 129–144. https://doi.org/10.2752/175174412X13190510222101

Greenebaum, J. B. and Dexter, B. (2017). Vegan men and hybrid masculinity. *Journal of Gender Studies*, 27(6), 637–648. https://doi.org/10.1080/09589236.2017.1287064

Guha-Majumdar, L., Niesen, P., & Kymlicja, W. (2022). Animal labour: a new frontier in interspecies justice? *Politics and Animals*, 8, 1–54.

Hamilton, C. L. (2019). *Veganism, sex and politics: tales of danger and pleasure*. Bristol: HammerOn Press.

Horta, A., & Albersmeier, F. (2020). Defining speciesism. *Philosophy Compass*, 15(11), 1–9. https://doi.org/10.1111/phc3.12708

Hunt, M. W. (2019a). Parental compromise. *Critical Review of International Social and Political Philosophy*, 25(2), 1–21. https://doi.org/10.1080/13698230.2019.1644582

Hunt, M. W. (2019b). Veganism and children: physical and social well-being. *Journal of Agricultural and Environmental Ethics*, 32(2), 269–291. https://doi.org/10.1007/s10806-019-09773-4

Intezar, Ackroyd and Sullivan. (in press). Bakhtin at the boundaries: exploring self-positionality in relation to socio-cultural ideologies. In K. Carriere (Ed.), *International Handbook on Cultural Political Psychology* (pp. xx–xx). Springer.

Ioannidou, M., Lesk, V., Stewart-Knox, B. et al. (2023). Feeling morally troubled about meat, dairy, egg, and fish consumption: dissonance reduction strategies among different dietary groups. *Appetite*, 107024. https://doi.org/10.1016/j.appet.2023.107024

Jahanbegloo, R. (2007). *Conversations with Isaiah Berlin*. London: Phoenix Press.

Jallinoja P, Vinnari, M., & Niva, M. (2018). Veganism and plant-based eating: analysis of interplay between discursive strategies and lifestyle political consumerism. In M. Boström, Micheletti, & P. Oosterveer (Eds.), *The Oxford handbook of political consumerism* (pp. 157–179). New York: Oxford University Press.

Kant, I. (1978). *Critique of practical reason*. Translated from the German by Lewis White Beck. Indianapolis: Bobbs-Merrill Educational Publishing.

Kennedy, E. H., Parkins, J. R., & Johnston, J. (2018). Food activists, consumer strategies, and the democratic imagination: insights from eat-local movements. *Journal of Consumer Culture*, 18(1), 149–168. https://doi.org/10.1177/1469540516659125

Kirsten-Effi, H., Seib-Pfeifer, L. E., Lüth, C. A. et al. (2020). Validation and application of a German version of the dietarian identity questionnaire: revealing

differences between omnivores, vegetarians, and vegans. *Food Quality & Preferences*, 86, 103988. https://doi.org/10.1016/j.foodqual.2020.103988
Klein, N. (2014). *This changes everything: capitalism vs. the climate*. New York: Simon and Schuster.
Ko, A. (2017). #AllVeansRock: the all lives matter hashtag of veganism. In A. Ko & S. Ko. (Eds.), *Aphro-ism: essays on pop culture, feminism, and black veganism from two sisters* (pp. 13–19). New York: Lantern.
Krattenmacher, J., Casal, P., Dutkiewicz, J. et al. (2023). Universities should lead on the plant-based dietary transition. *The Lancet Planetary Health*, *7*(5), e354–e355. https://doi.org/10.1016/S2542-5196(23)00082-7
Loughnan, S., Haslam, N., & Bastian, B. (2010). The role of meat consumption in the denial of moral status and mind to meat animals. *Appetite*, 55, 156–159. https://doi.org/10.1016/j.appet.2010.05.043
Luke, B. (1992). Justice, caring, and animal liberation. *Between the Species*, 8(2), 13. https://doi.org/10.15368/bts.1992v8n2.11
Lundahl, O. (2018). Dynamics of positive deviance in destigmatisation: celebrities and the media in the rise of veganism. *Consumption Markets & Culture*, 23(3), 241–271. https://doi.org/10.1080/10253866.2018.1512492
McIntyre, S. (2022). Veg(an) tales: vegan identity making in the United States. *Sprin Journal of Arts, Humanities and Social Sciences*, 1(6), 282–238. https://doi.org/10.55559/sjahss.v1i06.30
Milburn, J. (2022). Should vegans compromise? *Critical Review of International Social and Political Philosophy*, 25(2), 1–13. https://doi.org/10.1080/13698230.2020.1737477
Milburn, J. (2021). Zero-compromise veganism. *Ethics and Education*, 16(3), 375–391. https://doi.org/10.1080/17449642.2021.1927320
Moreno, L. A., Meyer, R., Donovan, S. M. et al. (2022). Perspective: striking a balance between planetary and human health-is there a path forward? *Advances in Nutrition*, 13(2), 355–375. https://doi.org/10.1093/advances/nmab139
Mosig, Y. D. (2006). Conceptions of the self in Western and Eastern psychology. *Journal of Theoretical and Philosophical Psychology*, 26(1–2), 39–50. https://doi.org/10.1037/h0091266
Narayanan, Y. (2018). Animal ethics and Hinduism's milking, mothering legends: analysing Krishna the butter thief and the ocean of milk. *Sophia*, 57(1), 133–149. https://doi.org/10.1007/s11841-018-0647-8
Oliveria, M. C. S. L. (2011). The Bakhtinian self and beyond: towards a dialogical phenomenology of the self. *Culture & Psychology*, 19(2), 259–272. https://doi.org/10.1177/1354067X13478988
Phua, J., Jin, V. S., & Kim, J. (2020). The role of celebrity endorsers' and consumers' vegan identity in marketing communications about veganism. *Journal of Marketing Communications*, 26, 813–835. https://doi.org/10.1080/13527266.2019.1590854
Pickett, S. (2021). Veganism, moral motivation and false consciousness. *Journal of Agricultural and Environmental Ethics*, 34(15), 1–21. https://doi.org/10.1007/s10806-021-09857-0
Plumwood, V. (2003). *Animals and ecology: towards a better integration*. Available online: https://openresearch-repository.anu.edu.au/server/api/core/bitstreams/4f5afcc2-6193-429d-89b0-5ee67d66f87f/content
Polish, J. (2016). Decolonizing veganism: On resisting vegan whiteness and racism. In J. Castricano & R. Simonsen (Eds.), *Critical perspectives on veganism* (pp. 373–392).

Basingstoke: Palgrave Macmillan. https://doi.org/10.1007/978-3-319-33419-6_17
Rosenfeld, D. L. (2018). The psychology of vegetarianism: recent advances and future directions. *Appetite*, 131, 125–138. https://doi.org/10.1016/j.appet.2018.09.011
Rosenfeld, D. L., & Burrow, A. L. (2018). Development and validation of the dietarian identity questionnaire: assessing self-perceptions of animal-product consumption. *Appetite*, 127, 182–194. https://doi.org/10.1016/j.appet.2018.05.003
Rosenfeld, D. L., & Burrow, A. L. (2017). The unified model of vegetarian identity: a conceptual framework for understanding plant-based food choices. *Appetite*, 112, 78–95. https://doi.org/10.1016/j.appet.2017.01.017
Saari, U.C., Herstatt, C., & Tiwari, C. (2021). The vegan trend and the micro foundations of institutional change: A commentary on food producers' sustainable innovation journeys in Europe. *Trends in Food Science & Technology*, 107, 161–167. https://doi.org/10.1016/j.tifs.2020.10.003
Sanders, C. (2008). Double-edged swords? Collective identities and solidarity in the environment movement. *The British Journal of Sociology*, 59(2), 227–253. https://doi.org/10.1111/j.1468-4446.2008.00191.x
Sanford, M., & Lorimer, J. (2022). Veganuary and the vegan sausage (t)rolls: conflict and commercial engagement in online climate-diet discourse. *Humanities and Social Sciences Communications*, 9(255), 1–13. https://doi.org/10.1057/s41599-022-01464-2
Scarborough, P., Clark, M., Cobiac, L. et al. (2023). Vegans, vegetarians, fish-eaters and meat-eaters in the UK show discrepant environmental impacts. *Nature Food*, 4, 565–574. https://doi.org/10.1038/s43016-023-00795-w
Schösler, H., de Boer, J., & Boersema, J. J. (2012). Can we cut out the meat of the dish? Constructing consumer-oriented pathways towards meat substitution. *Appetite*, 58(1), 39–47. https://doi.org/10.1016/j.appet.2011.09.009
Schouten, A. P., Janssen, L., & Verspaget, M. (2020). Celebrity vs. influencer endorsements in advertising: the role of identification, credibility, and product-endorser fit. *International Journal of Advertising*, 39(2), 258–281. https://doi.org/10.1080/02650487.2019.1634898
Shotwell, A. (2016). *Against purity: living ethically in compromised times.* Minneapolis: University of Minnesota Press.
Singer, P. (2011). *Practical ethics.* New York: Cambridge University Press.
Singer, P. (2009). *Animal liberation.* New York: Harper Perennial.
Singer, P. (1998). A vegetarian philosophy. In S. Griffiths and J. Wallace (Eds.), *Consuming passions: Food in the age of anxiety* (pp. 66–72). Manchester: Manchester University Press.
Sneijder, P., & Hedwig, F. M. (2004). 'Health should not have to be a problem': talking health and accountability in an internet forum on veganism. *Journal of Health Psychology*, 9(4), 599–616. https://doi.org/10.1177/1359105304044046
Sullivan, P. (2007). Examining the self-other dialogue through 'Soul' and 'Spirit.' *Culture & Psychology*, 13(1), 105–128. https://doi.org/10.1177/1354067X07073662
Taylor, A., & Taylor, S. (2020). Solidarity across species. *Dissent*, 67(3), 103–105. https://doi.org/10.1353/dss.2020.0071
The Vegan Society. (2019). Statistics. https://www.vegansociety.com/news/media/statistics#:~:text=Veganism%20in%20the%20UK,In%202018%2C%20the&text=The%20number%20of%20vegans%20in,150%2C000%20(0.25%25)%20in%202014. Accessed 20 December 2023.

The Vegan Society. (2021). Statistics. https://www.vegansociety.com/news/ media/statistics. Accessed 14 June 2024.

Tuttle, W. (Ed). (2019). *Buddhism and veganism.* Danvers: Vegan Publishers.

Vestergren, S., & Uysal, M. S. (2022). Beyond the choice of what you put in your mouth: a systematic mapping review of veganism and vegan identity. *Frontiers in Psychology*, 13, 1–12. https://doi.org/10.3389/fpsyg.2022.848434

Vettese, T. (2018). To freeze the Thames. *New Left Review*, 111, 62–86.

Willett, W., Rockstrom, J., Brent, L. et al. (2019). Food in the anthropocene: the EAT–lancet commission on healthy diets from sustainable food systems. *The Lancet*, 393(10170), 447–492. https://doi.org/10.1016/S0140-6736(18)31788-4

World Health Organization (WHO). (2015) 'Q&A on the carcinogenicity of the consumption of red meat and processed meat.' [Online 26th October 2015]. https://www.who.int/features/qa/cancer-red-meat/en/

Wrenn, C. L. (2017). Trump veganism: a political survey of American Vegans in the era of identity politics. *Societies*, 7(4), 32. https://doi.org/10.3390/soc7040032

Wright, L. (Ed.). (2019). *Through a vegan studies lens: textual ethics and lived activism.* Reno & Las Vegas: University of Nevada Press.

Wright, L. (Ed). (2018). Veganism studies and ecocriticism. *Special Cluster Interdisciplinary Studies in Literature and Environment*, 24(4), 737–802.

Wright, L. (2015). *The vegan studies project: food animals, and gender in the age of terror.* Athens: University of Georgia Press.

Yeh, H. Y. (2014). Voice with every bite: dietary identity and vegetarians. "The-Second-Best" boundary work. *Food, Culture, & Society*, 17(4), 591–613. https://doi.org/10.2752/175174414X13948130848502

2

POSITIONING THE *POLYPHONY*

Bakhtin: From Literature to the Social Sciences

Hopefully, as you will note by the end of this chapter, Bakhtin's writings and key concepts are forever shifting, and are intertwined in their meaning(s) (Morson and Emerson, 1990). This is not entirely surprising if we consider the full range of disciplines that have employed his work as conceptual and methodological scaffolding for underpinning research. Therefore, much like he professes in his writings, Bakhtin himself has also acquired a multiplicity of identities that permeates disciplinary boundaries between the Literary Studies, Humanities, Philosophy, and the Social Sciences. Before we move onto sketching out our onto-epistemology, I think it would be effective to address a pressing question for many: how do we reconcile the application of a literary theoretician to the human sciences? Perhaps because Bakhtin continually drew on literary sources, particularly Dostoevsky, to contextualise his abstract thinking, he has generally been associated with Literary Studies. In instances where academics from other disciplines have ventured into the Bakhtinian canon, their engagement has been limited to him facilitating the modernity versus postmodernity debate, depending on one's ideological inclination (Gardiner and Mayerfeld-Bell, 1998). Nonetheless, Bakhtin's earlier work, *Towards a Philosophy of Act* (TPA), is considerably philosophical, and the intellectual nucleus of his preceding works, such as, *The Problem of Dostoevsky's Poetics* (PDP), *The Dialogic Imagination* (DI), *The Problem with Speech Genres* (SG), and *Art and Answerability* (AA). In TPA, for instance, Bakhtin focuses on the abstract concepts of *Ethics* and *Aesthetics*, which explores our individual responsibilities towards others as human beings. TPA also foregrounds the *reciprocal dynamics* between art and life, which is later equated to a phenomenological

DOI: 10.4324/9781003384526-2

relationship between the *Author* and *Hero* in AA. Throughout his writings, Bakhtin argues for the distinction between two forms of existence, which help him permeate the boundaries between Literary Studies and Human Sciences: '*istina*' and '*pravda*.' While *istina* refers to theoretical truth(s), *pravda* is concerned with the non-theoretical moment(s) of truth between the *I* and *Others* who are now *concrete* and temporal individuals, and not simply an *Author* and a *Hero* within the pages of a novel. As Morson (1991) phrases it, for Bakhtin, 'genres themselves are forms of thought that have made valuable discoveries about time, society' (Morson, 1991: 1077). The multidisciplinary nature of Bakhtin's writings, and reading Bakhtin, offers an innovative insight into the boundaries between literature and the temporal world. For example, in addition to Dostoevsky, Bakhtin's works are also peppered with references to dramatic texts, particularly Shakespeare, when addressing the connection(s) between drama, society, and individual psyche: 'If one may speak of psychology here [within Bakhtin's commentary on the connection between theatre and society], then it is only of the "deep psychology" of life itself, the psychology of individuality as such' (Sandle, 2014: 523). This 'deep psychology' of the individual emerges and reveals itself within what Bakhtin terms as 'topographic gesture.' Here, I interpreter 'topographic gestures,' as a form of universal dialogical interactions, that

> locate the speaker [the *I*] within the whole of the cosmos but not in the universe studied by modern science, but rather in the concretely experienced, tangible space-time of human deeds and of the human body .... both tangibly present as levels of the medieval and Renaissance theater stage.
>
> (Sandle, 2014: 523)

What Bakhtin is referring to here is embodiment. What Shakespeare's actors depict, through their dialogical interactions, is how an individual consciousness manifests in a particular social time-space, and in order to understand said individual consciousness ('deep psychology') we need to analyse their dialogical relationships (*Dialogism*).

Sideward Glance

I would like to reiterate that *Dialogism*, or a dialogical methodology are applicable to both, a textual analysis, and a verbal conversation and or performance.

Developing a Bakhtinian Onto-Epistemology: As an Analytical Tool

Bakhtin defines *Dialogism* as a 'universal phenomenon, permeating all human speech and all relationships and manifestations of human life, everything that has meaning and significance' (Bakhtin, 1984: 40). In the next two sections, we will outline what *Dialogism* entails, and how it can be utilised as a practical methodological approach for textual analysis (such as interview transcripts) and used as a theoretical framework for conceptualising the *Self* and identity formation.

If we were to pick one quote that encapsulates the Bakhtinian canon, for me, it would be the following:

> I hear voices in everything and dialogic relations between them, and that focus of the human sciences should solely be the 'expressive and speaking being.'
>
> (Bakhtin, 1986: 169)

There are two noteworthy points alluded in the above quote, which are central to the overarching message of this project. First, that in a given social phenomenon, including individual consciousness, there is a presence and existence of another (the *Other*). Each of our *Utterances* not only hold *our* intensions, but are also endowed with the meaning-making of the *Others*; in this sense, an *Utterance* is also 'held to lie somewhere beneath or beyond the surface intention of its speaker or author' (Renfrew, 2015: 02). Importantly, said 'intensions' are continually in dialogue with each other. There is, therefore, a continual relationship between the *Self* and the *Other* on a linguistic plane. Second, that for an enriched understanding in social psychology, the human psyche, both individually and collectively, should be at the heart of psychological research. It is important to note that Bakhtin is not the sole intellectual sustainer of *Dialogism* and that he shares this accolade with Voloshinov, Mead, Vygotsky, Wittgenstein, and of course with the first proponent of a form of dialogism professed by Socrates. However, we will be undertaking a Bakhtinian approach. Indeed, in his ever-undulating concepts, the principle(s) of *Dialogism* are acknowledged as the golden-thread, which remains the constant locomotive within his intellectual canon (Holquist, 2002). *Dialogism*, then, refers to an *active* thinking, feeling, and being addressed (in conversation) and addressing others or multiple others (in conversation). Bakhtin recognises this process as one of *Addressivity* and *Answerability* (Bakhtin, 1990, 1986). *Utterances*, therefore, are distinct forms of 'living language' or describe anything that is said by the *Addresser* (*Author*) and *Addressee* (*Hero*) in a *dialogical* conversation:

> An utterance is never a reflection or an expression of something already existing and outside it that is given and final. It always creates something that never existed before, something that absolutely new and unrepeatable, and, moreover, it always has some relation to the value.
>
> (Bakhtin, 1986: 119–120)

Moreover, there is no limit to the length and form of an *Utterance*. They can be short as a single word or as long as a novel; it can be both spoken and written (Bakhtin, 1986; also see Renfrew, 2015), and all human interaction, must be understood in terms of *Utterances* (Bakhtin, 1986). An *Utterance*, or the word, therefore, is our unit of analysis, and the first link in the chain of our dialogical analysis. Furthermore, each dialogue, or dialogical interaction, consisting of *Utterances*, contains a *Voice*. Bakhtin (1984) defines *Voice* as an ideological position or value held by an individual, or the *Addresser* towards and *Addressee*. We will develop the role and position of the *Addresser* and *Addressee* in Chapter 3. Moreover, a *Voice* not only registers a certain 'intonation,' which provides texts and speech with a certain textual that coveys the *Addresser's* 'valuative attitude' towards the object they are referring to (Bakhtin, 1993: 32–33), but also contains *Speech Genres* (Bakhtin, 1986). For Bakhtin, *Speech Genres* are forms of *thinking*, and an insight into human experience.

If you have made it thus far into the chapter, I am sure you are beginning fully to recognise and appreciate the complexities that compose the Bakhtin's canon, and the intricacies involved in applying a dialogical methodology. To truly grasp Bakhtinian *Dialogism*, and apply it as a methodological stance, it is important for us to understand his notion of *Polyphony*, as for interactions to be truly dialogical they need to be polyphonic (Bakthin, 1984). Foregrounding the presence of *Polyphony* within lived experience(s) with Veganism is also a key endeavour in proceeding chapters, as it discloses the multiplicity of vegan identities. Akin to other Bakhtinian terminologies, the concept of *Polyphony* has also evolved and shifted depending on the text one reads. In *Problems with Dostoevsky's Poetics* (1984), for example, *Polyphony* is used to describe the *multi-voiced* nature of Dostoevsky's novels. It is also the opposite of *Monoglossia* where a text is *in-and-for-itself*; on other words, not *Polyphonic*. Considering our discussion in the previous section, it is not entirely surprising that, in *The Dialogic Imagination* (1981), *Polyphony* and *Monoglossia* transfer from a literary understanding of textual structure to a philosophical understanding of language and the formation of consciousness; *Monoglossia* refers to a more concrete complete 'whole' national language, which functions as building blocks for representing individual consciousness (Bakhtin, 1981: 66). Notably, novelistic structures of *Polyphony* and *Monoglossia* now describe structures in everyday language, life, and human consciousness. *Polyphony*, therefore, calls attention to the co-existence of a *plurality of Voices* that do not fuse into a single *Voice* within an *Utterance*, rather they exist in different registers, consequently generating a dialogic dynamism among them (Bakhtin, 1986, 1984). Finally, the *Speech Genres* within a *Polyphonic-form-of-thinking* (*Multivocality*) have the capacity for creating new truths (a *priori*) and shaping *Ideology*. *Speech Genres* within a *Polyphonic-form-of-thinking*, for instance, offer a change in authorial position(s), or an authorial *Voice*; remember, the whole point of *Polyphony* and, therefore, *Dialogism* is to offer the space to hear multiple *Voices*, opinions, and values. Hence, deconstructing the *'truth'* of an *Ideology* and presenting the potential and building blocks to shape a new one, or an altered version of one. We have already discussed the complexities of defining *Veganism* and vegan ideologies in Chapter 1. In the analysis chapters, *Speech Genres* are understood as *Polyphonic-form-of-thinking*, which offer an insight into understanding the different realms of individual experiences with *Veganism*. Specifically in terms of time, space, and place: the beginning, middle, and end of *Being* vegan. In the following section, we will cover how *Polyphonic Voices*, or existence of multiple *Voices* is a pivotal facet of the *Dialogical Self*.

Before doing so, however, I would like to exemplify not only how marginalised female *Voices* can be fore fronted with through a textual analysis, but also how a polyphonic text can encapsulate multivocality, I will analyse a Shakespearean text, *The Taming of the Shrew* (*The Shrew*) using *Dialogical* 'tools' to explore the text, particularly *Double-voiced* language. Additionally, to underscore the multivocality in the text of *The Shrew*, the section below also refers to excerpts from the anonymous text, *The Taming of A Shrew* (*A Shrew*), which supplements our argument on analysing *The Shrew* as a polyphonic piece of work. It is largely agreed that *A Shrew* was an inspectional source for Shakespeare and not a part of this canon (Sams, 1986).

Exemplifying a Polyphonic Analysis

The *Taming of the Shrew* is considered one of Shakespeare's early comedies, centring around marriage and male-female relationships within a patriarchal structure. A literal reading of the play would interpret the narrative as suggested in the title, the taming of a shrewish wife (Kate) by her husband (Petruchio). Drawing on Kate's 'final speech,' several twentieth-century scholars argue that upon their return Kate unconditionally obeys even Petruchio's most derogetory commands. From this interpretation, towards the end of the play, she is not simply an obedient woman and wife, she is acting as Petruchio's puppet, 'ventriloquising' the male stereotype of 'women's nature,' and men's expectation of what ideal wives ought to be. Boose (1991), however, points out that 'Ironically enough, if *The Shrew* presents a problem to male viewers, the problem lies in its representation of a male authority so successful that it nearly destabilises the very discourse it so blatantly confirms' (Boose, 1991: 179). Through a dialogical analysis, we can take this a step further and replace Boose's 'nearly' with totally. The reasons for this are the *Double-voiced* discourses readable within Kate's speech and her actions: words with a *Loophole*.

Sideward Glance

Here we outline the Bakhtinian definition of a word with a Loophole very briefly and will develop it further in this chapter in their simplest form; words with loophole prevent the finalisation of one's own words and another's words towards them. Hence, being recognised as *Double-voiced.*

The speech is 44 lines long and at the beginning Kate establishes a woman's supposed status in *'the chain of being'*: *'thy lord, thy king, thy governor'* (5.2.143). As the speech continues, however, the overemphasised and exaggerated declaration of male superiority *('thy life,' 'thy keeper,' 'thy head,'* and *'thy sovereign')* seems too grandiloquent to be taken seriously. Here speech begins to seem almost read as a form of satire The lines that follow appear to matter-of-factly list a woman's duty to her husband, and the consequences one faces when they refuse to do adhere to this duty. The ambivalence in Kate's words, however, increases as her preaching mixes religious and secular perceptions involving women. In her annotations on the play, Hodgdon (2010) proposes that the repetition of *'thy'* intensifies the force of Kate's speech. Having said that, what Kate is trying to reinforce with her multiple references to the word remains open to interpretation. I suggest that by using the word *'thy'* 13 times during her speech Kate is detaching herself from what she is saying. In other words, the wifely duties Kate outlines are applicable to others, such as Bianca (her sister), but not for her. For example, 'thy' is a possessive adjective corresponding to 'thou,' and in the second person, *'thou'* refers to 'ye,' 'you,' or 'yours' (Crystal and Crystal, 2002). In this context, Kate's line can be read as, 'your lord, your king, and your governor.' Thus, the repeated use of *'thy'* can be seen as a loophole through which Kate eludes the power of the other (her husband) to define her and her duties. Rather than include herself in her own statements, she questions them; the line, 'When *they* are bound to serve, love and obey,' is promptly followed by a question:

> *Why* are our bodies soft, and weak, and smooth,
> Unapt to toil and trouble in the world,
> But that our soft conditions and our hearts
> Should well agree with our external parts?
>
> (5.2.171–4, *emphasis added*)

The following lines, for the first time in the speech, Kate actually refers to herself:

> My mind *hath* been as big as one of yours,
> My heart as great, my reason haply more,

Read as a verb, *'hath'* can refer to the past tense; from this interpretation, Kate's mind had been as prideful as Bianca's (her once fair, now wayward sister). According to the *Oxford English Dictionary*, however, when read as an adjective *'hath'* or *'hathful'* can also mean scornful or mocking. Thus, reinterpreted in this light, one can argue that, similar to Bianca's, Kate's mind is scornful and mocking of the wifely duties she has just explained, and that her *'heart,'* which could be read as fighting spirit, is still potent and her mental reasoning even more so. The next few lines strengthen the argument of viewing the speech as a parody:

> Our strength as weak, our weakness past compare,
> That *seeming* to be most which we indeed least are.
>
> (5.2.180–1, *emphasis added*)

The use of the word 'seeming' (*Oxford English Dictionary* 3a) once again suggests a possible trace of ambiguity, irony or sarcasm in Kate's words.

Kate from *The Shrew* introduces another conditional clause or a *Loophole* into her speech: her hand is 'ready… *if* [Petruchio] please[s]' and '*may* it do him ease' (5.2.184–5, emphases added). Kate's use of the words 'may' and 'if' further suggests the ambiguous or open-ended nature of the final speech. The *Oxford English Dictionary* defines *'may'* as 'expressing ability or power,' therefore implying that Petruchio's *'ease,'* as Kate puts it, is indeed in her hand and she can withdraw that hand, and thus the ease, at will. We may perhaps, then, draw the conclusion from this that Kate is the one who has learned to deal with Petruchio rather than vice versa. Furthermore, in the case of actions, in contrast with *A Shrew*'s Kate's ultimate show of submission:

> And for a precedent I'll first begin,
> And lay my hand under my husband's feet.
> *She lays her hand under her husband's feet.*
>
> (14.141–2)

Kate from *The Shrew* introduces another conditional clause or a loophole into her speech: her hand is 'ready… *if* [Petruchio] please[s]' and '*may* it do him ease' (5.2.184–5, *emphases added*). Kate's use of the words 'may' and 'if' further suggests the ambiguous or open-ended nature of the final speech. The *Oxford English Dictionary* (*v^1* :15) defines 'may' as 'expressing ability or power,' therefore implying that Petruchio's 'ease,' as Kate puts it, is indeed in her hand and she can withdraw that hand, and thus the ease, at will. We may perhaps, then, draw the conclusion from this that Kate is the one who has learned to deal with Petruchio rather than vice versa.

Furthermore, even though Kate's hand is ready, in contrast to *A Shrew*, we are never entirely sure for what purpose. For example, *A Shrew's* Kate, as the stage directions make very clear, unequivocally 'lays her hand under her husband's feet.' With the lack of stage direction in the First Folio, however, and modern editions of *The Shrew*, it is not clear whether Kate actually performs the act of placing it under Petruchio's foot. Nevertheless, there is a range of interpretations we can draw from Petruchio's response: 'Why, there's a wench. Come on, and kiss me, Kate' (5.2.186). In some sense, Petruchio's 'Why' can be read as a predicate clause, which affirms Kate's status as a wench rather than a shrew because she has performed the act of placing her hand under his foot (see *Oxford English Dictionary* 5b). Many modern theatrical and screen adaptations, however, have chosen to show that Petruchio catches Kate's hand before she places it on the floor and demands a kiss instead. The noteworthy point here is the carnivalesque aspect of the language. In other words, the analysis above implies that, in contrast to *A Shrew*, the loopholes in Kate's speech make it more complex, as we can note contradicting accents in her *Voice*, thus generating a sense of unfinalisability.

Another factor that supports a carnivalesque reading is Kate's reaction to Petruchio's command that she throw her cap on the floor. Although most editors of *The Shrew* have followed Nicholas Rowe's (the first formal editor of Shakespeare) stage directions (*She pulls off her Cap and throws it down*), which presume that Kate has obeyed Petruchio's command, Shakespeare's First Folio contains *no* such stage directions (Moston, 1998). Judging by this, then, we cannot say for certain whether Kate obeys this particular command. Nevertheless, the meaning of 'cap' in Kate and Petruchio's relationship has changed or expanded since the symbol was first introduced into the discourse of the play. This underscores the theatricality of the whole taming plot. In Act 4, the cap raises the issue of who will decide which cap Kate will wear, and it stands for submission to her husband. Petruchio's command to dispose of Kate's cap – '*Katherine*, that cap of yours becomes you not: / Off with that bauble' (5.2.127–6), however, may instead be a sign that he is thereby liberating her from subordination to him. This could potentially imply, metaphorically at least, that he is 'winking' at her – urging her to give him a public display of obedience. At line 136, for instance, Petruchio addresses her by her chosen name: 'Katherine, I charge thee tell these headstrong women'; now that they have found equilibrium he asks the Kate from their first meeting to join him in carrying on the pretence (2.1.183). After her agreement to play along with him and deliver her final speech he reverts back to 'Kate' at lines 186–90: 'Come on, and kiss me Kate,' 'Come Kate, we'll to be.' Although, one could suggest that Kate's liberation is subject to Petruchio's will, rather than something she can exclusively attain, it is noteworthy that by addressing Kate with her preferred name, he is the first one to make peace. The potential reason for this could be that Petruchio's masculine reputation is subject to Kate's will, she can confirm his husbandry by lecturing the 'headstrong women' or refute it by remaining silent.

The final scene highlights women as being powerful rather than powerless and the male anxiety around harnessing this power. For example, prior to his command regarding the cap, Petruchio comments (5.2.125–6, *emphases added*):

> See where she comes, and brings your *forward* wives
> As prisoners to her *womanly persuasion*.

The noteworthy point I hope to have highlighted is that, at first reading the lines of the 'final speech,' generate negative monolithic meanings around the term '*womanly persuasion*' by suggesting that Kate is a prisoner to them. When we analyse the play under a *Dialogical* lens, however, the play's language holds a sense of ambiguity and open-endedness, and in doing so, foregrounds the *Polyphony* within a given text. Although defining the term *Dialogism* can be rather slippers, one aspect that remains consistent in the Bakhtinian understanding is that the meaning of an *Utterance*, or a *Word*, is not reducible to the intentions of the *Addresser*, nor is it dependent on the response of the *Addressee*. It not only emerges *between* the two (Holquist, 1981: 429–430) but is also an *addition* into the labyrinth of meaning(s) associate with a given *Word* or *Utterance*. Hence, as we move forward onto our analysis chapters, taking a *Dialogical* epistemology (Intezar and Sullivan, 2018) allows us to carve out a space for disclosing the *Polyphony* within the meaning-making process of social movements such as *Veganism*. It will also disclose the nuances within individual embodied and lived experiences.

Dialogism and Identity in Social Psychology: A Concept for Contextuality

In the previous section, we have outlined the use of *Dialogism* as an analytical tool, discussing the application of specific terminologies, which traditional psychological methodology may refer to as 'code' or 'themes,' within a given text. This section moves onto clarifying the framework applied for conceptualising the *Self* and identity throughout the analysis chapters, the *Dialogical Self*, which 'move beyond traditional egotism' in psychology (Bento, Cuncha, and Salgado, 2006: 21). If one was to propose a timeline, Psychology witnessed a 'dialogical turn' around the late 1990s, where *Dialogism* became a 'self-asserted' paradigm (Gillespie, 2010: 01). Specifically advocated by Markovà (2003a, 2003b) in terms of social psychology and relationship between the *Self* and *Other* in dialogical interaction. I would like to note here that there are a number of conceptual reiterations of the *Dialogical Self* in psychology (Olivera, 2013; Cresswell and Baerveldt, 2011; Salgado and Clegg; 2011; Sullivan, 2007; Hermans, 2004; Hermans and Kempen, 1993). The interpretation we adopt in this project does not strictly align with a specific iteration, rather, drawing on original texts, I etch my own understanding of the *Dialogical Self*, which does resonate with previous interpretations.

Positioning(s) of Identity in Contemporary Social Psychology

Much has been written about underpinning the psychology of identity, and although the fields of sociology and social psychology are most referred to in terms of identity research (Howard, 2000), scholars within the fields of anthropology and communication studies have also made significant contributions (Jung and Hecht, 2004; Mintz and DuBois, 2002). Despite its multidisciplinary nature, there is an overarching agreement in contemporary academia that, 'identity,' or 'identities,' are not singular and static. Traditionally, however, there are two major onto-epistemological positions in relation to researching identity. Abrams and Hogg (1999) argued that, with the stronghold of neuro-centric research methods in psychology, there has been a tendency for us to quantify even multidimensional concepts such as identity. Arguably, this could be an effect of subconsciously aligning with the Western traditions of thought and knowledge, where we feel that, for validity, all our explorations need to lead us to a *truth*. In his essay, *The Crooked Timber of Humanity*, Berlin (2013) described this as the West's obsession with *Monism*, which Bakhtin (1984) alludes to, in a rather accusatory manner, when he discusses it in the context of *Selfhood* and consciousness:

> The monist principle, that is, the affirmation of the unity of existence, is, in idealism, transformed into the unity of the conscious.
>
> (Bakhtin, 1984: 80)

In terms of identity, however, this particular thought structure is not sufficient, as 'Identity is never a *priori*, nor a finished product; it is only ever the problematic process of access to an image of totality' (Bhabha, 1994: 51). The second overarching onto-epistemological position derives from Mead's (1934) symbolic interactionism, and social constructionism (Leeds-Hurwitz, 2006). Traditional scholarship in social psychology has predominantly located identity within group membership (Tajfel, 1981). Since then, the psychological debate around the conceptualisation of identity is complex and multi-layered. Ting-Toomey (2010), for example, understands identity as 'the cultural, ethnic, societal, professional, relational, and individual images of self-conception' (Ting-Toomey, 2010: 455). Alternatively, others maintain that this is a limited interpretation, and that identity is not solely dependent on individual perceptions (Hecht, 2015; Hecht and Choi, 2012), but rather identity is 'inherently a communication process and must be understood as a transaction in which messages and values are exchanged' (Hecht, Jackson, and Ribeau, 2003: 230). Hecht posits that we talk our identities into existence through everyday rhetorical interaction. Our negotiations with others, therefore, have an integral function during our identity formation process. Essentially, as with the symbolic interactionist perspective, identity is anchored within communication, and is continually shaped and reshaped through personal and social experiences (Howard, 2000).

Sideward Glance

Although I have accredited the second onto-epistemological position to Mead (1934), I would also like to recognise that, Mead's pondering on Symbolic Interactionism, ultimately, derives from Husserl and his concept of Intentionality. Intentionality refers to the directness of mental experiences with a given object (symbol). For instance, one may think of or about an object or symbol. Intentionality also includes, and is sometimes seen as equated to, mental representations of an object. If you are interested in the Husserlian tradition and cognition, I would highly encourage you to read Dreyfus' (1982) Husserl, *Intentionality, and cognitive Science.*

The distinction between *personal* and *social* lived experiences proposes the existence of two separate cognitive schemas when conceptualising identity and identity formation. The first is 'group-schema,' and the second is 'self-schema' (Howard, 2000). While the former includes information about social expectations and norms, the latter refers to self-knowledge (one's personal characteristics and desires). It is through the symbolic interaction between our self-schema and group-schema, that we formulate and *negotiate our* identity and self-perception (Leeds-Hurwitz, 2006). Identity, therefore, can be perceived as both, a cognitive and affective understanding who and what one is, and by one's social roles, hence, one can adopt multiple identities. Moreover, individuals with multiple healthy identities have a higher life and health satisfaction, as multiple identities can help when one is in a static environment, as they can rely on another identity to strengthen their self-concept (McKenna and Bargh, 2000). However, what neither Hecht's and McKenna and Bargh (2000) concepts of identity do not acknowledge is the impact on one's self-perception if there is *tension between* one's multiple identities. In other words, *intra*-subjective tensions. Hecht (1993) refers to *external negotiations* with another, as does McKenna and Bargh (2000), but they do not elaborate to explain the impact if the negotiations, or tension, for attaining self-identity is *internal*. Talamo and Pozzi (2011), for instance, argue that identity and self-identity are a site for *inter-subjectivity*, or inward, and *inter-objective*, or outward (Moghaddam, 2003) tension. As discussed in Chapter 1, recent scholarship has shown that practising Veganism involves constant psycho-social negotiations (Buttny and Kinefuchi, 2020; Costa, Gill, Morda et al., 2019), which shapes one's identity, self-perception, and social networks (McDonald, 2000). Therefore, I propose that current identity theories, conceptually, underemphasise the exploration and importance of internal tensions. The *Dialogical Self* however, offers a framework for exploring the *inter*-subjective and *intra-subjective* identity tensions and negotiations.

Sideward Glance

Although you may already know the difference, I think it may be worth reiterating the difference between inter-subjective and intra-subject. The former, inter-subjective, refers to the process of meaning-making through interactions among individuals. The latter, intra-subjective, refers to meanings within the individual (within individual consciousness).

When writing about the *Self-Other* relationship, Bakhtin professes that:

> I am conscious of myself and become myself only while revealing myself for another, through another, and with the help of another.
>
> (Bakhtin, 1984: 287)

If I was to explain the quote above in one word, it would be *Outsideness*. Simply put, we perceive a sense of ourselves, our existence of *Being*, in relation to the *Other*. How we are seen and validated by the *Other* gives rise to our sense of consciousness. This is not to say, however, that individual consciousness, through a dialogical relationship with the *Other*, comes at the sacrificing of individual uniqueness. According to Bakhtin, there is no 'absolutely inconvertible relationship' between the *I* and the *Other*, and this is because the dialogical relationship between the *I* and *Other* is 'relative and convertible' (Bakhtin, 1990: 23). Essentially, one's consciousness and lived experience(s) are not concretely perceptible either by myself (*I*) or by another (*Other*); a reciprocal relationship between the two is pivotal. The section below will outline this process of *Self* and identity formation, as well as the retention of uniqueness. We will be referring to terminology such as *Utterance* and *Voice*, which by now, hopefully, you are becoming familiar with.

A Bakhtinian (1986, 1984, 1981) model of *Self* and identity hinges on the *tension* between *Voice(s)* that are representations of values (of the *Other*) within an individual's (the *I*'s) social discourse, through which they co-construct their identity and *Self*. We are sizeably influenced by the dominant ideological discourses (*Voices*) within the language of our given society (Bakhtin,

1986). Simultaneously, however, the individual *processes over* social ideological discourses (or *Voices*), which take on the semblance of one's own 'individual accents' (Bakthin, 1986: 86). In other words, social *Voices* are not passively accepted by the individual, rather, these *Voices* are *merged* with individual accents to create individual *Utterances.* A dialogical approach to identity not only draws our attention to the responses of the *Other* but also to our own embodied response to them. More uniquely, the 'individual accents' within our *Utterances* give form to something unrepeatable in what Bakhtin calls only 'once-occurrent event[s] of Being' (Bakhtin, 1993: 02). There are two exclusive events that occur during these moments. The first is that we fleetingly express and disclose our own distinctive *Self* and form our relational dynamics with the *Other* and our social structures. The second is that in such moments we also have the potential of *reshaping* the existing historical connotations and values embedded within a given *Utterance.* For example, the *Utterance* and the *Voice* rooted within words such as Veganism (or vegan ideology); practices and ideologies that shape the way in which we relate to ourselves, each other, and outer phenomenological structures. For a more detailed discussion on the reciprocal relationship between the mean-making of Veganism and the practitioner, please see Chapter 1.

Returning to our earlier discussion on the *Dialogical Self.* Thus far, we have established that the *Self* and identity are not only co-constructed but are also a dialogical experience of *multiple voices* (*Dialogism*). The *Self*, therefore, functions as a complex, *multi-voiced Self*, and does not adhere to concrete universal structures (Smythe and Jorna, 1998). In essence, the human mind is heteroglossic in nature, and forms during the ongoing tempestuous dialogical interaction between the *I* and *Other*. Moreover, this dialogical interaction of the *Self* is conserved within an interdependencies tri-matrix between the *I-for-myself*, the *I-for-other*, and the *Others-for-me* (Bakhtin, 1990). It is essential to note that, neither component exist in isolation, nor are they inanimate. They interact in a reflexive dialogue which *continually* re-shapes one's identity, sense of embodiment, and self-perception.

> dialogicality and dialogical subjectivity are not concerned with the *Ego* and *Alter* as abstract or schematic notions but with their *concrete manifestations*, for example, with the self versus another self, the self versus group, the group versus another group, the self versus culture and so on.
>
> (Marková, 2006: 125, *emphasis added*)

There is general consensus among Bakhtinian scholars that, in *Dialogical* onto-epistemology, there is an undeniable interdependence between the *Self* and *Other*. Marcovà (2006, 2003a) dubs this the *Ego-Alter* dynamics: 'Ego-Alter exists only within the realm of communication' (Marcovà, 2003a: 257). There is, however, a divergence in terms of the nature of the *I-for-myself* and the relationship between the *I* and *Other*.

Sideward Glance

Unless you are already familiar with the terms, I think it may be worth defining the concepts of *Ego* and *Alter* in psychology. In a nutshell, they can be interpreted as synonyms of the *I* and *Other*.

Dialogical subjectivity is not reducible to the *I* versus *Other*, where the *I* '"taking the role of the other" or the *Ego* being solely an actor in that interdependent relation' (Marcovà, 2006: 01). Instead, it is *reciprocal*, as examined by Hermans (2001), who conceived it as multiple symbolic and social representations that the *I* holds in relation to the *Other* and vice versa. Hermans (2001) coins this as collective *Voices* in the *Self*. Alternatively, dialogical scholars have also focused on dialogical subjectivity as involving *inter*-subjectivity, and have coined it as *the other-in-the-self* (Salgado and Ferreira, 2004). As Marcovà (2006) notes, the *Dialogical Self* has amounted to encapsulating a variety of meanings and different scholars have adopt different perspectives of dialogicality as an epistemology (see Linell, 2005).

The onto-epistemological position of the *Dialogical Self* appropriated in this project is as follows: the concrete person (the *I*) does not recede and is not *tabula rase* (*a la* Skinner). Instead, the *I* only gains meaning and creates meaning in a dialogical relationship with an *Other*. Likewise, the *Other* is also only meaningful in terms of a dialogically constituted counter-partner with the *I*. The *I-for-myself* (inner individual consciousness) becomes aware of the essential need of the *Other-for-me* (others in one's environment). As identity is a co-constructed and reciprocal process, the *I-for-myself* (the *I*) is equally needed by the *Other*. Therefore, the *I-for-other* generates re-shaping potential, by disrupting one's own ontological subjectivity. In other words, every time one enters a *dialogical* relationship with the *Other*, to construct the *Other's* identity and self-perception, the *I* exposes itself to the possibility of ontological change (the altering of one's identity and self-perception). An individual attains their identity and self-perception as they discover the *Other* either in *embodied* conversation between themselves and *Others*, or through *internal* dialogue between *Others' Voice(s)* and their own inner *Voice* (*I-for-myself*). The attitudes of *Others* that we interact with affect our conduct and self-perception, and vice versa. This potential shaping and re-shaping of one's identity and self-perception, not only distinguishes Bakhtin from other dominant identity theorists in social psychology, but also suggests that, during tension filled interactions, individuals experience *Threshold-moments* (Bakhtin, 1981). *Thresholds* are moments of *transitions and action*, where crisis events occur, and individuals must make *decisions* on how to *act*, or *postupok*, as favoured by Bakhtin, which ultimately impact identity and self-perception. The *Threshold-moment* contextualises two aspects overlooked by McKenna and Bargh (2000) and Hecht (1993): the *plurality* of individual lived experience, and that the identity *negotiations* between the *Self* and *Other* can be harmful. As explored in the analysis chapters, the interaction between the *I* and *Other*, within *certain* vegan ideologies, is monolithic or consisting of a 'single and unified' *Voice* (Hays, 2005: 9). I argue that the encounter(s) with a monolithic vegan *Voice*, where no alternate *Voice* is acceptable, places individuals practising Veganism on a *Threshold-moments*. The following chapters, therefore, have been structures to represent the three major *Threshold-moments* experienced by the interviewees: the period of *Becoming* vegan, the period of *Being* vegan, and the period after *leaving* Veganism. We also will continue to develop and explain Bakhtin's concept of *Dialogism* as we continue our analysis.

Methods

Recruitment

During the period of the global Covid-19 pandemic and 2024, I carried out in-depth semi-structured interviews. Each interview ranged between 30 and 90 minutes. A purposive sampling strategy was applied as participants were recruited with a pre-selected inclusion criterion; for example, at the time of the interview, participants needed to identify as 'former-vegans' for their experience and insight to align with the main aim of the project (Bergin, 2018; Blankenship, 2010). In terms of additional inclusion criteria, I deemed anyone 18 years old and above eligible to take part, however, anyone with a diagnosis of an eating disorder or dementia were not eligible to take part. Although the project was advertised on a global online platforms, all the participants that came forward can be considered from Western countries. Moreover, during the recruitment process, no particular emphasis was placed on demographic characteristics such as gender, ethnicity, occupation, and age, as, for richer data, I aimed to recruit a diverse population sample as possible. I chose to collect data through semi-structured interviews, as interviewing is one of the most effective methods for exploring the depth and nuances of my participants' opinions and personal experiences (Bergin, 2018). Similarly, the interviewing process offered the opportunities for fluid discussion, while remaining topic focused, which is more likely to take place during a one-to-one setting (Grow and Christopher, 2008). This was vital as before the interviewer began some participants revelated that they were initially very hesitant to come forward due to the nature of the research and thought that the posted research flyer may have been a 'fake,' or indeed, a 'trolling' tactic. An overall element of suspicion was also evident in the fact that a significant number of individuals expressed interest in the project, both vegan and non-vegan, and several informational emails were exchanged, however, only ten participants agreed to be interviewed. Keeping this in mind, for rapport building with the participant (Smith, 2019), and to reduces any 'power' dynamics that may occur in other approaches such as focus groups, I explained my motivations behind the research project, by relaying that I had also practised Veganism for a year, out of anthropological curiosity, which tended to receive nods of approval and appreciation.

The opening question were: 'how were you introduced to Veganism, or became aware of the dietary lifestyle?' This allowed participants to reflect, gather their thoughts, and bring their focus to the research topic (Richie, Lewis, and McNaughton et al., 2013). In order to encourage a detailed reflexive response, further prompts included: 'Could you tell me more about your thinking,' and 'How do you mean, can you expand on that' (Engward and Coldspink, 2020; Smith, Flower, and Larkin, 2009). Considering the research questions and the theoretical underpinnings, the interview questions were designed to explore the three aforementioned *Threshold-moments*: the beginning (*Becoming* vegan), the middle (*Being* vegan), the end (*leaving* Veganism). The ethical aspects of interviewing were also considered. Ethical points, for instance, were constantly reflected on during the data collection process, such as the well-being of the participant during the interview process. As mentioned in Chapter 1, discussions around food and eating habits can be a sensitive area of discuss, especially with diets such as Veganism, which can hold ethical and emotional values (Greenebaum, 2012a). Questions around identity and self-perception, therefore, were not asked directly, to ensure that participants were not uncomfortable. The phrasing of the questions was also kept neutral, an essential part of ethical research. During the interviews, I also paid constant attention to their tone of *Voice* and body language for signs of distress.

One of the aims of this monograph is to carve out a space for the passionate and multi-layered *Voices*, and narratives of the participants who took part in this study, as they moved through their vegan identities. Therefore, I think it is practical for me to 'introduce' you to the participants, even if it is only on the page. You will note that, for some participants, their demographic information is missing. This was because, as stated above, gathering demographic information was not an essential part of the project, however, was noted when participants chose to disclose it freely. The pen portraits presented below aim to capture an overview of the multifaceted nature of an individual's lived and embodied experience with and *within* Veganism. Hence, showcasing the complexities of personal identity, collective identities, and evolving perspectives. The purpose is to go beyond basic demographic information and outline a more nuanced understanding of the interviewees' interests, backgrounds, and experiences, which are developed further in the analysis chapters.

Participant Pen Portraits

Orlando

Orlando was the first interviewee, at the time of the interview, he resided in Mexico, and lived with his family. In total, Orlando had practised Veganism for two years, and had stopped six months prior to the interview. Orlando recollected that, in 2018, he was beginning to choose a career path, and was interested in health and nutrition. This also acted as one of the factors for his interest in Veganism. Towards the end of the interview, each participant was asked two question particular questions: (1) *'is there anything else you would like to share about your experience?'*; (2) *'If you had to sum up your experience with Veganism in one word, what would it be?'* Orlando wished to *Voice* two particular aspects of his journey. First, he revealed that his family, particularly his mother, had been very supporting of his lifestyle choices. He also mentioned that one of the major turning points for him to stop being vegan was the passing of his grandma:

> I think it will have been different because when I decided that I will be non-vegan again was when my grandma died, so if Covid hadn't happened maybe my grandma will still be here. But I was feeling bad, okay? So maybe my transition to a non-vegan will have been longer… Yes. But I don't think I will have been vegan if Covid hadn't happened.

Second, Orlando also wanted to clarify that during *his* journey he developed unhealthy eating patterns:

> Well I think another important thing maybe is that when, as I told you I wanted to lose weight when I started being vegan. I think I developed an eating disorder, so I think like that veganism was something to mask my eating disorder, to eat less or if something gave me food I will say "no thank you, I'm vegan" but it was because I was afraid of eating food, you know?

He expressed that this may have been because his local vegan community 'tend to separate foods into good and bad foods.' During, and after the interview, however, Orlando felt that he had a far more balanced relationship with food. When asked to summarise his experience in one word, Orlando responded with the following: '*I don't know. Maybe problematic.*'

Leigha

At the time of the interview, Leigha was in the process of studying an online MSc in *Psychology* and resided in Canada. Leigha recalled that she initially became interested in food when she was at school, '*from an assembly that a teacher did at school where he kind of likened food to the petrol or the fuel that you would put in a car so like what you put in your body.*' Her awareness of Veganism followed around 2012, once she began engaging with documentaries on health and well-being. In 2012, after university, Leigha also completed an online diploma in nutrition, and initially abstained from consuming meat as a challenge for Lent. Leigh also revealed that she has always been a picky eater: '*I don't know if you would say it's like a bit obsessive about food.*' For example, being cautious about eating certain meats, she travelled to Japan in 2016 to teach English, where her interest in nutrition shifted to the background. However, her interest in Veganism was reignited once she met the member of a local vegan group and was invited to meetings: '*I met this lady at a café, and it was just very random exchange but she sort of started that interest again.*' In its entirety, Leigha was vegan for three weeks, or as she phrased it, '*It was short-lived in a way compared to a lot of people.*'

> I suppose a final point is just to, it would be interesting to see how many people have ignored those feelings, whether they've had those, you know, because they're so much wanting to keep part of the community and the group yet their body didn't feel very good and I'm sure it's kind of under-reported, you know, because of the want to be part of the group and the community.

One of the reasons why Leigha's journey was short lived was due to health issues (see Chapter 3). When asked, '*If you had to sum up your experience with Veganism in one word, what would it be?,*' she mentioned that she was curious about others' experience.

Cordelia

The interview with Cordelia was particularly interesting, she had bought notes to the interview and was very detailed in her reflections. This was the longest interview and lasted approximately 90 minutes. At the time of becoming aware of Veganism, Cordelia was residing in the UK and '*still living at home with my mum and my stepdad at the time so I was quite excited to share the information ... so I didn't get a negative pushback from them.*' Although Cordelia's mother enjoyed '*playing Devil's advocate,*' she was agreeable: '*well actually-well actually, you know, so she was like okay, well if that's what you want to do and I think she trusted that because I like to research things deeply she thought well she must have really looked into this... I'm quite a headstrong person so I would have done it anyway but yeah.*' Chapter 3 explores Cordelia's research experience in more detail. She also continued to explain that her dad was already '*quite plant based heavy anyway,*' and felt that he had been '*a bit indoctrinated by the ideology that eating loads of plants is really good for you.'* Also, although he had reduced his meat intake, he remained cautious about Veganism: *'he was like, ooh you know, I'd never go vegan myself, I think veganism's a bit extreme but it's good that you're going more plant-based.'* In total, Cordelia practised Veganism for two years and had been post-veganism for three months: *'I think at my age, how old was I then, 21/22 when I turned vegan.'* It's also noteworthy that, since leaving Veganism, Cordelia had also encouraged her partner, who had also gradually become vegan after meeting Cordelia, to re-consider his vegan journey:

> … the day I said I'm not being vegan anymore, I said look, here's what I've learnt, please join me because I want you to get better, I'll cook it all for us and everything, I'm sorry, I explained and he found the transition more difficult than me, even though he'd been vegan less time … so moving back to a better connection with your food was difficult for him.

When asked, *'is there anything else you would like to share about your experience?'* and *'If you had to sum up your experience with Veganism in one word, what would it be?'* Cordelia was passionate in her response: *'I wanted to be vegan forever … I had every intention of doing it forever. One word. One word would honestly be "enlightening", it's been incredibly enlightening.'* She also expressed that she did not wish to be biase, as she was *'not vegan anymore.'* Nonetheless, she still wanted to try and be educational for others considering Veganism. She was happy to function as an 'anecdotal' case study to encourage others to consider different experiences with Veganism *'from another perspective and say, you know, look at both sides, really consider both sides … I'd just hate to think that I hadn't tried to educate someone on the other side of the coin.'*

Kate

The interview with Kate was the shortest, with several pauses throughout, and some inaudible speech. She started the interview with mentioning that: *'Yeah, even now like I still get like memory, my memory's still not that great, sorry if I like pause too long, I'm like trying to think.'* Her initial interest in Veganism was sparked at school. At the time of the interview, Kate had practised Veganism for seven years, and had been post-veganism for six months: *'So total, I don't know if I want to count like my age from 15 to 18 because it was on and off, so 18 till 25, so 18, 19, 20, 21, 22, 23, 24, 25, I say seven years.'* She clarified that she could not peruse Veganism completely between the ages of 15 and 18 as she was living at home and was financially dependent on her family who were not supportive of her diet. Once Kate turned 18, she remained at home, however, she became financially independent, which allowed her to become vegan, despite the disapproval of her family: '*I was 18 I was able to afford my own stuff because I got a job.*' When Kate turned 20, she moved out of the family residence and '*lived with relatives*' who were somewhat supportive: '*they would like buy stuff for me, but they weren't not [pause] and they would always make fun of me for being vegan.*'

Moreover, at 25, Kate was in Higher Education, going through '*career changes*' and in the process of making '*big life decisions,*' and '*trying to succeed.*' She was residing with her partner, who, interestingly, was still vegan: '*so he's still vegan, and then my partner's sister's family, they're mostly vegan, his sister eats like fish and eggs every now and then.*' Kate also reflected that during her vegan journey she was the '*militant vegan,*'

> I definitely was the, the like the veganism, the vegan that like, the leader with my friends and I would like [pause] them to go vegan and so, and they were really, they liked the idea and a lot of them did try to go vegan, and my best friend she was vegan, she went fully vegan with me, it was just them, but then [pause] *they all fell off before I did.*

Kate's use of the word, '*fell*' is noteworthy in itself as it implies that moving away from Veganism, or *Being* vegan equates to a lapse in moral standing. When asked, '*is there anything else you would like to share about your experience?*' and '*If you had to sum up your experience with Veganism in one word, what would it be?*' Kate stated that: '*My experience, it was, honestly this is going to sound really mean, but it was felt kind of like a cult .... I'm glad I'm not vegan anymore.*'

Regan

The interview with Regan, and her general experience with Veganism, was significantly different than with other interviewees. At the time of our conversation, Regan resided in Hawaii and felt that she '*grew up in quite a, liberal upbringing,*' as she perceived Hawaii to be the '*forefront of liberalism.*' Hence, animal ethics as environmentalism were concept that had been embedded within her phenomenology ('*we would talk about like morals and ethics and, you know, conservation and those sorts of things in school*'), and several of her friends were '*vegetarian from birth.*' She did not class herself as '*an activist,*' but did identify as '*a young person who's politically active.*' In total, Reghan had practiced Veganism twice: initially when she had been 17 and then for the second time once she had left university. Regan explained that one of her school friends, who had been vegetarian, became vegan once she had: '*she had become vegan after I had been vegan, after, yeah, so she did convert to veganism shortly after, I guess.*' Regan's drive for *Becoming* vegan had always been 'moralistic,' and I found her use of the word '*convert*' poignant which is discussed further in Chapter 6. In terms of wider support, she explained that:

> I didn't have too much in the way of family and I've always been quite independent, so I've been cooking my own food since I was about 6 years old.

Hence, her family was '*mostly supportive, yeah, indifferent.*' Regan eventually stopped *Being* vegan due to health reasons. When asked, 'is there anything else you would like to share about your experience? and *'If you had to sum up your experience with Veganism in one word, what would it be?'* Regan's response was, '*I think it's more of like a philosophical debate than more of like an actual like pragmatic and like practical approach to eating.*' This is reflective of the argument outlined by Dutkiewicz and Dickstein (2021), as discussed in Chapter 1. Once again, we will return to this line of though in Chapter 6.

Portia

At the time of the interview, Portia resided in Canada, and lived with her family. In total, she had been vegan for two years, and had stopped *Being* vegan for two years prior to the interview. Similar to a number of other interviewees, Portia had practices Veganism twice:

> I went vegan briefly when I was 16, and that lasted only about two months, but then I went, so the second time around that's when it lasted longer, that was when I was in second year university …

When she became vegan for the first time, Portia explained that it was due to social media fitness and beauty influencers, and that during that period she was exceedingly impressionable: '*when I was young I was very, I'm still fairly impressionable but when I was a teenager I was very, very impressionable.*' Although she had several vegetarian friends, during her vegan journey, Portia relayed that she experienced a number of emotional tensions with her family and cultural heritage: '*from my culture we eat a lot of meat, so I'm Hungarian and it's a very big base of the food, so it wasn't very well received in my family at all.*' Portia continued the explain that, when she became vegan at 16, she,

> … went back to Europe to visit my family, and since I was younger I wasn't really in a position where, not to like say I couldn't make my own food or go shopping, I definitely could, I just wasn't responsible enough at that time where I could commit to eating vegan while I'm visiting my family in Europe, so I just stopped [laughs].

The second time Portia chose to become vegan was strictly due to moralistic views, and she explained that this was probably why she continued *Being* vegan for a longer period of time, despite experiencing health issues. When asked, '*is there anything else you would like to share about your experience?' and 'If you had to sum up your experience with Veganism in one word, what would it be?'* Portia recalled that it '*was a learning curve, I think I learned a lot about like what my body likes, what I like to eat ... I think I would say that I'm just like an individual and I don't have to follow.*' Portia regaining a sense of individuality is explored further in Chapter 5 through a dialogical lens.

Bianca

The interview with Bianca was illuminating for a number of reasons. It was evocative of the curious 'final statement' remark from Leigha, '*it would be interesting to see how many people have ignored those feelings ... of honouring what your body whats.*' As discussed in Chapters 4 and 5, Bianca's journey of being vegan was fraught with tension, indeed her one word summarise her experience with Veganism was, 'struggle.' For instance, Bianca was very candid about both her mental *('every single night, if I even managed to get to sleep, I would think about dying')* and physical experiences *('I was having heart palpitations as well and they started to get more and more frequent')*. In total, Bianca had been vegan for six years and had been post-vegan for three months. At the time of the interview, she resided in Australia with her partner, who had also gradually become vegan (*'shortly, shortly after we'd been living together, yeah, he just decided that one day he was just vegan, like he just sort of like, "Yeah, I'm vegan now"'*), but had also live in London. Notably, when Biance decided to stop being vegan, her partner remained vegan but was supportive of her decision: '*Erm... so, yeah, I think he was on board with it, because he kind of just wanted me to get better.*'

Although Bianca's initial interest in Veganism began due to health driven motivations. However, the longer her vegan journey continues, and she began to engage with vegan social media, Bianca's motivations gravitated towards animal ethics, and ethical algaculture was still an essential value for her.

> So, yeah, so we sourced it from a local fishmonger and I'd, I even went so far as to like dig into like his Facebook page, his website, and like I was trying to find like all of these little details to make sure it wasn't, you know, like fish farms and things like that ...

Towards the end of her interview, Bianca mentioned that she did not want her vegan journey to be, '*all for nothing, basically.*' And that if she could speak to her former self, or anyone interested in becoming vegan, that they should '*just research*' and not to '*just research the good stuff about it,*' but also to explore and acknowledge '*all the bad stuff about it so that you know both sides. And then you can really make your own decision.*'

Goneril

Arguably, the interview with Goneril was a good representation of Bianca's point about '*doing research*' that also includes all the '*bad stuff*' before making one's decision about '*eating vegan.*' Although, notably, this sentiment was not limited to Bianca. Goneril recalled that her motivations to become vegan, to a certain degree, were environmental and a challenge for herself. She went on to explain that she was a long-distance runner and the positive health discourse surrounding Veganism was another reason why she became interested in the dietary life-style. For example, Goneril explained that, in her opinion, '*A lot of people say it's like quite culty and I do agree,*' which she explained was '*really appeal[ing] to like my generation that's, … that's just very, very fixated on climate change and environmental impact, as we should be.*' She continued to explain that once she had become vegan her athletic performance began to drop:

> I thought I, like I didn't really realise that it was up to what I was eating, I thought it was something else. I didn't, I really didn't feel great, like I got quite ill, like I lost my period for like half a year and I just was always thinking about food …

Goneril also expressed a discontentment with the lack of, or lack of accessibility to, academic and scientific research on the negative impacts of a plant-based diet:

> Oh, absolutely not. Absolutely not. There's like zilch out there, like maybe I saw a couple of articles about your periods stopping because of veganism, which happens to a lot of people, which is not a good sign, like people can ignore it and say, oh it's fine, this is part of the diet, it's like no, it's your body telling you like you can't sustain a pregnancy, that like you could go infertile, it's not safe. I think that there's just not enough information about it, there's like all of these like green websites saying benefits of going vegan, like cost analysis of vegan but there just is not enough information about like health impacts and stuff like that.

Interestingly, Goneril also mentioned that, unlike others she had read about on social media, she did not feel any emotional side-effects such as depression or heightened anxiety, generally and around food. She went on to explain that she stopped being vegan once she returned home for the seasonal period and her mother intervened.

> Oh my God, my mum spent like a week just being like have milk, have cheese. I think we had, I think we had like sausages and it was just the best thing ever and I was just, yeah. It was just like no, you're not doing this anymore …

When asked to summarise his experience in one word, Goneril chose 'confusing': *'I think confusing. Confusing, I think that's it.'* She expanded on this by explaining that, while being vegan, she was continually questioning herself *'why has this happened* [decline in health],' even thought she was eating the *'healthiest [she'd] ever eaten.'* Finally, although she would not deter anyone else from pursuing a vegan diet, she would urge them to *'understand that it just doesn't work for everybody, like some people just can't sustain it.'*

Puck

At the time of the interview, Puck was living independently. The factors of living independently and also being financially independent were significant in Puck's vegan journey, and this is something that is discussed further in Chapter 6. Puck had been vegan for six years and post-vegan for six months. When asked how he was introduced to Veganism, they reflected that they were 16 the first time '*the seed was planted*,' through vegan documentaries and certain Channels in her YouTube recommendation list:

> my young brain was like, you know what, I like this, I really like this, it really resonates with like my morals and everything, so I was like binge watching YouTube.

The discourses of animal ethics and morality were key factors of Puck deciding to become vegan. He also mentioned that his decision was almost instantaneous: '*like, okay, let's go for it, and it was cold turkey, I gave up everything like immediately, and it was just very sudden.*' Puck mentioned that, overall, his immediate family was not supportive of his decision: *'I tried to like talk to my family about it, and reasonably so they were like, that sounds unhealthy, like don't do that.'* Nonetheless, as Puck was ethically motivated, he chose to become vegan regardless, and found it a *'pretty alone'* experience. Moreover, the aspect of 'vegan privilege,' in terms of finance, also came through strongly during Puck's interview. Especially in terms of their employability, or lack thereof, during the Covid-19 global lockdowns. I acknowledge that the concept of 'vegan privilege' is highly contested within certain academic circles (Greenebaum, 2016). The purpose of our discussion, however, is to foreground individual experiences with *Being* Vegan, and not necessarily a commentary on the use of concepts such as 'vegan privilege.' Nonetheless, we will explore the definitions of the term further in Chapter 6.

When asked, *'If you had to sum up your experience with Veganism in one word, what would it be' and 'is there anything else you would like to share about your experience?'* Puck chose the word 'complicated,'

> Complicated *[laughs]*. It was complicated for a lot of reasons, if I had to pick a statement … morally it's complicated, ethically it's complicated, it's complicated to learn how to make food that doesn't involve meat dairy and eggs, and it's even more complicated coming back to it, you know, there's just so many reasons.

After a pause, Puck also wished to emphasise that their being vegan, '*taught [them] a lot about compassion*.' He was grateful for learning about factory farming, however, did not thing he should have been exposed to it '*at a young age*'; especially as several of the vegan documentaries he engaged with used highly emotive language. For example, Puck went on to reflect on the detrimental emotional impact certain phrases had on them while they were engaging with pro-vegan social media at an impressionable phase in their life:

> this bothers me now that I'm an adult, but like when I was 16 I didn't think so far into it, but like the use of the words like slavery, and like comparing like the Holocaust to the factory farming, it's just so messed up. The word, oh I hate this, the word, they use the word rape talking about the dairy industry, and like because of my life I was like, whoa, I can't do that to somebody else, like that's horrible. But like just those very like bad buzzwords, they really get into your skin.

Despite the obstacles, the most positive aspect Puck took aways from being vegan was mindfulness: *'when consuming animal products, and I do think it helps me consume those more mindfully.'*

Gertrude

One aspect that set the conversation with Gertrude apart from others was her situational time-space, in the sense that she, at the time of the interview, tentatively referred to herself as a 'stay at home mom' (the other being the fact that the interview took place during an insurrection in the United States and Getrudes exclamation that, '*One of the protestors is on Nancy Pelosi's desk right now*'): '*I'm now a stay at home, I don't know if you'd call it stay at home mom, I don't know what we call them. I'm certainly not the most domestic [laughs].*' Familial responsibilities meant that she could not wholly commit to being vegan: '*I still think if I were living by myself I would probably be, if not 100%, mostly vegan. But I do not live by myself and I do not have control over a lot of the situations.*' Her geographical location also proved to be an obstacle in terms of accessibility to vegan product:

> I live in A *[laughs]*, everyone eats meat all the time, do you know how many steakhouses we have here, you can't go a block without hitting a steakhouse *[laugh]*, and G, I lived in G, like churches in G, steakhouses here *[laughs]*.

Although Gertrude reflected that she did not practise Veganism '*long enough for it to be an integral part of [her] identity*,' in comparison to other interviewees, not being '*100% vegan*' was exceedingly difficult for her and her sense of *Self*. Gertrude felt that she ought to be committing to being vegan, however, could not and, to a certain degree, was able to reconcile her internal quibble: '*I want to take care of my husband who's a hardcore carnivore … I can only handle so much and right now I'm focusing on my family*' Gertrude's intra-subjective tensions are discussed in Chapter 6 at length.

> Yeah, I think I probably would be by this point a hard-core vegan who would never even consider a different lifestyle, if I had started this when I was 18 I think I probably would have gone in a far different direction, and been much less flexible, you know, I have to live in a grey, a world of grey, not white and black, but I think I would prefer *[laughs]*, some part of my brain prefers that, I could live in a black and white world, where I could make these decisions and say, this is right, and this is wrong.

When asked to sum up her experience, Gertrude felt that it could not be summarised in a single word, however, did highlight the perils of social media (see Chapter 5). The quote above encapsulates her thoughts about her experience if her situational time-space has been different.

Data Analysis

Now that we have determined our unit of analysis, the *Utterance*, this section will focus on how certain *Utterances* within the data will be selected. Considering the focus of this project and its dialogical methodology, we appropriate *Voice* as identity-shaping, when it becomes embodied in dialogue. Therefore, we will be locating the *Utterances* emerging from the interview transcripts. More specifically, we will be examining whether each *Utterance* is a *Single-voiced* or *Double-voiced*. Moreover, we will also analyse the presence of the *Other* within each *Utterance*. By this we mean the socio-ideological *Voice* of Veganism, the *Voice* of the *vegan-other*, or the *Voice* of the *none-vegan-other*. While analysing the transcripts, we will be applying Sullivan's (2012) method of illustrative *Sound bites. Sound bites* refer to which give *Utterances* a 'textured feeling of heaviness and lightness and colour as discourse [or *Utterances*] becomes lived experiences' (Clark and Holuquist, 1984: 10). *Sound bites* can be found within a larger and lengthy data set, and such an analytical approach also aligns with the *Dialogical Self* conceptual framework. The identified *Sound bites*, for instance, which will encompass a particular *Speech Genre* endowed *Utterance*, can be considered as a *Threshold-moment*, where the participants experience a moment of crisis concerning their vegan journey. Additionally, presenting the identified *Sound bites* as a 'table of dialogue' is a useful way of foregrounding the multiplicity within a dialogical analysis (Sullivan, 2012). In doing so, the analysis process will also move beyond surface-level analysis to understand the context in which certain *Sound bites* frequently appear, by simultaneously mapping the emerging *Single-voiced* or *Double-voiced Utterances*, against dimensions of the tri-part *Dialogical Self.*

Exemplifying Soundbites

I think, perhaps, an illustrative example could be useful. Let us use the participants's responses to the questions posed at the end of each interview and their responses: (1) *'is there anything else you would like to share about your experience?'*; (2) *'If you had to sum up your experience with Veganism in one word, what would it be?'* We have discussed them at length above, and you will note that the responses varied in length, yet captured profound emotive value. Table 2.1 illustrates how we can capture this in a snapshot.

TABLE 2.1 Example of *Sound bites*

Interviewee	*Word for Overall Experience*	*Final Statement*
Orlando	Problematic	*'tend to separate foods into good and bad foods.'*
Cordelia	Enlightening	*'from another perspective and say, you know, look at both sides, really consider both sides.'*
Portia	Learning curve	*'I think I would say that I'm just like an individual and I don't have to follow.'*
Bianca	Struggle	*'just research'* and not to *'just research the good stuff about it.'*
Kate	Cult	*'I'm glad I'm not vegan anymore.'*
Puck	Complicated	*'it taught me a lot about compassion.'*
Goneril	Confusing	*'understand that it just doesn't work for everybody.'*
Leigha	–	*'it would be interesting to see how many people have ignored those feelings.'*
Gertrude	–	*'I have to live in a grey, a world of grey, not white and black, but I think I would prefer.'*
Regan	–	*'It's a philosophical debate than … [a] like practical approach to eating.'*

If you are already comfortable with the use and application of *Sound bites*, please feel free to move onto the next section of this chapter.

Table 2.1 encapsulates the *Sound bites* within the data and we can now determine the *Speech Genre(s)* emerging from the *Sound bites*. We could argue that one of the *Speech Genres* is *Tension*. A sense of tension, for example, between what the interviewees expected in juxtaposition with what they actually experience while *Being* vegan. There are, of course, multiple *Speech Genres* visible through the *Sound bite* table above, and you as the reader may identify a different one, that is after all the essence of *Polyphony*. Indeed, as you read through the participants's quotes, I highly encourage you to engage with them through a *Dialogical* epistemology.

Chapter Summary

This chapter has engaged in detail with Bakhtinian concepts that will inform the discussion and analysis in proceeding chapters. We began by outing the complexities of adopting a *Dialogical* methodology, not only because Bakhtin's concepts can seem immensely abstract but also because, during the course of his career, they meld, shifting, and intertwine in meaning. This is further convoluted by the multi-disciplinary identity of Bakhtin himself. Nevertheless, the sections above have attempted to explain the onto-epistemology we will take, and pinned-down mobile terms such as *Utterance*, *Voice*, *Speech Genres*, and the *Dialogical Self*, which will be utilised as discursive tools of enquiry. In doing so, the aim is to re-think our recent understanding of social phenomena, specifically Veganism, and bringing the *Polyphony* within embodied and individual lived experiences to the foreground.

References

Abrams, D., & Hogg, M. A. (1999). *Social identity and social cognition*. Malden, MA: Blackwell Publishers.

Anonymous. (1998). *The taming of a shrew*. Cambridge: Cambridge University Press.

Bakhtin, M. (1993). *Toward a philosophy of the act*. Austin: University of Texas Press.

Bakhtin, M. (1990). *Art and answerability: early philosophical essays*. Austin: University of Texas Press.

Bakhtin, M. (1986). *Speech genres and other late essays*. Austin: University of Texas Press.

Bakhtin, M. (1984). *Problems of Dostoevsky's poetics*. Minneapolis: University of Minnesota Press.

Bakhtin, M. (1981). *The dialogic imagination: four essays*. Austin: University of Texas Press.

Bento, T., Cuncha, C., & Salgado, J. (2006). Ambiguity and the dialogical self: in search for a dialogical psychology. *Studies in Psychology*, 27(1), 19–32. https://doi.org/10.1174/021093906776173216

Bergin, T. (2018). *An Introduction to data analysis: quantitative, qualitative and mixed methods.* London: Sage Publication.

Bhabha, H. (1990). *Nation and narration.* London: Routledge.

Blankenship, D. C. (2010). *Applied research and evaluation methods in recreation.* Champaign: Human Kinetics.

Boose, L. (1991). Scolding brides and bridling scolds: taming the women's unruly member. *Shakespeare Quarterly*, 42(2), 179–213. https://doi.org/10.2307/2870547

Buttny, R., & Kinefuchi, E. (2020). Vegans' problem stories: negotiating vegan identity in dealing with omnivores. *Discourse & Society*, 31(6), 565–583. https://doi.org/10.1177/0957926520939689

Clark, K., & Holuquist, M. (1984). *Mikhail Bakhtin.* Massachusetts: Harvard University Press.

Coldspink, S., & Engward, H. (2020). Lodgers in the house: living with data in the interpretive phenomenological analysis research. *Reflective Practice*, 21(1), 41–53. https://doi.org/10.1080/14623943.2019.1708305

Costa, I., Gill, P. R., Morda, R. et al. (2019). More than a diet: a qualitative investigation of young vegan Women's relationship to food. *Appetite*, 143, 1–8. https://doi.org/10.1016/j.appet.2019.104418

Cresswell, J., & Baerveldt, C. (2011). Bakhtin's realism and embodiment: towards a revision of the dialogical self. *Culture & Psychology*, 17(2), 263–277. https://doi.org/10.1177/1354067X11398308

Crystal, D., & Crystal, B. (2002). *Shakespeare's words: a glossary and language companion.* New York: Penguin.

Dreyfus, H. L. (1982). *Husserl, intentionality, and cognative science.* Massachusetts: Massachusetts Institution of Technology.

Gardiner, M. E., & Mayerfeld-Bell, M. (Eds.). (1998). *Bakhtin and the human sciences: no last words.* London: Sage Publications.

Gillespie, A. (2010). The dialogical turn: turning the corner? *Theory & Psychology*, 20(3), 461–463. https://doi.org/10.1177/0959354310364279

Greenebaum, J. B. (2012a). "Face-Saving" strategies of vegetarians and vegans. *Humanity & Society*, 36(4), 309–325. https://doi.org/10.1177/0160597612458898

Grow, J. M., & Christopher, S. A. (2008). Breaking the silence surrounding Hepatitis C by promoting self-efficacy: hepatitis C public service announcements, *Qualitative Health Research*, 18(10), 1401–1012. https://doi.org/10.1177/1049732308322603

Hays, C. B. (Ed.). (2005). *The silence of the wives: Bakhtin's Monologism and Ezra 7–10: Bakhtin and the biblical imagination consultation.* Philadelphia: Philadelphia Press.

Hecht, M. L. (2015). Communication theory of identity: Multilayered understandings of performed identities. In D. O. Braithwaite & P. Schrodt (Eds.), *Engaging theories in interpersonal communication: Multiple perspectives Volume II* (pp. 175–189). Thousand Oaks, CA: Sage Publications.

Hecht, M. L., & Choi, H. (2012). The communication theory of identity as a framework for health message design. In H. Cho (Ed.), *Health communication message design* (pp. 137–152). Thousand Oaks, CA: Sage Publication.

Hecht, M. L., Jackson, R. L., & Ribeau, S. A. (2003). *African American communication: Exploring identity and culture.* Mahwah: Lawrence Erlbaum.

Hermans, H. J. M. (2004). The dialogical self: between exchange and power. In H. J. M. Hermans & G. Dimaggio (Eds.), *The dialogical self in psychotherapy* (pp. 13–28). East Sussex: Brunner-Routledge.
Hermans, H. J. M. (2001). The dialogical self: toward a theory of personal and cultural positioning. *Culture & Psychology*, 7(3), 243–281. https://doi.org/10.1177/1354067X0173001
Hermans, H., & Kempen, H. (1993). *The dialogical self: meaning as movement.* San Diego, CA: Academic Press.
Hodgdon, B. (2010). *The taming of the shrew*. London: Arden Shakespeare.
Holquist, M. (2002). *Dialogism: Bakhtin and his world.* London & New York: Routledge.
Howard, J. A. (2000). Social psychology of identities. *Annual Review of Sociology*, 26, 367–393. https://doi.org/10.1146/annurev.soc.26.1.367
Intezar, H., & Sullivan, S. (2022). Metamorphosis from exalted person to cultural symbol: a case study of the GOAT in tennis. *Culture & Psychology*, 28(3), 395–412. https://doi.org/10.1177/1354067X211044990
Intezar, H., & Sullivan, P. (2019). Carving a dialogical epistemology for investigating altruism: a reply to Mitchell and Eiroa–Orosa. In R. H. Mitchell (Ed.), *Cultivating new post-secular political space* (pp. 1–5). Routledge. https://doi.org/10.1080/23269995.2018.1511766
Intezar, H. (2014). *Shakespearean Polyphony. An exploration of female voices in seven selected plays using a dialogical framework.* Unpublished PhD. Thesis. University of Bradford.
Jung, E., & Hecht, M. (2004). Elaborating the communication theory of identity: identity gaps and communication outcomes. *Communication Quarterly*, 52(3), 265–283. https://doi.org/10.1080/01463370409370197
Leeds-Hurwitz, W. (2006). Social constructionism and symbolic interactionism. In D. O. Braithwaite & L. A. Baxter (Eds.), *Engaging theories in family communication* (pp. 229–242). Thousand Oaks, CA: Sage Publications.
Linell, P. (2005). *The written language bias.* London: Routledge.
Marková, I. (2006). On the 'inner Alter' in dialogue. *International Journal for Dialogical Science*, 1(1), 125–148.
Markovà, I. (2003a). *Diagonality and social representations.* Cambridge: Cambridge University Press.
Markovà, I. (2003b). Constitution of the self: intersubjectivity and dialogicality. *Culture & Psychology*, 9(3), 249–259. https://doi.org/10.1177/1354067X030093006
McDonald, B. (2000). Once you know something, you can't not know it: an empirical look at becoming vegan. *Society and Animals*, 8(1), 1–23. https://doi.org/10.1163/156853000510961
McKenna, K. Y. A., & Bargh, J. A. (2000). Plan 9 from cyberspace: the implications of the internet for the personality and Social Psychology. *Personality and Social Psychology Review*, 4(1), 57–75. https://doi.org/10.1207/S15327957PSPR0401_6
Mintz, S. W., & Du Bois, C. M. (2002). The anthropology of food and eating. *Annual Review of Anthropology*, 31(2), 99–119. https://doi.org/10.1146/annurev.anthro.32.032702.131011
Moghaddam, F. M. (2003). Interobjectivity and culture. *Culture & Psychology*, 9(3), 221–232. https://doi.org/10.1177/1354067X030093004
Morson, G. S. (1991). Bakhtin, genres, and temporality. *New Literary History*, 22(4), 1071–1092. https://doi.org/10.2307/469079

Morson, G.S., & Emerson, C. (1990). *Mikhail Bakhtin: the creation of a prosaics.* Stanford, CA: Stanford University Press.
Oliveria, M. C. S. L. (2011). The Bakhtinian self and beyond: towards a dialogical phenomenology of the self. *Culture & Psychology*, 19(2), 259–272. https://doi.org/10.1177/1354067X13478988
Renfrew, A. (2015). *Mikhail Bakhtin.* London: Routledge.
Ritchie, J., Lewis, J., McNaughton, C. et al. (2013). *Qualitative research practice: a guide for social sciences students and researchers.* London: Sage Publications.
Salgado, J., & Clegg, J. W. (2011). Dialogism and the psyche: Bakhtin and contemporary psychology. *Culture & Psychology*, 17(4), 421–440. https://doi.org/10.1177/1354067X11418545
Sams, E. (1986). The timing of the shrews. *Notes and Queries*, 32(1), 33–45.
Sandler, S. (2014). Bakhtin on Shakespeare: excerpts from "Additions and Changes to Rabelais". *PMLA*, 129(3), 522–537. https://doi.org/10.1632/pmla.2014.129.3.522
Smith, J. A. (2019). Participants and researchers searching for meaning: conceptual developments for interpretative phenomenological analysis. *Qualitative Research in Psychology*, 16(2), 166–181. https://doi.org/10.1080/14780887.2018.1540648
Smith, J. A., Flowers, P., & Larkin, M. (2009). *Interpretive phenomenological analysis: theory, method and research.* London: Sage Publications.
Smythe, W. E., & Jorna, R. J. (1998). The signs we live by: the relationship between semiotics and psychology. *Theory & Psychology*, 8(6), 723–730.
Sullivan, P. (2012). *Qualitative data analysis: using a dialogical approach.* London: Sage Publications.
Sullivan, P. (2007). Examining the self-other dialogue through 'Soul' and 'Spirit.' *Culture & Psychology*, 13(1), 105–128. https://doi.org/10.1177/1354067X07073662
Tajfel, H. (1981). Human groups and social categories: Studies in social psychology. Cambridge: Cambridge University Press.
Talamo, A., & Pozzi, S. (2011). The tension between dialogicality and interobjectiveity in cooperative activities. *Culture & Psychology*, 17(3), 302–318. https://doi.org/10.1177/1354067X11408131
Ting-Toomey, S. (2010). Mindfulness. In R. L. Jackson II (Ed.), *Encyclopedia of identity*, Volume I (pp. 455–458). Thousand Oaks, CA: Sage Publications.

3

THE BEGINNING, HOW IT ALL BEGAN

> *I thought well this is like a Holy Trinity of, you know, everything points to this as being the perfect diet so solidifying this idea in my head that nothing else was right apart from being vegan.*
>
> (Cordelia)

In Chapter 1 we outlined the three main 'forms' (or ideological positionings) of *Veganism*, and individual motivational drives for adopting a vegan diet: animal ethics, health, and environmentalism. However, there is limited social psychological research available that specifically focuses on how motivational drives intertwine and *fluctuate* for vegans who have been practising Veganism. This may be because scholarship predominantly focuses on the practitioners's second *Threshold-moment*, *Being* vegan, and the motivation(s) underpinning their choice (Dhont and Ioannidou, 2021; Janssen, Busch, Rödiger et al., 2021; Braunsberger and Flamm, 2019). Here, we start at the beginning. This chapter is the first of three, examining empirical data derived from ten interviews with participants who identify as 'former vegans.' Each chapter captures a distinct *Threshold-moment* in their journey.

Sideward Glance

A 'Threshold-moment' can be understood as an abstract doorway, where the participants need to make a life choice(s) that potentially impact one's sense of self and identity.

DOI: 10.4324/9781003384526-3

Tables 3.1 and 3.2 highlight the *Primary* and *Secondary Speech Genres* from the participants's first *Threshold-moment*. For further context, during the conversations, this is when they first became aware of Veganism and discuss what influenced them to make their final decision to begin practising Veganism. If you have read Chapter 2, you will note an addendum in my reference to *Speech Genres*: the addition of *Primary* and *Secondary*. For accessibility and continuity, I thought it best that we outline them in this chapter, rather than in Chapter 2.

For instance, in *Speech Genres and Other Late Essays* Bakhtin (1986) differentiates between *Primary* and *Secondary Speech Genres*. While the former captures the simple 'everyday' position of an individual within a particular sphere of communication (in other words, the *spoken Speech Genre*), the latter are '*more complex* and comparatively highly developed and organised' forms of 'cultural communication' (Bakhtin, 1986: 62, *emphasis added*).

TABLE 3.1 *Sound bites* for the *Primary Speech Genres of Self-focus*

Primary Genre of Self-focus	*Secondary Genres*	*Utterances*
1.	Health and fitness	*I was getting into nutrition .... veganism as a healthy lifestyle, it was the best thing a human could do to be healthy (Orlando).*
		I went to the gym so that to me, I was like okay, this is about nutrition .... I think in terms of my health I wasn't actually that good prior to it [veganism] (Cordelia).
		... at the time I was like really insecure about like my weight, which doesn't make a lot of sense, I was very small (Puck).
	Animal Ethics	*... And also I knew about the environmentalism and ethical stuff (Orlando).*
	Environmental Concerns	*It was just the like environmental kind of idea behind it (Goneril).*
	Sense of Identity	*... I was really impressionable at the time (Kate).*
		I think I had quite a poor sense of self and my ego has always been unsure of who I am or what I represent, what my identity is so .... I was, you know, trying to figure something out, have something to, you know, make a difference in the world (Cordelia).
		... at first I don't think it was the lifestyle that attracted me, it was just that I see these role model like people and I want to be more like them. So I also wanted to become vegan ... (Portia).

TABLE 3.2 *Sound bites* for the *Primary Speech Genre of External Influence*

Primary Genre of External influence	*Secondary Genres*	*Utterances*
2	Vegan literature	*Well I guess I've been aware of veganism since my early 20s … I read a book that I'd been putting off reading for a long time that I had called Eating Animals by Jonathan Safran Foer, that kind of opened my eyes to animal agriculture, which I had been almost wilfully ignorant about … (Gertrude).*
	Pro-Vegan Media	*I think I saw a documentary in school that was called Cowspiracy and before that, like (Goneril).*
		…probably say my awareness began, probably 2017 that it was more present on social media and things like that, so I'd see videos come up quite often either on recipes or people discussing veganism or maybe the lesser nice part of it of all the animals getting harmed and things like that, there was a huge bout of Facebook showing all these animal cruelty videos and things so that was probably where I first started seeing it (Cordelia).
	Social Media Influencer	*The first time when I went vegan, that was 100% social media influence, second time around it was more of an ethical route, but I was still very much influenced by social media (Portia).*
		… so I found a few YouTubers and then a couple of documentaries, which kind of set the ball rolling for me (Bianca).

Also, in comparison to *Primary Speech Genres*, *Secondary Speech Genres* are, generally, locatable within the *written* text, and due to their complexity, *Secondary Speech Genres* tend to absorb *Primary Speech Genres.* What grants each form of *Speech Genre* with its respective properties, you may ask. For Bakhtin, *Primary Speech Genres* take place in 'unmediated speech communion,' and are *a moment* of the *whole* (Bakhtin, 1986: 62). My conversations with the interviewees, and the *Speech Genres* that emerge from within them, for instance, can be perceived as *Primary*, as they became visible during a *moment* of *spontaneous* speech, on the part of the interviewee. The *Secondary Speech Genres*, however, become apparent (in writing) once the interviews have been transcribed, describing a more complex and nuanced description of the interviewees' experience, hence, encapsulating the *whole*. At this point, some Bakhtinian scholars may pause and argue that I have exercised some creative liberty while applying *Speech Genres* within the onto-epistemologicall framework developed for this monograph. Especially as, for Bakhtin (1986), *Secondary Speech Genres* are located within literature and texts such as the novel, dramatic texts, scientific research, and genres of socio-political commentary. That I do not deny. In Chapter 2, however, we discussed Bakhtin's trans-disciplinary identity at length, particularly the 'dialogical turn' in psychology, where Bakhtin's writings on the *Author* and *Hero* relationship within the Dostoyevskian novel have been applied to the conception of *Self* consciousness through the *Other*. I guess I am taking a similar liberty here, as I argue for the presence of *Primary* and *Secondary Speech Genres* within the oral interview process and interview transcripts, respectively.

Sideward Glance

If you wish to peruse Bakhtin's (1981) work on Primary and Secondary Speech Genres, I recommend reading the following essays: Epic and Novel and From the Prehistoric of Novelistic Discourse.

To exemplify the application of *Primary* and *Secondary Speech Genres* further, let us consider the participants's *Utterances* during their first *Threshold-moment* (Tables 3.1 and 3.2). In my conversations with the interviewees (what Bakhtin may refer to as, a 'sphere of communication'), *Self-focus* and *External-influence* emerge as *Primary Speech Genres.* These *Primary Speech Genres,* however, begin to form a more significant and *whole* meaning of the interviewees's lived experience(s) with Veganism when considered in the context of their respective *Secondary Speech Genres.* For *Self-focus,* the *Secondary Speech Genres* were *Health and fitness*, *Animal ethics*, *Environmental concerns*, and a *Sense of identity.* While the *Secondary Speech Genres* for *External-influence* were *Vegan literature*, *Pro-vegan Media*, and *Social Media Influencers.* Additionally, *Secondary Speech Genres* not only constitute the *whole* of a given *Primary Speech Genres* but also present an interconnection between various *Primary Speech Genres* (Bakhtin, 1986, 1984, 1981). Indeed, the potentiality of a given *Utterance* is best revealed and determined through the analysis of both types of *Speech Genres.* If we were to apply that here, in our case, *Self-focus* and *External-influence* are representative of the *Dialogical* dynamics within the *Becoming* of self-consciousness. The former *Primary Speech Genre* is representative of the *I-for-myself*, while the latter underscores the relevance of the *Other-for-me*. When they are viewed simultaneously, both *Primary Speech Genres* are illustrative of the *I* and *Other* relationship (see Chapter 2).

The final point I would like to convey about *Speech Genres* is that, as with any Bakhtinian concept, they are not reducible to a common denominator or singular in meaning.

> Literary language [or transcripts] is not represented in the novel as a unitary, completely finished-off and indisputable language-it is represented precisely as a living mix of varied and opposing voices, developing and renewing itself.
>
> (Bakhtin, 1981: 49)

In this sense, then, *Speech Genres* are boundless, not only because the potentiality within human interaction is inexhaustible, but also because each 'sphere of communication' comprises a repertoire of *Speech Genres.* They differentiate and evolve as a given 'sphere of communication' develops and becomes more complex. Simply put, *Speech Genres*, both written and oral, are *heterogeneity* at its extreme. Furthermore, *Secondary Speech Genres* tend do subsume *Primary Speech Genres*:

> During the process of their formation, they [*Secondary Speech Genres*] absorb and digest various primary ... genres that have taken form in unmediated speech communion. These primary genres are altered and assume a special character when they enter into complex ones. They lose their immediate relation to actual reality and to the real utterances of others.
>
> (Bakhtin, 1986: 62)

Cordelia's *Utterances*, presented at the beginning of this chapter, for example, are multi-faceted. Her initial motivational drives were health-focused (*'The health perspective, I've always had an interest in that'*); however, she also expressed her love for animals (*'but I like animals, I am an animal person, so naturally I think it felt right'*), and while *Being* vegan learnt more about environmentalism (*'learnt more about the environmental impacts of perhaps factory farming but you're told it's animal agriculture in general'*). The *Speech Genres* within the *Utterances* that constitute Cordelia's consciousness around the phenomenon of Veganism are not finite and closed. The emergence of the *Secondary Speech Genre*, and therefore, the content of the *Primary Speech Genre* may reposition and rearrange. For accessibility and readability reasons, however, below, *Primary* and *Secondary Speech Genres* have been discussed separately.

The Primary Genre of Self-focus

One of the points of discussion in Chapter 1 was the recent ascendency of a 'post-vegan' narrative (Giraud, 2021: 136), partly driven by discourses of global (Moreno, Meyer, Donovan et al., 2022) and individual health (Christopher, Bartkowski, and Haverda, 2018). Wright (2018) refers to health motivated Veganism as the popularised and de-politicised branch of Veganism, which poses the danger of decentralising the original connection between Veganism morality, and animal ethics. Nonetheless, the *Utterances* of the interviewees during our conversation disclosed that they were aware of the contemporary multi-valued social-linguistics underpinning Veganism and that, despite the multi-vocality, their awareness of animal ethics remained a constant. Having said that, for some participants, animal ethics maintained a more peripheral role at the beginning of their vegan journey. Their awareness of the multiplicity of meaning surrounding Veganism, not only situated them in a *Polyphonic* space of understanding, but also placed them at their first *Threshold-moment*: 'To be, or not to be, [vegan].' From a classical Social Psychology perspective (Erickson, 1968), such moments of ambiguous deliberation can be understood as a moment of 'crisis,' or an obstacle one needs to overcome, in order to achieve a sense of *Being* or *Selfhood*. Under a dialogical onto-epistemology, existing in a *Polyphonic* state of ambiguity is not an obscure occurrence, one which needs to be overcome. Rather, this sate of ambiguity is necessary for *inter*-subjective and *intra*-subjective processes, such as the formation of one's self-consciousness and identity. In the analysis below, we explore the *Utterances* and *Voice(s)* of the interviewees during their first *Threshold-moment*, their discovery of Veganism, and what motivated them during their decision-making.

Sideward Glance

Bakhtin coins the categories of 'I-for-myself,' 'Other-for-me' and 'I for-the-other,' in order to present his concepts of the 'Spirit' and 'Soul,' in a more tangible manner. The I-for-myself is a representative of the Spirit, while the I-for-other, and Other-for-me are grounded within the Soul (see Chapter 2 for a detailed discussed). We will be referring to Bakhtin's tri-part *Dialogical Self* throughout the analysis chapters.

Secondary Genre: Health and Fitness

The subjects of nutrition and health are dominant discourses within online vegan communities (Lupton and Feldman, 2020), and recent scholarship has also identified a number of possible reasons for the perpetual connection between health and Veganism on online platforms. First, in Western cultures, meat consumption has predominantly been considered as an essential source of nutrition and nourishment (Hayley, Zinkiewicz, and Hardiman, 2015; Cole and Morgan, 2011), creating associations between a vegan diet and weak(er) physical health. Online platforms, therefore, become mediating spaces where vegan practitioners may continuously negotiate with non-vegans concerning the health benefits of *Being* vegan (Oliver, 2020; Greenebaum and Dexter, 2017). Second, to "save face" during said negotiations vegan practitioners may also attempt to re-orientate vegan discourses away from controversial aspects such as ill-health, and more towards rhetoric of healthy eating (Greenebaum, 2012a).

It is not surprising, then, that a number of interviewees were drawn to Veganism because of their interest in health and nutrition.

> The health perspective, I've always had an interest in that, even over the course of me being vegan … it's something that perhaps I'd like to go into in the future but I like animals, I am an animal person so naturally I think it felt right and whilst (Cordelia).

> I don't know, when did I first hear of veganism? It's probably after I, you know, I started watching more documentaries about health and things like that … so after university I did like an online course in nutrition, like a nutrition diploma (Leigha).

While taking an online course Leigha recalled the diversity, or in Bakhtinian terms, the *Polyphony*, within the tutors's *Voice*(s): '*it was interesting because you kind of think like, you kind of assume that everyone will be vegan*,' as that was considered the '*most healthy way to be and stuff*.' Leigha reflected her gratitude for encountering multiple perspectives: '*it was nice in a way that some of the teachers weren't, you know, some of the teachers were saying you needed to eat more meat and, you know, like more protein*.' Particularly as, otherwise, she felt that she would have experienced a higher degree of pressure, to become vegan or reduce her meat consumption: '*I think there would have been a feeling of pressure to kind of conform, yeah*.' What eventually prompted her to *Become* vegan and abstain from consuming meat was a challenge she took on for Lent:

> So when I was, I was at university and I was like maybe 20, maybe, yeah, 20, 21, something like that and I decided to for Lent give up meat. I mean, I'm not particularly religious but I guess like from '18, '19 or even before that just like it was kind of this idea of I'm going to try and give something up and challenge myself… And then this particular year I was like oh, okay, I'll give up meat. So I didn't go fully vegan but I went vegetarian so I was having like cheese and stuff like that.

Leigha, however, began re-consume meat after Lent and did not consider Veganism again until she was working in Japan:

> But yeah, the veganism came when I was in Japan, I think it was 2016, and I think I'd started like watching more documentaries and just learning more about just kind of educating myself a bit more about it. And I mean, I guess you could say that the documentaries are quite powerful, some of them, in their persuasion. But equally, I had some basis of nutrition knowledge and so I sort of was like okay, you know, there's some fact to it.

> Yeah, and it's interesting that you mention it in that sense because, you know, there's, I mean, there's many different arguments for many different diets, you

> know, for the paleo diet and oh, we're hunter gatherers and all that kind of thing. I remember a lesson in the class, the nutrition class that I did here and it compared, you know, like a dog digestive system with a cow's digestive system with a human digestive system and it kind of, you know, just showed the differences of, you know, a herbivore, a carnivore and an omnivore. And you know, the human digestive system is somewhere in between those two extremes and I think that in kind of like honouring what your body is being omnivore, you know, because that's how the digestive system. So yeah it's, as I say, I'm still going to place a lot of importance on plants and vegetables but the body does need, in my opinion, the body needs some quality meat animal product.

Gertrude, in contrast, expressed her mystification regarding those who associate Veganism with health, not only in their motives for *Becoming* vegan but also their understanding of it.

> I didn't do it for the health, a lot of people do it to lose weight which I think is amazing, because I gained weight since I started being vegan but people do … Oh for sure, I don't think there is such a thing as a health vegan. I don't think that's a category, because it's not healthy, really.

For other interviewees, the interest in nutrition that led them to Veganism was more nuanced, in the sense that it was tied to emotions around embodiment. For example, they disclosed weight '*insecurities*,' which contributed towards a poor sense of embodiment and a negative self-perception. Several interviewees expressed their desire to address their weight concerns in a healthy, sustainable manner:

> I was kind of trying to find a way that would be better to lose weight, but in a healthy way. It's weird because I never really saw any documentaries when I first discovered it. I actually just did like a Google search of like healthier ways, like healthy diets you incorporate into fitness (Bianca).

> I found out about a podcast that was talking about veganism as a healthy lifestyle, so I thought it was the best thing a human could do to be healthy. I was trying to lose some weight and I did (Orlando).

> … and at the time I was like really insecure about like my weight, which doesn't make a lot of sense, I was very small, and so I had this person telling me that like you can have all of these really good foods and like you can eat as much as you want, and like you're going to have this banging body and I was like, cool, like I'm 16, of course I'm going to do it (Puck).

At this point, if you have become familiar with Bakhtinian philosophy, it will come as no surprise that, for Bakhtin, a sense of embodiment emerges from an *inter*-subjective dialogue between the between *I* and *Other*: 'Inner determinateness-the embodiment of meaning in mortal flesh-is born and dies in the world and for the world' (Bakhtin, 1990: 111). From this, it may seem that Bakhtin is implying that the experience of embodiment is entirely socially constructed and there is no 'real' corporal sense of embodiment. There is, essentially, no *intra*-subjective sense of embodiment, and that the *I* is simply a vessel for language to take form. When the matter of embodiment is considered in light of Bakhtin's (1984b) thoughts in *Rabelais and His World*, it seems to me that, such interpretations fall short. Bakhtin, for instance, (1984b) proposes that the 'biological' cannot be 'separated from the social,' and in doing so, centralising the corporality of the body. Principally, embodiment is not solely abstract and created through social dialogical interactions with the *Other* but is also *experienced within* the body (Cresswell and Baerveldt, 2011; also see Cresswell and Teucher, 2011).

Sideward Glance

For those wondering how the concept of the embodiment links with Dialogism. In *Rabelais and His World Bakhtin* (1984b) refer to the corporality as the 'Grotesque Body,' which is a symbol of renewal, death, and social unity. Scholars have argued that Dialogism and inter-corporeity are intertwined. Dialogical relationship cannot take place between dis-embodied minds, and the Grotesque Body can be perceived biosemiotic conception of sign.

(Ponzio, 2016)

During Bianca's, Puck's, and Orlando's, first *Threshold-moment*, their motivations for *initially* considering Veganism was based on health and self-empowerment. A sense of empowerment which was located within their corporal body. In relation to the academic discourses concerning Veganism, the *Utterances* emerging from within the *Secondary Speech Genre* of *Health and Fitness* offer insight into the positionality of post-feminist discursive practices (Gill, 2016, 2007), where self-empowerment is embedded within a 'makeover paradigm' that extends beyond the body to constitute a remaking of subjectivity. Although postfeminist scholarship focuses on women's bodies, the rise of social movements, such as 'Heganism,' has been coined to capture the rejection and re-construction of hegemonic masculinity (Randall, 2018; Potts and Parry, 2010).

> ... by emphasising strength, control and personal empowerment as masculine, by regarding compassion to be an act of courage and rebellion in a society that socializes men to be stoic and uncaring and by asserting men's crucial role in bringing legitimacy to the vegan movement.
>
> (Greenebaum and Dexter, 2017: 640)

The purpose is to demonstrate how forgoing meat also clashes with connotations attached to performing masculinities. Greenebaum and Dexter (2017) continue to argue that once one begins to explore the rhetoric of male vegan practitioners, their language and experiences readily align with masculine stereotypes around health and physical strength. Moreover, some scholarship focus on self-empowerment and self-gain distils the original ethos of Veganism: animal ethics and critique of oppressive social structures (Wright, 2015). Nonetheless, the concept of embodiment is important within the interviewee's vegan journey, be it from a nutritional perspective, a health perspective, or a sense of self-empowerment. Hence, as you continue through the analysis chapters, you will note that embodiment is a re-occurring theme at each *Threshold-moment*.

Secondary Genre: Environment

The *Secondary Speech Genre* of *Environmentalism* also emerged within the *Utterances* of several participants. During the analysis process, I chose to differentiate between the *Secondary Speech Genres* of *Animal Ethics* and *Environmentalism*, as I found a distinct difference within the *Utterances* concerning these two *Speech Genres*. Particularly in terms of the dialogical tensions between the *I-for-myself* and *I-for-others* when it came to *inter*-subjective and *intra*-subjective exchanges. What we mean by this, as discussed below, is that the *Utterances* of interviewees who were *environmentally* driven remained *Double-voiced*, while the *Utterances* of those who were motivated by *Animal Ethics* were predominantly *Single-voiced*.

Sideward Glance

We have already considered before, however, as a quick reminder, a Single-voiced Utterance refers to where the Voice(s) of the I and Other have aligned and fused. The Utterance is no longer Polyphonic. For Bakhtin, the monological is marked by the reduction of multiple Voices to one Voice: 'within monological world contradictory accents collide in a single voice'.

(Bakhtin, 1973: 67)

Amongst the interviewees, Goneril was the only participant whose motivational drive remained *Environmental* throughout her vegan journey.

> ... It was just the like environmental kind of idea behind it.... I can really cut down on my waste and things like that, it was just kind of like a personal challenge but it went too far. Yeah.

Similarly, for Leigha, whose motivations were nutrition orientated, *Becoming* vegan was a personal challenge: '*kind of this idea of I'm going to try and give something up and challenge myself*.' Goneril's vegan journey was also a '*personal challenge*,' thus, both interviewees remained outside the 'vegan as social movement' paradigm. For Goneril, *Becoming* vegan centred around personal *Environmental* responsibility and taking accountability for her actions (Ghaffari, Rodrigo, Ekinci et al., 2021; Hussar and Harris, 2010). Additionally, Leigha was the only participant who knew that, for them, *Being* vegan would be for a limited period of time: '*I gave it up but then I sort of went back. And it wasn't really a lifestyle that I was kind of like thinking I would continue*.' Perhaps, this is why, throughout their vegan journeys, both Goneril's and Leigha's *Utterances* remained *Double-voiced*, which will be explored further in Chapter 4.

Secondary Genre: Animal Ethics

In the context of dietary lifestyles, research has demonstrated that vegetarians and vegans are strongly motivated by animal ethics and the abstinence from meat consumption (Hopwood, Bleidorn, Schwaba et al., 2020). In comparison to vegetarians, those practising Veganism, however, apply the same staunchness when it comes to other animal by-products such as dairy and eggs. It is important to note that, for the interviewees, the *Secondary Speech Genre of Animal Ethics* represented a variety of motivations. Animal ethics, for instance, compromised of *Utterances* that expressed concern for animal rights or animal welfare. More specifically, the interviewees's desire to reduce animal suffering, their opposition their exploitation, and viewing animals simply as food, which they found morally objectionable Effectively, to abolish *Speciesism*. I would like to take a moment to define *Speciesism,* as the concept is a cornerstone for those prompting animal ethics and animal liberation. The term '*Speciesism*' was initially coined by Ryder (1971) to describe the biased delegation of different rights and ethical considerations to individuals depending on their species. In other words, the doctrine that human beings possess social and moral priority over other species and can utilise them as a means to ends for their own benefit. The animal liberation activist, Yourofsky (2010) defines *Speciesism* as:

> The unethical, unprincipled point of view that the human species has every right to exploit, enslave and murder another species because we believe that our species is so more special, so more superior than the other ones, that we're the only ones that count, and we're the only ones that matter.
>
> (Yourofsky, 2010)

Portia transitioned in and out of the Veganism twice, each time driven by different motivational factors at each *Threshold-moment*. Initially, at 16, her motivation arose from social media influencers, and then at 18, when Portia's primary motivation shifted to animal ethics.

> I would say I was definitely most drawn to the ethics actually, because I remember that's what actually kept me going for so long, I just felt really bad, I was like, it's like it's been two years, I just feel so terrible if I eat this, that's what really kept me going, and yeah.

During our conversation Gertrude's concern for *Animal Ethics* and her views on the role of animals in society became evident from the beginning. Many of the participants who were initially motivated by *Animal Ethics* also expressed their attitude towards *Speciesism*. While *Speciesism* had been theorised broadly, for the purpose of our discussion here and in Chapter 4, we will define it as the individual and collective attitudes with regards to human-human relations and human-animal relations.

> I think that's for me it was just totally [animal] ethical … I don't think there is such a thing as a health vegan. I don't think that's a category, because it's not healthy, really. *I feel that my desire, I feel like my, I honestly feel like my health is not as important as these animals suffering.*

Both Gertrude's and Portia's *Utterances* are particularly noteworthy because, for those practising Veganism motivated by animal ethics, in comparison to interviewees with a different motivational drive for *Becoming* vegan, there is a greater degree of *tension* within their *I-for-myself* during their vegan journeys. The reason for this being that, at their first *Threshold-moment*, the *Voice* within their *Utterances* is already *Single-voiced*, leading to a sense of self-finalisation, or the de-centralisation of the *I-for-myself*. Having said that, Gertrude's response to the relationship between Veganism and identity formation is significant from a dialogical perspective, as it foregrounds the co-existence of multiple *Voices* within Gertrude's *I-for-myself*. This means that Gertrude potentially encountered a multitude of *Voices* and values. Nonetheless, she seemed to hold a strong, and potentially monolithic, understanding and perspective of vegan ideology, which we explore in Chapter 6.

> I wasn't vegan long enough for it to be an integral part of my identity, I think my… I think identity is a very interesting issue because I don't think you have one identity … You have all different parts of your brain saying, I'm your identity, I'm your identity, and there's the part of my brain saying wife, mother, that's your identity, and the other part saying, well you're a kind person who doesn't cause harm, that's your identity, and those are clashing. But I have all these different, so I think that I would not say identity, veganism is part of my identity, I made a conscious decision not to be vegan.

From a Bakhtinian dialogical perspective of *Self-Other* relations, self-finalisation is detrimental on an ontological plane, as the *I-for-myself* must remain *Unfinalisable*. This is only attainable when the *I-for-myself* can continually engage with itself while in dialogue with the *Other*. In other words, one's *Voice* remains *Double-voiced*, preserving a separation between self-consciousness and the *Other*. As the analysis in Chapter 4 unfolds, we will explore how the *I-for-myself* can only remain *Unfinalisable* through an open dialogical interaction; while doing so, it can transgress through several changes and continue to maintain ontological security.

Sideward Glance

You may already be aware of terms such as ontology and ontological security and/or insecurity. Ontology, in a broader sense, refers to philosophical underpinnings of understanding the nature of existence, including ourselves.

Secondary Genre: Identity Uncertainty

Identity was also a prominent *Secondary Speech Genre* that emerged from my conversations with the interviewees and was strongly connected with the *Secondary Speech Genre* of animal ethics. The exploration in this chapter has focused on how becoming aware of Veganism placed the interviewees at a *Threshold-moment*. I have, however, specifically coined this *Secondary Speech Genre* as *Identity Uncertainty* because I hold that interviewees such as Portia and Kate were, perhaps, *already* at a *Threshold-moment prior* to becoming interested in Veganism. For example, prior to her interest in animal ethics at 16, Portia's motivations were identity-based, and Veganism became a medium for self-construction, albeit through social media '*role models*,' who served as Portia's *Others-for-me* (Feng, Chen, and Kong, 2020; Doyle, 2016). Portia's *Utterance*, '*I don't think it was the lifestyle [Being vegan] that attracted me … I wanted to be more like them*,' illustrates this dynamic.

> I became aware of it because of social media, probably like most people when I was young I was very, I'm still fairly impressionable but when I was a teenager I was very, very impressionable, and I was following a lot of beauty groups on YouTube, fitness influencers, all sorts of people, and they were all vegan (Portia).

Similarly, Kate was also initially drawn to Veganism because her favourite Punk artists practised Veganism and promoted animal ethics thought their song lyrics: '*I had these like idols that I followed … and all of the like musicians they were vegan.*' Towards the end of our conversation, Cordelia also reflected on how *Being vegan* had given her a sense of purpose and identity:

> I think I had quite a poor sense of self and my ego has always been unsure of who I am or what I represent, what my identity is so I think quite classically it gave me that sense of identity, it was something to say, you know, *I am a vegan, this is what I stand by*, this is my ethical point of view, so definitely that, that was the first thing (Cordelia).

From the participants interviewed for this project, those motivated by animal ethics were more aware of what *Being* vegan signifies in terms of their identity and self-perception in the eyes of the *Other* (them as an *I-for-others*), particularly in terms of in-group cohesiveness. In other words, how would, or could, the vegan and non-vegan *Other* perceive them? From a Dialogical perspective, consciousness, or what contemporary psychology may term self-identity, is accomplished and perceived against the backdrop of the consciousness that *another has of it.* When applying Bakhtinian terminology, it would be the *I-for-myself* against the backdrop of *I-for-the other.*

However, for those who were not motivated by other vegan practitioners, Veganism *itself*, or the ideological stance they adopted, became a form of the *Other* (*Others-for-me*). It is also noteworthy that a wealth of research suggests that adolescence is a period in which one becomes more socially conscious and develops a sense of *Self* and identity that is independent of their family. One way of doing so is by adopting a dietary lifestyle that is parallel of their families (Golden, Schneider, and Wood et al., 2016). Conversations with the interviewees, to a certain extent, suggest that, for some, consumer food freedom and accountability through Veganism became a means of distinguishing their self-identity (the *I-for-myself*) (Bauman, 1995). Puck, for instance, recalled their family's response to them wanting to *Become* vegan:

> It was definitely just me, I tried to like to talk my family about it, and reasonably so they were like, that sounds unhealthy, like don't do that, I did it anyway. So yeah, my family was like not okay with it, but they couldn't stop me, you know?

Goneril, who had started university, also expressed a desire to becoming '*self-sufficient*': '*I just wanted to just do it for myself and just kind of, you know, prove my capabilities, show I can, you know, be sufficient.*'

Thus far, we have explored the participants's motivational drive for *Becoming* vegan. Although their motivational drives were diverse, albeit overlapping, their *Others-for-me*, or the external *Voices* that influenced them to *Become* vegan remained consistent.

The Primary Genre of External Influence

In Chapter 2, we outlined the reciprocal nature between the *I* and *Other*, emphasising that it is interwoven to the extent that the *Other*, or the perception of the *Other*, is always bracketed within the *Self*. As our discussion above suggests, all the participants's *I-for-myself* experienced a *Threshold-moments*, or a moment of crises, relating to, and often overlapping, concerns about health and fitness, animal ethics, environmental factors, and identity uncertainty. According to Bakhtin, during such moments of 'crises,' the *I-for-myself* seeks confirmation from the *Other-for-me* for affirmation. The *Secondary Speech Genres* within the participants's *Utterances* implied that the presence of the *Other-for-me* manifested through *Vegan Literature*, *Pro-Vegan Media*, and *Social Media Influencers*.

Much like the *Secondary Speech Genres* within the *Primary Genre of Self Focus*, the *Secondary Speech Genres* encapsulated within the *Primary Speech Genre of External Influence* are also overlapping. To illustrate this, I have quote Kate's initial *Utterances* below from the beginning of our conversation. You will be able to note the emergence of all three *Secondary Speech Genres*. At the age of 14, she was introduced to Veganism by a perceived knowledgeable other and *Vegan Literature*. From there she engaged with *Pro-Vegan Media*, and then finally *Social Media Influencers*.

> So I became aware of the vegan lifestyle when I was 15, it was in my biology class, my biology teacher was talking about how like there's vegetarians and then there's like omnivores and then I don't know, it just like sparked an interest in me especially at a young age, and then I was like vegetarian/vegan on and off until I was 18 and I watched *Earthlings* for the first time and that made me go completely full vegan and ever since then I was just following this like no animal products like lifestyle. I was also into that community, I don't know if you heard [name censored], she was present at that time (Kate).

Secondary Genre of Vegan Literature

The *Secondary Speech Genre* of *Vegan Literature* is particularly distinct from that of *Pro-Vegan Social Media* and Social *Media Influencers*, as it carried a higher degree of authenticity for the interviewees, and influencing their attitudes towards *Becoming* vegan. According to the Vegan Society (2021), for instance, a search for vegan literature on a certainer popular online bookstores in August 2018 generated approximately 994 titles, which grew to 2,779 by 2019. There is also a growing body of scholarship focusing on the medicalised rhetoric of Veganism, particularly in the context of health (Trauth, Stanescu, Levin et al., 2022). Although the medicalised health rhetoric of Veganism may initially be perceived as distinctive from the ethical and moral rhetoric surrounding Veganism, the discussion in this chapter and some of the interviewees's *Utterances* imply that this is not entirely the case.

> And then I read a book that I'd been putting off reading for a long time that I had called *Eating Animals* by Jonathan Safran Foer… *And when I read that I, he does not advocate for veganism, but he talks a lot about the animal agriculture side to it, and basically how to not be a hypocrite if you believe this is wrong* (Gertrude).
>
> … and then he posted about a book called *How Not to Die* by Michael Greger. I don't enjoy saying that man's name because he caused me a lot of pain! *I was like okay, this is about nutrition and its non-fiction science based, supposedly, book and I was like right, I want to buy that so I bought it* (Cordelia).

Arguably, the vegan literature that the interviewees engaged with, or rather the authors of said literature, were regarded as 'elite advocates' (Christopher, Bartkowski, and Haverda, 2018). In their analysis of popular advocacy films, they also identified two distinct duplications of Veganism: 'holistic veganism' and 'health veganism' (Christopher, Bartkowski, and Haverda, 2018: 64). For Cordelia, engaging with *Vegan Literature*, presented Veganism as the '*only*' logical and '*scientifically*' backed dietary lifestyle. She felt that she had found the *'Holy Trinity,'* as Veganism encompassed ethics, health, and environmental principals. The *Vegan-other-for-me*, in this case vegan literature, influenced Cordelia's *I-for-myself* to the extent that not *Being* vegan was no longer an option. Rather, it became compulsory. The same can be argued for Gertrude, who actively postponed engaging with *Vegan Literature*:

> But you have to understand I was already knowing that when I read this book I was going to become a vegan eventually … which I had been almost wilfully ignorant about, because I didn't want to change my eating habits.

Secondary Genres of Pro-vegan Social Media and Vegan Social Media Influencer

While, at the *Threshold-moment*, most participants found validation for their uncertain *I-for-myself* through identification with social media influencers (*Other-for-me*), an overarching commonality between all participants was that they were heavily influenced by vegan literature (McDonald, 2000), or those perceived to be 'experts.' Simultaneously, the *Utterances* within the *Secondary Speech Genres* of *Pro-Vegan Media* and *Vegan Social Media Influencers* were intrinsically interconnected. For example, once 'discovering' Veganism, all interviewees had engaged with vegan documentaries such as Earthling, Cowspiracy, and Blackfish, before or after they became vegan. For clarity, the former refers to participants's engagement with films and documentaries promoting Veganism such as, *Forks over Knives* (2011), *Vegucated* (2010), and *Cowspiracy* (2014). While the latter refers to particular social media Influencers who, at the time of the interviews, were practicing Veganism.

> The first time when I went vegan, that was 100% social media influence, second time around it was more of an ethical route, but I was still very much influenced by social media (Portia).

> I had a lot of friends who did who started a pro-vegan page and he would do statuses and a lot of them would ring bells for me and I'd think, oh actually, I can see where you're coming from (Cordelia).

Bianca's use of phrase *'set the ball rolling'* is meaningful because, for participants who discovered pro-vegan social media, it pervaded all their online activity. To the extent that, for some, it not only became their primary *Other-for-me* but also functioned as a *Single-voiced* echo chamber: *'... even on Instagram ... all the pages I followed were usually mainly about the diet and the food you ate'* (Cordelia). This, however, is an aspect we will explore further in Chapter 4.

At the beginning of this Chapter, we also discussed the interviewees's heavy engagement with *social media influencers*, particularly those on Instagram and YouTube. This is not particularly surprising, as several studies, in the past five years, have explored how Veganism and vegan nutrition have emerged as popular trends on platforms such as Instagram and YouTube (Phua, Jin, and Kim, 2020), where influencers claim to pursue an ethical vegan lifestyle and promote it to their followers. In her article, Sitko (2023) explores the business ties of *social media influencers* who promote Veganism and questions the authenticity of their communication with their audience. She also refers to Veganism as a 'multidimensionality' movement, which I read as another term for *Polyphony*. Sitko (2023) concludes that, 'the potential of influencers' impact in the area [Veganism] can be evidenced by the reactions of recipients,' and that each influencer promotes a particular, if not multiple version(s) of Veganism (Sitko, 2023: 64). Similarly, Santos, de Brito-Silva, and da Coata et al. (2023) examine how social media influencers promote vegan cosmetics and shape individual digital behaviour. Our analysis in Chapters 4 and 5, will take this a step further. We will not only explore how various representations of Veganism were internalised and interpreted by our interviewees and how the *Vegan-other-for-more* influenced their self-perception, but also how this fluctuated at each *Threshold-moment*.

Chapter Summary

There is a lot of pre-occupation in current scholarship concerning the distinctions between defining Veganism, and the 'type' of vegan one *Becomes*.

In this chapter, as we have discussed that these 'types' are not simply definitional differences. Rather, each approach is *positivistic* within their own respective vegan community (Greenbaum, 2012a). As you may already know, within psychological research, positivistic or *Positivism*, is generally represents a research philosophical stance, and *Positivism* is often connected with experimental and quantitative epistemology (Phillips and Burbules, 2000). Ontologically, *Positivism* champions the existence of *priors* (facts), and that lived experiences of individuals are the same within a given community, with a given *prior.* The community factor is key in such a context as research emphasises the importants of group and community within the formation of vegan identities.

However, through exploring the *Speech Genres* within the interviewees's *Utterances*, at their first *Threshold-moment*, we have sought to convey is their multiple-faceted motives for *Becoming* vegan, and that the boundaries between the 'type' of vegan they choses to become are, perhaps, more permeable than what current research proposes. One potential reason for this being that, at this *Threshold-moment*, participants experience *Polyphonic* vegan *Voice(s)*. This was reflected not only in their shifting motivational drives but also in how several of the participants's *Voice(s)* remained *Double-voiced*. The *Speech Genres* during this *Threshold-moment* of 'discovering' Veganism are also indicative of how the interviewees's *I-for-myself* was at, or placed at, a 'given moment' of uncertainty (Bakhtin, 1984: 30). As Bakhtin notes, *inter*-subjectivity occurs at such *Thresholds* where the boundary between one's own and someone else's consciousness communicates with an *Other*. The analyses disclosed how, after engaging with a variety of *Others*, the interviewees were faced with a choice: to *Become* vegan, or not to *Become* vegan. Of course, it goes without saying that they did chose the former.

Finally, this chapter has also been illustrative of the process of applying a *Dialogical* analytical framework. As we move forward to our second analysis chapter, it is important to note that consciousness of the *Self* is achieved and perceived *against the background* of the consciousness that another has of the *Self* (or of us): the *I-for-myself* against the background of *I-for-the-other*. It is a complex 'paradox' in which *Others* may attempt to finalise the *I*, and the *I* incorporates the *Finalisation* of the *Other*. However, it must also remain *Answerable*. That is why it is possible for one to be simultaneously 'social' and 'individual.' During this process, it is essential that the *I-for-myself* does not become *Finalised*:

> In order to live and act, I need to be unfinalized, I need to be open for myself … I have to be, for myself, someone who is axiologically yet-to-be, someone who does not coincide with his already existing makeup.
>
> (Bakhtin, 1993: 13)

One's *Voice* and self-consciousness must continue to be in a perpetual state of *Becoming* and *Unfinalisability*. This is not to say, however, that some of the participants did not specifically seek this sense of finalisation:

> I think I had quite a poor sense of self and my ego has always been unsure of who I am or what I represent, what my identity is so I think quite classically it gave me that sense of identity, it was something to say, you know, I am a vegan, this is what I stand by, this is my ethical point of view (Cordelia).

In the following chapter, we will explore individual lived experiences, in terms of *Selfhood* and self-identity, in relation to Veganism and the vegan *Other*.

References

Bauman, Z. (1995). *Life in fragments: Essays in postmodern morality.* Oxford: Blackwell.

Bakhtin, M. (1993). *Toward a philosophy of the act.* Austin: University of Texas Press.

Bakhtin, M. (1990). *Art and answerability: early philosophical essays.* Austin: University of Texas Press.

Bakhtin, M. (1986). *Speech genres and other late essays.* Austin: University of Texas Press.

Bakhtin, M. (1984b). *Rabelais and his world.* Bloomington: Indiana University Press.

Bakhtin, M. (1981). *The dialogic imagination: Four essays.* Austin: University of Texas Press.

Braunsberger, K., & Flamm, R. (2019). The case of ethical vegan: motivations matter when researching dietary and lifestyle choices. *Journal of Managerial Issues*, 31(3), 228–245.

Christophe, A., Bartkowski, J. P., & Haverda, T. (2018). Portraits of veganism: a comparative discourse analysis of a second-order subculture. *Societies*, 8(3), 1–21. https://doi.org/10.3390/soc8030055

Cole, M., & K. Morgan. 2011. Vegaphobia: derogatory discourses of veganism and the reproduction of speciesism in UK. *The British Journal of Sociology*, 62(1), 134–153. https://doi.org/10.1111/j.1468-4446.2010.01348.x

Cresswell, J., & Baerveldt, C. (2011). Bakhtin's realism and embodiment: towards a revision of the dialogical self. *Culture & Psychology*, 17(2), 263–277. https://doi.org/10.1177/1354067X11398308

Cresswell, J., & Teucher, U. (2011). The body and language: M. M. Bakhtin on the ontogenetic development. *New Ideas in Psychology*, 12, 106–118. https://doi.org/10.1016/j.newideapsych.2010.05.001

Dhont, K., & Ioannidou, M. (2021, November 4). Vegan for the animals. The Vegan Society-The Expert Series Autumn/Winter 2021. https://www.vegansociety.com/get-involved/research/research-news/expert-series-autumnwinter-2021-vegan-animals

dos Santos, R. C., de Brito-Silva, M. J., da Costa, M. F. et al. (2023). Go vegan! Digital influence and social media use in the purchase intention of vegan products in the cosmetics industry. *Social Network Analysis and Mining*, 13(49), 1–13. https://doi.org/10.1007/s13278-023-01034-7

Doyle, J. (2016). Celebrity vegans and the lifestyling of ethical consumption. *Environmental Communication*, 10(6), 777–790. https://doi.org/10.1080/17524032.2016.1205643

Erikson, E. H. (1968). *Identity, youth and crisis*. New York: W. W. Norton & Company.

Feng, Y., Chen, H., & Kong, Q. (2020). An expert with whom I can identify: the role of narratives in influencers marketing. *International Journal of Advertising*. https://doi.org/10.1080/02650487.2020.1824751

Ghaffari, M., Rodrigo, P. G. K., Ekinci, Y. et al. (2022). Consumers' motivations for adopting a vegan diet: a mixed-methods approach. *International Journal of Consumer Studies*, 46(4), 1193–1208. https://doi.org/10.1111/ijcs.12752

Giraud, E. H. (2021). *Veganism: politics, practice, and theory*. London: Bloomsbury Academic.

Golden, N. H., Schneider, M., Wood, C., et al. (2016). Preventing obesity and eating disorders in adolescents. *Paediatrics*, 138(3), e20161649. https://doi.org/10.1542/peds.2016-1649

Greenebaum, J. B., & Dexter, B. (2017). Vegan men and hybrid masculinity. *Journal of Gender Studies*, 27(6), 637–648. https://doi.org/10.1080/09589236.2017.1287064

Greenebaum, J. B. (2012a). "Face-Saving" strategies of vegetarians and vegans. *Humanity & Society*, 36(4), 309–325. https://doi.org/10.1177/0160597612458898

Hayley, A., Zinkiewicz, L., & Hardiman, K. (2015). Values, attitudes, and frequency of meat consumption. Predicting meat-reduced diet in Australians. *Appetite*, 84, 98–106. https://dx.doi.org/10.1016/j.appet.2014.10.002

Hopwood, C.J., Bleidorn, W., Schwaba, T. et al. (2020). Health, environmental, and animal rights motives for vegetarian eating. *PLoS One*, 15(4), 1–20. https://doi.org/10.1371/journal.pone.0230609

Hussar, K. M., & Harris, P. L. (2010). Children who choose not to eat meat: a study of early moral decision-making. *Social Development*, 19(3), 627–641. https://doi.org/10.1111/j.1467-9507.2009.00547.x.

Janssen, M., Busch, C., Rödiger, M. et al. (2016). Motives of consumers following a vegan diet and their attitudes towards animal agriculture. *Appetite*, 1(105), 643–651. https://doi.org/10.1016/j.appet.2016.06.039

Laing, R. D. (1960). *The divided self: an existential study in sanity and madness*. U.K.: Penguin Books.

Lupton, D., & Fieldman, Z. (Eds.). *Digital food cultures*. New York: Routledge. https://doi.org/10.4324/9780429402135-7

Moreno, L. A., Meyer, R., Donovan, S. M., et al. (2022). Perspective: striking a balance between planetary and human health-is there a path forward? *Advances in Nutrition*, 13(2), 355–375. https://doi.org/10.1093/advances/nmab139

Oliver, C. (2021). Vegan world-making in meat-centric society: the embodied geographies of veganism. *Social & Cultural Geography*, 24(5), 831–850. https://doi.org/10.1080/14649365.2021.1975164

Phillips, D. C., & Burbules, N. C. (2000) *Post-positivism and educational research*. Oxford: Rowman & Littlefield Publishers.

Phua, J., Jin, S. V., & Kim, J. J. (2020). Pro-veganism on Instagram: effects of user-generated content (UGC) types and content generator types in Instagram-based health marketing communication about veganism. *Online Information Review*, 44, 685–704. https://doi.org/10.1108/OIR-06-2019-0213

Ponzio, A. (2016). Otherness, intercorporeity and dialogism in Bakhtin's vision of the text. *Language and Semiotic Studies*, 2(3), 1–17. https://doi.org/10.1515/lass-2016-020301

Potts, A., & Parry, J. (2010). Vegan sexuality: challenging heteronormative masculinity through Meat-Free Sex. *Feminism & Psychology*, 20(1), 53–72. https://doi.org/10.1177/0959353509351181

Randall, T. (2018). Heganism. *Between The Species*, 22(1). Retrieved from https://digitalcommons.calpoly.edu/bts/vol22/iss1/6

Rosalind, G. (2016). Post-feminism?: New feminist visibilities in postfeminist times. *Feminist Media Studies*, 16(4), 610–630. https://dx. doi.org/10.1080/14680777.2016.1193293

Rosalind, G. (2007). Postfeminist media culture: elements of a sensibility. *European Journal of Cultural Studies*, 10(2), 147–166. https://doi.org/10.1177/1367549407075898

Ryder, R. D (1971). Animals, men and morals. London: Oxford Group.

Sitko, B. (2023). The promotion of veganism by influencers. A case study of selected Instagram profiles. *Social Communication*, 1, 24–34.

Trauth, E., Stanescu, V., & Levin, S. et al. (2022). Rhetoric of vegan/vegetarianism, and health, medicine, and culture: a dialogue. *Rhetoric of Health & Medicine*, 4(2), 246–273. https://doi.org/10.5744/rhm.2021.2006

Wright, L. (Ed.). (2018). Veganism studies and ecocriticism. Special cluster *Interdisciplinary Studies in Literature and Environment*, 24(4), 737–802.

Wright, L. (2015). *The vegan studies project: food animals, and gender in the age of terror*. Athens: University of Georgia Press.

Yourofsky, G. (2010). *The most important speech you will ever hear.* Accessed 30th May 2024. https://www.humanedecisions.com/the-most-powerful-speech-you-will-ever-hear/

4

THE MIDDLE, HOW IT ALL WENT?

> *Complicated [laughs].*
> *It was complicated for a lot of reasons, if I had to pick a statement*
> *I would say good in the beginning but not worth it.*
>
> (Puck)

The topic of 'purity politics,' coined by Shotwell (2016), has been a hotly contested subject, not only in recent scholarship but also in broader vegan activism. Shotwell (2016) notes that there is no utopian state of time and space of *Being* or practice to which we as a society must (re)turn. There is a quantifiable time-space of *priori* that we can hope to achieve as a society, one which addresses oppressive structures such as colonialism, disease, and climate change. Moreover, as Giraud (2021) phrases it, 'purity politics' also frames the vegan individual within a certain light for the *Other*: as a self-satisfied and self-righteous individuals. Giraud (2021) further notes that this framing of superiority is further re-inforced by popular social media representations of Veganism and *Being* vegan. In the vegan context, the meaning of purity politics, in a very dialogical manner, has begun to transform, and perhaps should now be understood axiologically. The reason for this is that, historically, in terms of consumption habits, 'purity' has been centred around the individual for health benefits. In the context of *Being* vegan, 'purity' and 'impurity' have categorised food and defined the boundaries concerning prohibited foods (Arppe, Mäkelä, and Väänänen, 2011). Recent scholarship, however, questions placing accountability for food, animal ethics, and agricultural energy systems on the shoulder of *individuals*, suggesting that Veganism should be perceived as a *collective* political movement to

DOI: 10.4324/9781003384526-4

overturn systematic oppressive structures (Cochrane and Cojocaru, 2022). Therefore, to a certain extent, parting ways with 'purity' while retaining the 'political.' Such debates are fractious, continuous, and indeed polyphonic. What unifies them, however, is that they pursue their arguments at a macro and structural level, with the goal of eliminating animal exploitation through agriculture and consumption. In Shotwell's words, such an approach evokes the recognition 'that individual purity or actions aiming toward it are not going to solve the collective, complex problems in which we are differentially complicit' (Shotwell, 2016: 202).

Having said that, Barad (2007), maintains that 'the effect of boundary-drawing practices that make some identities or attributes intelligible (determinate) to the exclusion of others' (Barad, 2007: 208, 2003). In a world that is in constant change, however, which is embedded with multiplicity, Veganism, and those practising Veganism, are unable to preserve total purity. Of course, this is not to say that *Being* vegan can be understood as, or include, indulging in the 'impurities' imposed by the prescribed boundaries. I would argue that what Shotwell (2016) and Barad (2007) are referring to is what Bakhtin (1993: 106) refers to as an 'ideal form,' or a *symbolic form* of Veganism. Bakhtin writes,

> ... as such, and because of the fact that the various cultural forms enjoy autonomy, no particular ... is reducible to the universal, the ideal form: But the text (as distinct from the language as a system of means) can never be completely translated, for there is no potential single text of texts.

It is true that in the quote above, Bakhtin is referring to *Utterances* within texts. However, in Chapter 2 we outlined Bakhtin's stance on the interwoven nature of language, social realities, and individual consciousness (*Being*). On an elemental level, a 'pure' symbolic form of Veganism, or any other social phenomenon, has no ontological reality. Under a *Dialogical* lens, language and the symbols it constructs can never become singular and demand for us to understand them within the various social setting ('sign system') that aggregate them.

Sideward Glance

For those of you who are philosophically inclined, you will have noticed that Bakhtin's thinking here is akin to Cassirer's Symbolic Form. For Cassirer, the Symbolic Form is also structured and conceived within language. It is through their use of language that a given culture creates a symbolic for and gives it meaning.

(see Intezar and Sullivan, 2022)

Despite the acknowledgement of *Polyphony* within the meaning-making of Veganism or defining what *Being* vegan entails, as we explore in this chapter, the notion of 'purity politics,' or indeed the term 'purity' itself, has the potential to become problematic for those practising Veganism, especially in terms of their sense of *Self.* The primary purpose of this chapter is not to contribute to the existing literature around Veganism and purity politics. Rather, the aim is to explore the experiences of those practising Veganism at a micro level and highlight how they negotiate *intra*-tensions of *Selfhood* and group identity within popular vegan culture, as well as broader cultural settings. For example, how they negotiate the boundaries of *Being* vegan. Furthermore, although some conceptual and theoretical scholarship acknowledges the *Polyphonic* nature of Veganism, there is limited research on how such approaches are experienced 'in action.' For example, how collective movements can become a part of one's *Selfhood*, self-perception, and identity. Does experiencing and participating in collective moments / movements alleviate individual responsibility or *intra*-subjective tensions?

Towards the opposite point of the axis, in their recent theoretical piece on individual resistance to vegan advocacy, de Groeve, Bleys, and Hudders (2022) propose that such resistance to vegan advocacy is ideological and identity-based. Despite agreeing with vegan ideology in private, they argue that one may continue to consume animal products as it may conflict with one's ideology of carnism; potentially, threating one's moral identity as a consumer of animal products. The majority of carnists, therefore, revolt against dietary changes, specifically the cessation of animal product consumption, because 'they are motivated to protect their identity as consumers of animal products when confronted with an "outgroup" of veg*n advocates,' leading to stigmatisation of said advocates (de Groeve, Bleys, and Hudders, 2022: 04).

Sideward Glance

For several scholars focusing on sustainability, Veganism, and animal ethics, Carnism can be understood as the 'dominant' *socio-cultural perspective, where consumption of animal products is legitimised. Joy (2020, 2011) define* Carnism *as an ideological stance which endorses* Carnism *and* Speciesism.

What is overlooked in current scholarship, they continue, is a thorough exploration of how carnist ideological stances toward Veganism and vegan activism derive from identity-based motivations. We will return to the discussion on ideology-based motivation in Chapter 6. Here, however, I want to focus on for those practising, Veganism can not only become an identity-based motivation but also magnify a sense of individual responsibility towards animal ethics.

Especially in cases neither factor was the salient motivational drive for *Becoming* vegan. Puck's *Utterances* below, for instance, encapsulates the experience of a number of the interviewees (though not *all* I must stress):

> I want to say it was like 90/10, with heavy on the ethics, because I am such a sensitive person, and I get very passionate about things very quickly, so when I kind of latched onto that it was like ethics all the way, and like the health benefits are good, I used to say it was like the icing on the cake, you know, so like the health benefits were there, but I at 16 was not very worried about my health because who is as a teenager.

There has been academic interest in the intersection between identity and Veganism for some time, as mentioned in Chapter 1. In their systematic review of vegan identity, Vestergren and Uysal (2022) propose a poignant question: is Veganism a part 'of a social identity, or a social identity in *itself*' and suggest that the answer is likely dependent 'on the social context' (Vestergren and Uysal, 2022: 02). They also advocate for the need of a 'fine-grained exploration' of vegan identity. This chapter builds on this by beginning to explore the *inter*-subjective and *intra*-subjective tensions experienced by those practising Veganism. We discuss how, during their second *Threshold-moment*, the interviewees not only experienced disruptions in group cohesion (MacInnis and Hodson, 2021), but this also created disruptions within the *I-for-myself* (ontological insecurity). For instance, the first *Threshold-moment* of *Becoming* vegan presented a *Polyphonic* landscape. However, recent academic and activist initiatives call for Veganism to become a more *inclusive* and a practice-based ethos, offering a sense of unification within the cacophony of *Polyphony*. Arguably, for some participants, this unification manifested in Veganism becoming an ideology-based-ism, hence, leading to a unification of *Double-voiced Speech Genres* to *Single-voiced Speech Genres.*

In Chapter 1, we discussed a key passage in Bakhtin's writings, which emphasised that dialogical *Utterances* are, and must remain, 'contradiction-ridden, tension-filled unity [of Veganism] of two embattled tendencies in the life of language' (Bakhtin, 1981: 272). It is important to note that, for Bakhtin, contradictory *Voices* are not a catastrophe. Indeed, they are simply the nature of our social fabric, as language is *living*. In this sense, it is not a matter of championing one *Voice* over the other; it is not about 'liberating plurality or "heteroglossia" over the restrictively unitary "monoglossia"'(Reed, 2014: 09). The goal is to find an equilibrium these embattled forces. There are, therefore, incontrovertible tensions and frictions between the diverse interpretations and meanings that our social consciousness has placed on a given concept, such as Veganism, and an immutable tension between the living *Utterance* and the *understanding* of *said Utterance*. In Chapter 2, we also outlined the relationship between social language and the *Dialogical Self*. What impact, then, does the unification of *Voices* and *Speech Genres* in relation to concepts such as Veganism have on individual identity and *Selfhood*? In proceeding sections, we being to explore the *Utterances* from the interviewees second *Threshold-moment* (*Being* vegan). Once the interviewees took the decision to become vegan, the *Utterances* within their *Primary Speech Genres* deviated away from the *Primary Speech Genre* of *Self Focus* and towards a sense of anti-self-consciousness or a *decentring* of the *Self*. For example, the two *Primary Speech Genres* emerged during the participants's *Threshold-moment* of *Being* vegan: the *Intra-conflict of the I-for-myself* and *Denial*. The *Intra-conflict of the I-for-myself* consisted of the *Secondary Speech Genres* of *Collective Identity and the Vegan-other-for-me*, the *Non-vegan-other-for-me*, and *Vegan Social Media*, while the *Primary Speech Genre* of *Denial* encapsulated the *Secondary Speech Genres* of *Physical Health* and *Mental Health*.

Maintaining a *Double-Voiced* Speech Genre

It is important to note that some participants's *Utterances*, and therefore *Speech Genres*, remained *Double-voiced*, or heteroglossic. You may remember that in previous chapters, we discussed the concepts of *Finitisability* and *Unfinalisability* as the corner stones of Bakhtin's work, and how the latter offers an aspect of openness, which is essential for the *Self* and identity construction. Within a dialogical interaction between the *I-for-myself* and *I-for-other*, the *I-for-myself* should always maintain *Answerability*. This means that the *I-for-myself* needs to *continually* experience and understand a phenomenon, such as practising Veganism, from their *own life experience*, rather than ascribe entirely to the *Voice(s)* of the *Other*. Hence, avoid becoming finalised with a monolithic *Voice*. Ruby (2012) and Salehi, Diaz, and Redondo (2020) have argued that there is a higher probability of those practising Veganism to remain vegan for a long term if they: (1) have social support, (2) if they are motivated by animal ethics, and (3) if they are knowledgeable about nutrition. To a certain degree, this aligns with Goneril's and Leigha's experiences, respectively. The quote below, for instance, reveals Goneril's resistance towards being *Finalised*, and a *Single-voiced* consciousness. Additionally, while engaging with vegan social media, Goneril chose to limit her interests to food preparations and nutrition: '*Well, the like YouTubers that I used to watch that would show you like easy ways to make this vegan thing, like student vegan meals, that kind of thing. That's basically it.*'

> Yeah, definitely but I did have these kind of online voices that I was listening to but *I was alone in it*, yeah. *Yeah. Yeah, I try not to get involved in that* [animal ethics], in the kind of… I mean, I get it, animals rights and like environmental, you know, protest and stuff but I just didn't really want to be part of that quite aggressive front that happens a lot in veganism, I just wanted to just do it for myself and just kind of, *you know, prove my capabilities* …

Leigha's experience was similar in the sense that she only encountered the *Vegan-other-for-me* once she had already practised Veganism and had decided to stop. She explained that she '*had some basis of nutrition knowledge*' prior to trying Veganism, and while engaging with vegan documentaries, she acknowledged that '*you know, there's some fact to it.*' Moreover, while interacting with an *Other* practising Veganism, Leigha was hesitant to enter into a dialogue with them, by refraining to adding her *Voice* and sharing her experience:

> I remember she told me that, you know, she was vegan and dah dah dah and I remember, I think *I was a bit sceptical in saying like oh, you know, I tried that and I didn't feel very good.*

From a *Dialogical* epistemology, Leigha's experience is indicative of the closed, totalising *Speech Genres* surrounding certain definitions of Veganism. From a socio-institutional perspective, Bakhtin identifies this as a *Single-voiced Genre* (Bakhtin, 1981). As we have discussed elsewhere, the function of *Single-voiced Genres* is to accomplish 'the task of cultural, national and political centralization of the verbal-ideological [such as certain definitions of Veganism] world in the higher official socio-ideological levels' (Bakhtin, 1981: 273). A key characteristic of the *Single-voiced Genre* is the failure to recognise other *Genres.* In other words, the *Voice* of the *Other*, which leads to the alienation of multivocality and, thus, *Polyphony*: resulting in static, ahistorical and, fundamentally, unified world-view of socio-institutional authority. A closed totality. We elaborate on unifying *Speech Genres* and socio-cultural ideologies in Chapter 6. What I would like to highlight here is how meaning-making and identity construction can take place within online vegan communities.

Scott (2020) and Sneijder and Hedwig (2005), for example, have analysed online discourses within online vegan forums. This is particularly noteworthy as all the participants interviewed in this study had, both implicitly and explicitly, engaged with vegan social media. Indeed, it remained a steady consistent thread throughout their vegan journey. The analysis of online vegan communities disclosed, in Bakhtinian teams, the critical *vegan-other-for-me*, as they attempt to finalise the *Answerability* of the *I-for-myself* by constructing solutions to their individual health issues. The empirical data from this project would extend Sneijder and Hedwig's (2005) analysis to include the practitioners's lifestyle as a whole and imply that finalisability rhetoric also applies more broadly in the context of identity and self-perception, not simply in terms of health. Scott (2020) also notes that, in terms of health, practising Veganism is understood as an individualised process, where one is responsible for their own health risks. The individualisation of health and Veganism in online discourse is somewhat contradictory to the call for collective political solidarity in the context of animal ethics.

Scholarship concerning dietary lifestyles and meat consumption often places emphasis on consumers developing cognitive dissonance strategies (Ioannidou, Lesk, Stewart- Knox et al., 2023) and choosing to morally disengage (Graça, Calheiros and Oliveira, 2016, 2015) with animal suffering. My conversation with Gonaril, as well as other participants, was indicative of a more nuanced cognitive process, which did not necessarily involve the development of cognitive dissonance.

> ... *I wasn't like emotional*, like I know that a lot of people, I've looked up a lot of stuff online about people that were vegan and got really ill because of it and a lot of people got depression and anxiety, just heightened anxiety, I didn't get that but, you know, like my body was just not, like really giving me signs that this wasn't a suitable diet for me. *But mentally like I felt fine.*

As we discuss in the next section, however, several of the interviewees who were motivated by animal ethics during their first *Threshold-moment* did experience emotional turmoil during their second *Threshold-moment*. Arguably, this could be because of their *I-for-myself* did not having maintained a *Double-voiced Speech Genres*.

Primary Genre: Intra-conflict of the I-for-myself

For a dialogical ontological perspective, the *Self*, should not be totalised and resists *Finalisation*, where one's *Voice* becomes signalised and fuses with that of the *Other*, which insulates one from existing as a 'non-being,' where one is empty, 'determined, predetermined, bygone and finished, that is essentially not living' (Bakhtin, 1990: 16). This is not to say that Bakhtin is advocating for a conflict-free dialogical exchange between the *I* and the *Other* in terms of identity and self-formation. The purpose, rather, is to 'provide a way of thinking about shifts between levels of identity' without reducing it to a *single consciousness* (Nielsen, 2002: 25). The social psychology of the relationship between food and identity, and indeed identity and Veganism, is now a well-trodden landscape in academia. Scholarship in the last decade or so has developed this further by emphasising the collective boundary building between different understandings of dietary food groups, especially vegetarianism and Veganism (MacInnis and Hodson, 2021; Neuman, 2020). There is limited research, however, on *inter*-subjective tensions among those practising Veganism. For example, health and environmentally driven vegans are sometimes perceived as 'not sufficiently vegan' by those who are motivated by animal ethics (Greenebaum, 2012b), and there is even more limited qualitative research concerning intersectionalities within lived experiences, vegan identity, and *intra*-subjective tensions (Table 4.1).

TABLE 4.1 *Soundbites for the Primary Speech Genre of Intra-conflict*

Primary Genre	*Secondary Genre*	*Quotes*
Intra-conflict of the I-for-myself	Collective Identity and the Vegan-Other-For-Me	*... so I really wanted to go to where all these people were because I kind of felt like they're the only ones that would really understand me* (Bianca).
		...my local vegan group encourages vegans to stop seeing their non-vegan family. I remember they would tell us to stop eating in the same table and if possible to avoid them completely (Orlando).
	The None-Vegan-Other-For-Me	*I still kind of felt like, you know, a bit of an outcast, like I wasn't really there enjoying the food with them, I still felt a bit separated* (Bianca).
		I stopped seeing my non-vegan friends ... I just used the 'I'm vegan' to stop seeing them but it was an excuse to be honest. But yes, I was not comfortable with non-vegan people (Orlando).
	Vegan Social Media	*[Laughs] F brainwashed me, okay. F, okay, so when I was younger I was like, wow, this person is so passionate, like they really care about animals* (Puck).

Sideward Glance

Before moving forwards, I would like to highlight that scholarship focusing on Veganism and identity emphasises different subgroups of identity, which is often determine by the researchers' epistemological positioning. Identity Theory (IT), for example, is generally associated with Sociology, while Social Identity Theory (SIT) is allied with Psychology. In this chapter, when I refer to Collective Identity, we position ourselves with the conceptual framework proposed by Davis, Love, and Fares (2019), who amalgamate IT and SIT by integrating collective identity with group and social identity base. Please see Glossary for further definitions.

Collective Identity and the Vegan-Other-For-Me

Participants's *Secondary Speech Genres* disclosed three predominant *Others-for-me* who carried 'contradiction-ridden' *Voices* for their *I-for-myself*, often manifesting as ontological insecurity and, therefore, causing high levels of *inter*-subjective and *intra*-subjective tensions. This was particularly the case for those who had developed a strong sense of collectiveness once they became vegan. Classical and contemporary social psychological research has demonstrated that social groups and the shared social identities they offer us (the *I-for-myself*) help us accomplish basic psychological needs (Greenaway, Cruwys, Haslam et al., 2016). Although they do conclude that psychological needs are not reducible to one particular facet and actually refer to them as 'blanket' universal needs, we can relate 'psychological needs' here to a sense of identity or affirmation for the *I-for-myself*. For a number of interviewees, Veganism offered a sense of identity and a positive sense of *Self*:

> … it gave me that sense of identity, it was something to say, you know, I am a vegan, this is what I stand by, this is my ethical point of view (Cordelia).
>
> Yeah, it was a big part of my identity (Kate).
>
> Definitely, it was definitely like an identity (Puck).

Other participants reflect that they began to form friendships simply based on the premises that the encountered *Other* was also vegan:

> so I found that I have made friends with vegans very easily, so like I would become friends with someone just for that reason. I'd just be in class, I'd figure out me and another classmate, we'd figure out we're both vegan and then we're just friends like that (Portia).

After initially becoming vegan, some participants experienced a boost in self-perception, not only for altruistic reasons but also because they felt physically better (Vögele and Gibson, 2010) and experienced health benefits.

> I felt really good at the beginning because I was trying to lose some weight and I did (Orlando).
>
> I did feel good as a vegan and there was a lot of positives that I reaped which I'd say were just detoxification and not eating and drinking and everything, the lifestyle I had before (Cordelia).
>
> And erm… like it was good at first and, you know, I started to see some really good results. But then, yeah, it was like a, kind of a slow decline from then (Bianca).

In Chapter 1, we outlined the complex and contradictory academic perceptions of the connection between Veganism, identity, and personal gain. Recent social psychological research, however, has argued for the positive relationship between Veganism and identity, implying that those practising Veganism for personal benefits were, mentally, less conflicted. For instance, Costa, Gilla,

Morda et al. (2019) focus on how Veganism has helped individuals 'heal' their relationship with food and initiated an inner transformation, where it became 'more than a diet.' Others, such as Stuart, Thomas, Donaghue et al. (2013), Vestergren, Drury, and Chiriac (2019), and Judge, Fernando, and Begeny (2022), focus on how Veganism can and has become a cornerstone of some activist identities. Research has also highlighted how vegan practitioners have experienced *inter*-group tension and actively chose to avoid discussing *Being* vegan or revealing their vegan identity, as they were aware of the negative discourses surrounding Veganism, especially in relation to other dietary groups (Buttny and Kinefuchi, 2020). This was also the case for Bianca:

> And I kind of kept it a bit private because *[sighs]*, I don't know, I feel like I was kind of slightly afraid of people judging me for it. I just didn't really want the attention from it. So, I mean, if somebody asked me, then I would tell them.

Although there has been academic discussion on *inter*-group tensions for those practising Veganism Giraud (2021) and vegan stigmatisation (Markowski and Roxburgh, 2019), a number of participants from the study, who chose to join a vegan community, disclosed experiencing *intra*-group tensions that have largely been underemphasised in vegan scholarship. Intra-group tensions, which also led to *intra*-subjective tension for the *I-for-myself*. Portia, for example, recollected that she did not wish to disclose *Being* vegan because she felt that her vegan friendship group displayed a sense of superiority, which she did not identify with:

> No, but I did, I found that like [laughs], like I found that a lot of vegans have, I don't, yeah, I don't want to say that they have a superiority thing necessarily, *but I feel like they tend to look at people who aren't vegan in a different way* (Portia).

Classical social identity theory (Tajfel and Turner, 1979) proposes that the motivational drives for individuals to become members of certain groups is to project and hold a positive image of the groups they identify with. Additionally, individuals adopt various strategies to achieve and maintain said positive image (Ellemers and Haslam, 2011); we will return to the point a little later when we discuss the *Primary Speech Genre* of *Denial.* Some group members, for instance, can claim their group is superior to others by maintaining that it has a range of positive features. Research has supported the notion that those who practise and promote Veganism may project a sense of moral and ethical distinction in the context of Sustainably (Bramble and Fischer, 2016; Ulusoy, 2014), and that this conviction of high moral standing is greater in relation to animal ethics (Simons, Vierboom, Klink-Lehmann et al., 2021; Napoli and

Ouschan, 2020). In their research on dietary identities, Kirsten, Seib-Pfeifer, Lüth et al. (2020) note that, compared to omnivores and vegetarians, vegans are not only more likely to centralise their diet to their sense of identity but are also more likely to adhere to their dietary boundaries. Moreover, they also propose that, in comparison to other dietary groups, vegans also perceive their dietary in-group more favourably while simultaneously evaluating other dietary out-groups more negatively. Puck's *Utterances* are insightful in relation to framing dietary ideologies, which we discuss further in Chapter 6.

> And also I think veganism is *portrayed as* this very like prestigious and very like high horse kind of thing to do, which is and isn't, because there is a lot of *privilege behind being able to be vegan, so I think the way it's initially framed to people was like a really big issue for me, because I didn't feel morally superior to anybody, so I really do think it's like there is this stigma* around people who are vegan that we're like hateful and you're doing this wrong, I'm doing it right kind of thing.

Ellmers (2017) also proposes that 'reality constraints may force individuals to acknowledge that the group they identify with actually is not doing very well in terms of achieving important outcomes or in building a positive social image' (2017: 179). Nonetheless, individuals still maintain their membership in their selected group, even if their identity and self-identity (*I-for-myself*) may not be perceived favourably by other dietary groups or the wider public in general. Kirsten-Effi, Seib-Pfeifer, Lüth et al.'s (2020) paper also highlights a more statistically extreme response by those practising Veganism when it came to sentiments of being peripheralised and judged more negatively by other dietary food groups. There is ample of research arguing for the stigmatisation Veganism as a concept, and how those practising Veganism are often stigmatised (de Groeve and Rosenfeld, 2022; Markowski and Roxburgh, 2019). Despite expressing that he did not identify strongly with a vegan identity and being conscious of the rhetoric of 'superiority' associated with Veganism, Orlando chose to join a local vegan community.

> Yes, I was not comfortable with non-vegan people. I remember them [*Vegan-other-for-me*] being really pushy about it on holiday season, like Christmas and New Years. For example, the first Christmas dinner with the family (we have a big party with my aunts, uncles, cousins, etc) I went but didn't eat on the same table because I didn't want to eat close to them.

Orlando's *Utterances* and his conscious action of distinguishing his consumption space from the *Non-vegan-other* illustrate what Lara (2021) refers to as the 'organic process' of everyday food practises becoming a construction of self-identity (*I-for-myself*). Moreover, the politics of *institutional* vegan ideology (see Chapter 6) and compassion towards other species instils a sense of vegan of responsibility. Orlando's experience also reflects Bakhtin's (1990), emphasis on the *inter*-subjective nature of identity formation and the *Self*, which is often underemphasises in contemporary social psychological research. The *I-for-myself*, for instance, is continually evaluating and calculating *Voices* (from the *Other-for-me*), which influences and shapes the *I-for-myself*'s inner experience (or *Spirit*), as the *I-for-myself* perceives itself through the eye of the *Other*. The is a form of vivification, where the *Other* bestows upon the *I* a sense of validation (*I-for-others* or *Soul*). Here, for Orlando, that would be the authentication of *Being* vegan. Orlando's *Utterances* disclose how his communication with the *Vegan-other-for-me* altered his communication with, and perspective of, the *Non-vegan-other-for-me*. Applying a dialogical epistemology allows us to extent this another analytical step further. Orlando's *Utterances*, for example, are indicative of *intra*-group and *intra*-subjective tensions, as his *I-for-myself* is placed in a dialogically agitated and tension-filled environment of *Polyphony*. *Intra*-group tensions arose as Orlando did not entirely agree with the *Voice* (note I am using the singular here) emerging from the *Vegan-other-for-me*, and *intra*-subjective strain arose as Orlando hesitated to salinities *Being* vegan.

> I wanted to introduce myself because of what I do or what I like to do, not of my lifestyle ... They [*Vegan-other-for-me*] were blasting out that they were vegan. They knew new people and they started like "I'm vegan" ... I remember one time ... we had to introduce ourselves ... I remember those two or three vegan people they all say their name and that they were vegan.

Nonetheless, Orlando chose to be a part of the local vegan community, which is not entirely surprising, as sociological research has emphasised importance social networking to gain support and motivation for maintain the vegan identity and ideology (Cherry, 2015, 2006). The *intra*-subjectivity tension for Orlando could also be a result of the fact that, initially, during his first *Threshold-moment*, Orlando's motivation for *Becoming* vegan was not based on animal ethics. Rather, the predominant *Secondary Speech Genre* within his *Utterances* was *Health and Fitness* (see Chapter 3). Interaction with the *Vegan-other-for-me*, however, manifested a shift in Orlando's *Voice*: *'I remember we talk about food and animal welfare and animal cruelty and how to stop it.'* Whereas Orlando's first *Threshold-moment*, consisted on *multivocality*, his second *Threshold-moment* was monolithic in nature, therefore, driven more towards *Finitisability*. Although Orlando began to physically distance himself from the *Non-vegan-other* and began to assume a *Collective Identity* and *Voice*, he was clear in expressing that he did not attempt to *'turn anyone else vegan.'* Despite his *intra*-subjective conflicts, Orlando allows himself dialogical space, or what Bakhtin (1990) refers to as a *Loophole*, thus preventing his *I-for-myself* from becoming *Finalised*. This, however, was not the experience of other participants I conversed with.

Secondary Speech Genre of Vegan Social Media

In comparison to other interviewees, one of the most interesting aspects of my conversation with Bianca and Puck was the fact that the *Voice* (again in the singular) of their *Vegan-other-for-me* was based entirely online.

> I think a lot of vegans will know the person that I'm talking about, but I kind of fell into the YouTuber F.... I don't know how it happened, I never like actively searched, I think it just one day came up on my recommended videos (Bianca).

> So you may have heard of this person, her name's F .... [Laughs] brainwashed me, okay. F, okay, so when I was younger I was like, wow, this person is so passionate, like they really care about animals (Puck).

Despite Bianca and Puck's *Vegan-other-for-me* consisting entirely of online vegan communities, they developed a strong sense of a vegan identity. Bianca's lived experience, and indeed the experience of several other interviewees such as Portia, Puck, and Kate, not only raise a reflexive question around identity formation and spatial proximity, but also the need to acknowledge the social psychology and dialogical relationships within online spaces. Classical social psychology studies, as well as research from other disciplines such as sociology and anthropology, place significant emphasis *on shared group temporal places and spaces.* In other words, group dynamics are linked with close physical proximity (Santos and Buzinde, 2007). However, contemporary research has begun to identify a shift in individual behaviour, where online spaces are becoming as corporal and as significant in forming an identity and a sense of *Self.*

> I kind of fell into like her little community, and that's kind of where my like social circle started to really break down, that's where I started to lose a lot of friends because I was kind of slowly being brainwashed by her and her partner at the time (Bianca).

Bianca's recollective *Utterances* convey how, for some of the interviewees, the tendency was for them to become increasingly detached from their physical time-space and the *Non-vegan-other-for-me*. The formation of dialogical relationships within online spaces, and the exaltation of certain influencers is a largely underexplored area. When scholars have explored the area of dietary group identity and social media, it was largely been from a marketing epistemology position. Although there is some research in the area of dialogical relationships within online spaces, it is in the context of athletes and fandoms (Intezar and Sullivan, 2021; Intezar, 2020).

Bianca's use of the term '*brainwashed*' and Puck's light-hearted reference to the '*internet making her vegan*' are noteworthy *Utterances* as they are indicative of the *supposedly* dialogical relationship between their *I-for-myself* and the *Vegan-other-for-me*. Hence, they not only re-framing Veganism through celebrity culture (Sitko, 2023; Phua, Jin, and Kim, 2020) and social media influencers (Schouten, 2020), but also emphasise how said individuals can be perceived as more accessible and reliable (Sedmak and Svetina, 2023). While some participants were a part of a local vegan community (Portia, Kate, Orlando, and Reghan), Bianca's and Puck's *Vegan-other-for-me* remained predominantly online, and both interviewees appeared to experience the greatest degrees of detachment from the *Non-Vegan-other-for-me*. The group membership, however, did not offer them a positive sense of identity and platform were they could express their Voice. Puck, for instance, relayed that they became a 'lurker.' In this *Threshold-moment*, Bianca expressed her belief that she only felt '*seen*' via the online vegan influencers and the communities they had created, even though she has not interacted with them directly: '*so I really wanted to go to where all these people were because I kind of felt like they're the only ones that would really understand me*.' Despite this, similar to Orlando, there were still signs *intra*-conflict between Bianca's *I-for-myself*, *I-for-other*, and *Other-for-me*: '*at the same time, like there was something in me … I wanted to but something just was not going to let me go*.'

We noted earlier that *Vegan Social Media*, and more specifically vegan social media influencers, is a significant motivational marker for those practising Veganism, as they function as 'experts' with whom followers can build a connection (Feng, Chen, Kong, 2020; van Driel and Dumitrica, 2020). This came through particularly strongly during my interview with Bianca:

> I really wanted to do the things that some of these people were doing. Like I wanted to move to Thailand, for instance. I just wanted to be where these people were and I was actually eating an extremely high fruit diet whilst I was watching her, in particular.

We will discuss the 'authenticity,' or the struggle to remain authentic, of influencers in Chapter 5. For now, the analysis above emphasises the *Voice* of the *Vegan-other-for-me*, regardless of whether they were in an online and/or corporal time-space. During their vegan journey, the *Voice* of the *Other* took prominence, to the extent that the *Voice* of the *I-for-myself* began to fuse into a *Single-voiced Utterance*. During our conversation, Cordelia relayed that, from a '*from a place of care*,' her mother often liked to play '*Devil's Advocate*,' and that

> … veganism they kind of *give you the equipment to respond to anything*, even if it's *not ideologically or logically sound or scientifically correct*, you *have these almost feedback loops* where someone says something and you've always got an answer that opposes it as to why veganism would work.

Cordelia's use of the word '*feedback loops*' is remonstrant of Bakhtin's notion that, an idea only becomes dialogical and living 'when it enters into genuine dialogic relationships' with the ideas of *Others* (Bakhtin, 1984a: 88). Without such encounters, words and ideas are monolithic, as 'they do not recognize someone else's thought' (Bakhtin, 1984a: 79). As you may have become familiar with by now, for Bakhtin, the purpose of a *Voice*, above all, is to consolidate the presence of an autonomous subject, and this is only possible when one's *Voice* maintains its own *separate* intonation. Otherwise, the *Voice* of the *I-for-myself* becomes homogenised, potentially leading to self *Finitisability*, as reflected in Bianca's *Utterances*:

> I just started to kind of repeat everything that they [vegan-influencers] would say, even if I didn't believe it myself, I was kind of, like I said brainwashed into what they were telling me.

In the final section of this chapter, we will explore the dialogical tension(s) between the *I-for-my-self*, *I-for-others*, and *Others-for-me* during the latter stages of the participants's second *Threshold-moment*, as they struggled to maintain multivocality and 'therefore' began to experience an *Unfinalised* sense of *Self* within their experiential time-space. This theme also came though strongly during my conversation with Gertrude. For the sake of maintaining anonymity, I am paraphrasing the italicised *Utterances* below:

> *and she [*the Vegan-other-for-me*] knows that my family, especially my husband, are not vegan.* But she doesn't really care about that part of it, you know, it's really to *the Vegan-other-for-me* it is first morality, morality comes first, your internal morality comes before your relationships.

Sideward Glance

A reminder: as covered in Chapter 2, an individual's inner lived experience can be perceived inwardly in two distinct forms: either by the I-for-myself (my own lived experience) or, by the Other-for-me (the lived experience of a particular unique Other). For us, here, that would be the None-vegan-other-for-me.

Non-Vegan-Other-For-Me

Contrary to Goneril, who actively chose not to engage with vegan social media or become a part of a local vegan community, and Leigha, who actively chose not to enter into a dialogue with other vegan practitioners, the *Speech Genres* within the *Utterances* of other participants revealed *intra*-subjective conflict and *inter*-subjective tensions between the *Voice* of the *I-for-myself* (note,

I am using the singular once again) and the *Voices* of the *Non-vegan-other-for-me*. I have referred to the *Voice* of the interviewees's as singular because, hopefully, the analyses above and in Chapter 3 have showcased the gradual shift within their *Utterances* as they transcend from *Double-voiced* to *Single-voiced*. Bianca, for instance, actively refrained from socialising or conversing with *Non-vegan-other-for-me* and social groups as she '***knew that, you know, people would kind of try and persuade me to eat meat.***' For those who did maintain non-vegan friendship groups at the beginning of their journey, such as Puck, Portia, and Kate, their *I-for-myself* struggled to reach an equilibrium between the *Voice* of the *Vegan-other-for-me* and the *Non-vegan-other-for-me*:

> …. my family did not support my diet (Kate).
>
> …. I tried to like talk to my family about it, and reasonably so they were like, that sounds unhealthy, like don't do that, I did it anyway. So I was pretty alone in it (Puck).
>
> … my family didn't really take it well because they strongly believed that you need meat to survive (Portia).
>
> …. when are you going to join the right side again, when are you coming out for a steak with me like the good old days, oh I miss the old C (Cordelia).
>
> My housemates knew that I was basically vegan and they kind of took the mick out of me because I'd be making like oat milk and they'd be like, what on earth are you doing but like in a funny, like in a funny way, they weren't like annoyed at what I was doing (Goneril).

Several studies have illustrated how vegans are encouraged to develop strategies for overcoming vegan stigma and have the skills to respond to the questioning of their choices by friends and family (Niva, Vainio, and Jallinoja, 2019; Twine, 2014). The process of developing 'stigma strategies' is particularly thought-provoking from a Bakhtinian perspective, especially in the context of individual *Selfhood* and maintaining one's *Voice*. Earlier, for instance, we discussed that, from a dialogical perspective, Bakhtin proposes that, if self-consciousness and identity of the *I-for-myself* are to be established through dialogical relationship between the *Self* and *Other*, then the relationship must be *reciprocal*. One's *Voice* must always remain, 'yet-to-be-determined.' In other words, the *I-for-myself* should always have *Answerability*. One could argue that interviewees *did* possess the option of *Answerability*. However, it was not only limited towards the *Non-vegan-other-for-me*, but also is vacant of the *I-for-myself's* unique intonation. The *Speech Genres* within Cordelia's *Utterances* are *Single-voiced*, and therefore, her *Utterances* are full of 'empty possibility' (Bakhtin, 1990: 145). This, however, was not limited to Cordelia. During our conversation, Bianca also expressed a similar experience.

Thus far, we have been discussing the dialogical relationship between the *I-for-myself* and the *I-for-others*. We have also explored the dialogical(or lack thereof) relationships between the interviewees's *I-for-myself* and the *Vegan-other-for-me*. We can also touch on the facet of the relationship between the *I-for-myself* of the participants and the *Non-vegan-other-for-me*. As the final point of this section on the *Primary Speech Genre* of *Intra-conflict* of the *I-for-myself*, what I would like to consider is the experience of the interviewees from a different perspective: how the *I-for-myself* of the participants became the *Vegan-other-for-me* for their non-vegan family and friendship groups. We can contextualise this within the discourse of 'responsibility,' embedded within ethical considerations for animal ethics and well-being, whether it is collective political responsibility (Cochrane and Cojocaru, 2022) or individual responsibility (Turner, 2019).

Sideward Glance

Recent studies have also focused different dietary groups in relation to the diffusion of responsibility. For example, dietary groups such as omnivores diffusing individual responsibility by referencing structural factors such as industries, Culture, and governmental policies. We will return to this line of discussion in Chapter 5.

A number of the interviewees, for example, reflected on their attitude towards their non-vegan friendship groups and family. Although *Orlando*, for example, chose not to try and '*turn others vegan*,' and Goneril opted to '*keep away*' from activism, this was not the case for other participants. Elsewhere, we have touched on how several of the participants were aware of the negative discourse surrounding Veganism itself and those practising Veganism. Also, remember that, from a Bakhtinian perspective, self-consciousness is only attainable through the lens of how the *I-for-myself* believes the *Other* might see them and how the *I-for-myself* might *want* the *Other* to see them (*I-for-other*). The *Secondary Speech Genres* within the *Utterances* analysed above revealed tension between the participants's *I* and the *Non-vegan-I-for-others*. One of the strategies for several of the participants to overcome this tension was to become a *Vegan-I-for-other* for their non-vegan acquaintances in order to attain a more stable inner experience for *themselves*.

> I was like one of them like militant vegans and I was just like you know everybody has to be vegan because this is the only way (Kate).

> I tried to get both my parents, my sister, my friends, my ex-boyfriend to go vegan I would always really rude actually … they'd be drinking coffee and I would bring up that something about the cows (Portia).

This is not surprising, as work by Ellemer, van Rijswijk, Roefs et al. (1997) notes that there are also limits in the extent to which groups, such as vegan practitioners and vegan activist, can build a positive self-identity (*I-for-myself*) as well as a social identity (Turner, Hoggs, and Oakes, 1987). Classical social psychology theory proposes that our group memberships are essential in determining how the *I* (the *I-for-myself*) perceives itself and establishes its values.

Portia's and Kate's *Utterances* align with the discourse of 'vegan responsibility,' which is framed as a supposedly self-less endeavour for animal welfare and ethics. However, I would also propose considering vegan activism or 'vegan responsibility' from a more self-centred perspective of the *I-for-myself*. Bakhtin understands the *Spirit* as continual and *Unfinalisable*, and dialogue with the *Other* can momentarily *stabilise* the *Spirit* by offering affirmation in the form of a *Soul*, which the *I-for-myself* incorporate within itself (Morson and Emerson, 1990). What if, however, the affirmation bestowed upon the *Spirit* is not a 'gift' that *stabilisation* but rather one of *destabilisation* in the form of negative stereotypes or contradictory values? Would the *I-for-myself* not attempt to persuade the *Non-vegan-other-for-me*? Especially as Bakhtin (1993, 1990) argues that the dialogical interaction between the *I* and *Other* should be exclusively positive, constructive, progressive, as it is the source of the dynamic that perpetuates our *Becoming* and self-identity.

Moreover, the dominance of the vegan *Voice* can also be questioned by what Mlicki and Ellemers (1996) refer to as 'reality constraints,' or what we will refer to as lived reality. In the context of this project, a time-space where the individual reality of the participants's *I-for-myself* is paradoxical to the 'gift' 'promised' by the *Voice* of the *Vegan-other-for-me*, especially if their lived reality does not align with their embodied experience of *Being* vegan. In the next section, we will discuss the *Primary Speech Genre Denial*, which illustrates the continued tension between the interviewees's *I-for-myself*, *I-for-other*, and *Other-for-me*. The *Utterances* within the *Primary Speech Genre* of *Denial* are composed of the *Secondary Speech Genres* of *Physical Health* and *Mental Health*, which placed participants upon their third and final *Threshold-moment* in their vegan journey (Table 4.2).

TABLE 4.2 *Soundbites for the Primary Speech Genre of Denial*

Primary Genre	*Secondary Genre*	
Denial	Physical health	*I just, I became so sick, like I was incredibly bloated all the time ... 24/7 (Bianca).*
		I wasn't really being honest with myself, that I missed eating meat, because on social media you see all these people who are like, I don't eat meat, I'm totally fine without it (Portia).
	Mental health	*I started dreaming about dying ... every night (Bianca).*
		I actually developed psychosis, I developed psychosis I want to say back in March or April, which I [laughs] literally, I just thought I was having like a mental breakdown because of quarantine and everything, it turns out I had a B12 deficiency (Puck).

The Primary Speech Genre of Denial

Crafa and Nagel (2020) highlight how culturally dependent social phenomena, such as Veganism, shape neural pathways (for arguments on viewing Veganism as a cultural movement, please see Chapter 1). Although they specifically focus on mental health, there is room to argue that their work also notes the relationship between the '*feedback loop*' and the regulation of human behaviour.

The following *Utterances* suggest that the rhetorical '*feedback loops*' some of the participants referred to from their *Vegan-other-for-me* were '*misanthropic*' and '*self-blaming*' if they doubted the efficacy of Veganism:

> I remember lots of people feeling sick being vegan and I remember how the group made them feel bad about it (Orlando).
>
> .... there were a lot of things that I chose to overlook or blamed on external matters (Cordelia).
>
> But even with all of these symptoms, like I still thought it was the right diet, so I just, I kept on pursuing it, basically. But I still believed that veganism was still the diet, there were just different ways to do it. *I was still letting myself become more and more brainwashed* (Bianca).
>
> Oh yeah. Yeah, I was completely, like I was so... I was completely shutting out all the signs that I was getting. I thought this is nothing to do with it, this is something else (Goneril).
>
> I just felt really bad, I was like, it's like it's been two years, *I just feel so* terrible if I eat this, that's what really kept me going, and yeah. *And I still kept remaining firm with myself that it wasn't because I didn't, or it wasn't veganism's fault* (Portia).

Towards the end of their second *Threshold-moment* of *Being* vegan, a number of participants, regardless of their motivational drives for *Becoming* vegan, experienced intense *intra*-subjective tensions between the *I-for-myself* and the *I-for-other*. The monolithic *Voice* of the *Vegan-other-for-me* had cemented certain cognitive attitudes towards food (Baranova, Loughnan, and Bastian, 2011), resulting in a *Finalised* sense of *Selfhood*.

Secondary Speech Genre of Physical Health

With the drive for sustainability and the continual popularity of Veganism, especially among adolescents (Williams, Vardavoulia, Lally et al., 2023), there is also a growing incentive to seek adequate nutritional information for long-term success. As discussed in Chapter 3, during the participants's first *Threshold-moment*, many interviewees discovered Veganism through social media and vegan literature. Vieira (2020), however, argues that it is easy to 'encounter advice by popular social media personalities and best-selling authors whose claims may not be evidence-based and might even result in adverse outcomes (Vieira, 2020: 100)' In Chapter 1, we discussed how in recent years, Veganism has been embedded within a discourse of health, which is rooted in scientific arguments about the dietary benefits of Veganism. The *Secondary Speech Genres* in Chapter 3 revealed that, along with concerns about animal welfare, sustainability, and the environment, personal health was also a primary motivational factor for *Becoming* vegan. On the one hand, research has emphasised the positive health befits associated with a vegan diet in various areas and across one's lifespan (Sebastiani, Barbero and Borrás-Novell, 2019; Chlebowski, Mortimer, Crandall et al., 2018; Melina, Craig, and Levin, 2016). On the other hand, studies have also noted the development of nutritional deficiencies within meat-free diets, leading to cognitive impairment and mental health disorders (Bali and Naik, 2023; Kapoor, Baig, Tunio et al., 2017).

Scholarship on the health benefits of Veganism is conflicting, and it is not the purpose of this project to comment on clinical studies. Rather, it aims to highlight individual experiences across one's vegan journey. While *Being* vegan, all the interviewees experienced a degree of general health issues: some short-term, others long-term, which contradicted to the vegan *Voices* and discourses associated with health benefits. The quotes in this final section are extensive; however, I felt that they were worth quoting at length as they are essential for conveying the participants's *Voices* concerning their health, and for you, as the reader to be able to engage with their *Utterances*.

> Well, it was just the belief that this was the diet. I just, I became so sick, like I was incredibly bloated all the time, I mean, throughout my whole vegan journey, my time being vegan, I was just 24/7 bloated from, especially when I went to bed, even if I'd have fasted, I would wake up bloated. I have heart palpitations and severe anxiety (Bianca).

> I started to realise with every meal that I ate, I wasn't satiated, I was hungry but I was full, if that makes sense, like no matter how much I ate I didn't feel satisfied, and I was laying in bed one day and I was so tired that I couldn't get out of bed. I was so tired, and I had just eaten like half hour prior (Puck).

> I got back from university after about 4 months and I was like pale as a sheet, just pasty, like really puffy and I just got really ill and then they just said, like my mum just said look, you look like shit, just stop this, just you know, just give it up, so yeah (Goneril).

For Bakhtin, the *Self* is social on an *embodied* plane in which *inter*-subjective exchanges are anchored. Cresswell and Baerveldt (2011) note that from a Bakhtinian approach, 'the corporeal experience of life cannot be separated from the *sociality of life* because these are two moments of the *same* experience' (Cresswell and Baerveldt, 2011: 266, *emphasis added*). As I have tried to reiterate throughout our discussions, reciprocity is key, and that the *Spirit's* embodied, *felt* experience is *expressed* within social phenomena and symbolic forms (Cresswell and Teucher, 2011). The noteworthy point here is that, despite embodied discord, several participants continued to deny negative impact, for them, of *Being* vegan, leading to the discord between the vegan *Voices* their *I-for-myself* had adopted and their phenomenological experience. There are several interpretations outlining the centrality of embodiment in Bakhtin's understanding of the *Self* and phenomenology (Cresswell and Baerveldt, 2011).

For Bakhtin (1990), *Speech Genres* within language utilised by certain communities (in our case, vegan communities) involve generic *stylisation* of language; for example, intonation and the emotion it evokes. Language, therefore, encapsulates emotionality, *Ideology*, and how we embody it. To a certain degree, the *stylised* language used by a community socialises our living experiences of certain symbols and language, or our embodiment of them. Essentially, through *stylised* community language, the *I-for-other* constructs how the *I-for-myself ought* to feel, and it performs precisely in that manner. The research around vegans, vegetarians, and the heightened emotion of disgust when around meat, and therefore its avoidance, is an example of this (Becker, Kozmer, Aulbach et al., 2022; Hamilton, 2006; Fessler, Arguello, Mekdara et al., 2003). *Physical Health* was a recurring *Secondary Speech Genre* within the interviewees's *Utterances* and was often mentioned in relation to how their *embodied* experiences sharply differed from that of the *Vegan-other-for-me*, or the stylised *Speech Genres* within the vegan community they ascribe to. Nonetheless, as the *Utterances* above emphasise, participants continued to deny their own embodied experiences.

I acknowledge that much of the current research around the vegan diet focuses on physical factors such as nutritional deficiencies and cognitive decline, and not necessarily on social, psychological, and philosophical factors factors such as ontological insecurity. Nevertheless, emerging research argues for an increase in the risk of experiencing mental health issues for following a vegan diet or abstaining from meat consumption. I must stress, however, that the literature in this area, like in others, is conflicting (Dobersek, Wy, Adkins et al., 2021; Li, Cao, Xie et al., 2019), but it was a clear *Secondary Speech Genre* within the *Utterances* of the interviewees.

Secondary Speech Genre of Mental Health

Once participants began to experience contradictions between the *Voice* of the *Vegan-other-for-me* and their embodied reality, this often manifested as emotional distress, including '*obsessive thoughts*' around food, '*anxiety*,' '*brain-fog*,' dreams about dying, thoughts of '*self-harming*,' '*psychosis*,' '*mood swings*,' and '*depression*'. Much of their disquiet centred around the potential re-consumption of meat and no longer *Being* vegan.

> so learning that my psychosis was possibly a B12 deficiency, and also I was like, and I was like, this isn't how I'm supposed to feel after I eat, like I don't feel good (Puck).

> And the depression, I'd cry all the time over everything, I was constantly crying, the anxiety which I've not really been an overly anxious person but I was anxious, I was very anxious. I didn't know how I'd manage the mental gymnastics of trying to justify eating animal products again. I was just incredibly anxious. I think the… *I think a lack of B12, even though I was supplementing, definitely affects your mental state along with a myriad of other things* (Cordelia).

> I could barely sleep, … *I started to have a lot of nightmares about dying. And I know that sounds really morbid, but it was like every single night*, if I even managed to get to sleep I would think about dying, sorry, dream about dying. And now, I haven't had a single dream where I've died or a nightmare like that and I can't help but think maybe it's like the brain's way of saying like something's wrong (Bianca).

Participants continued to experience *intra*-subjective struggles, which eventually led them towards their third *Threshold-moment*, as they felt an emotional and physical sense of depletion, which forced them to begin their transition out of *Being* vegan.

In a meta-analysis Dobersek, Wy, Adkins et al. (2021) noted 'obsessive thoughts' as a side effect of a meat-free diet in comparison to a diet that included animal products. This was also experienced by two participants in particular:

> my family knew that something was quite wrong because I suddenly always was thinking about food because I just wasn't feeling nourished, I was just always thinking about it and like if there was stuff in the fridge I'd be like, we could make this and this and this and this and I'd just be like completely focused on food and what to do with food (Goneril).

My conversations with Bianca, Cordelia, and Puck, however, were particularly insightful as they described the re-consumption of animal products as a moment of euphoria, both physically and emotionally. Bianca relayed her '*last straw*' moment, and her experience also questions research that suggests there are no differences in 'perseverative thinking' between vegans and other dietary groups (Brytek-Matera, 2020: 2).

the last day that I was vegan, I was, I'd been thinking about salmon the whole few days. And I was so desperate, I was thinking, I had money, you know, I could have bought it, but I was still thinking about all the ways that I could get it, either like buy it, I was even thinking about stealing it, just ways that I could have it physically with me so I could eat it. And then my boyfriend came into the living room where I was sat, and it just, I came out with it, I was like, "I don't think I can be vegan any more". Like I was thinking of robbing a fishmonger just so that I could eat some fish. So we kind of went, even though our first meal was fish, like it made me feel better, and I actually did have the best night's sleep I ever had in those six years that night. But the next morning, so we'd bought some locally sourced eggs as well because we wanted to have them for breakfast... So it was just, I remember, as soon as I put that first bite in my mouth, like I was just smiling like this and I just felt my brain, it was like the fog had just left me and I could think again. And I felt, this sounds so silly, but, you know, when your body is so depleted and you give it what it wants, it's like you've been brought back, you know. And I just felt so happy and I just felt like my body was like thanking me. So, yeah, I feel like the eggs really kind of saved me. I think the fish gave me the night's sleep I needed, but the eggs truly saved me.

I love talking about this [laughs], so I work at Starbucks, so I went and I got my like free meal for the day, I had an Impossible sandwich because I wasn't ready to eat meat yet, so it was cheddar cheese, one of those like egg patty things, and the vegan sausage, I had two cake pops and a Frappuccino, I [laughs] took one bite of the birthday cake pop and I started crying, it was so delicious, it was so good, and then I had the Impossible sandwich and oh man, there's no way to describe this feeling if you've never had it before, but getting like that nutrients from an egg for the first time in six years, it was wow, it was mind blowing. Not only was it fantastic tasting, but I could just feel the like chemicals rush to my brain, like finally thank you, I needed this. So that's what I ate, and it was fantastic (Puck).

Oh my gosh, when I introduced eggs because I said to my mum, after researching all this I said, please could you bring over some eggs and she was like yeah, that's fine. Had two eggs and I felt my eyes like dilate, the pupils dilate and the whole room was like crystal clear and I was like whoa, that felt ... and she said, oh it's probably because you were overtired and I get that when I'm tired. I went no, I know the difference between being overtired and my body reacting to something I've just eaten and it was immediate and I thought, right, okay, I'm going to have more eggs (Cordelia).

The need to justify the re-consumption of meat is suggests the extent to which Veganism had become embedded in participants's identity and self-perception, to the extent that not *Being* vegan caused ontological insecurity. From a dialogical perspectives, this is not surprising, especially for participants who had, what Bakhtin terms, as finalised sense of *Self*. In order to foreground their *I-for-myself*, or to re-gain a *Double-voice*, participants extricated themselves from the *Voice* of the *Vegan-other-for-me*. For some, this was curated purposefully; for others, it was more serendipitous, driven by the Covid-19 pandemic and global lockdowns.

Chapter Summary

The analysis in this chapter has revealed that a unified definition of Veganism is questionable on a practical level, particularly for those practising it themselves. The vegan *Voice* can become totalising – and the *Self* from a dialogical perspective, should never be static. My conversations with the interviewees also imply that, regardless of the motivation behind their first *Threshold-moment*, *Being* vegan had a wider impact scale. Several participants sough social connections - people to share ideas with, whether in-person or online; they became a part of a vegan community. Moreover, as their involvement in this community increased, they also become more aligned with the idea of being an 'ethical vegan,' particularly in terms of environmental and animal-rights concerns.

References

Arppe, T., Mäkelä, J., & Väänänen, V. (2011). Living food diet and veganism: individual vs collective boundaries of the forbidden. *Anthropology of Food*, 50(2), 275–297. https://doi.org/10.1177/0539018410396618

Bakhtin, M. (1993). *Toward a philosophy of the act*. Austin: University of Texas Press.

Bakhtin, M. (1990). *Art and answerability: early philosophical essays*. Austin: University of Texas Press.

Bakhtin, M. (1984a). *Problems of Dostoevsky's poetics*. Minneapolis: University of Minnesota Press.

Bakhtin, M. (1981). *The dialogic imagination: four essays*. Austin: University of Texas Press.

Bali, A., & Naik, R. (2023). The impact of a vegan diet on many aspects of health: the overlooked side of veganism. *Cureus*, 15(2), e35148. https://doi.org/10.7759/cureus.35148

Barad, K. (2007) *Meeting the universe halfway: quantum physics and the entanglement of matter and meaning*. Durham, NC, London: Duke University Press.

Barad, K. (2003) Posthumanist performativity: toward an understanding of how matter comes to matter. *Signs: Journal of Women in Culture and Society*, 28(3), 801–831.

Becker, E., Kozmer, S., Aulbach, Am, A. et al. (2022). The relationship between meat disgust and meat avoidance—A chicken-and-egg problem. *Frontiers Nutrition*, 9, 958248. https://doi.org/10.3389/fnut.2022.958248

Bramble, B., & Fischer, B. (Eds.). (2016) *The moral complexities of eating meat*. New York: Oxford University Press.

Bratanova, B., Loughnan, S., & Bastian, B. (2011). The effect of categorization as food on the perceived moral standing of animals. *Appetite*, 57(1), 193–196. https://doi.org/10.1016/j.appet.2011.04.020

Brytek-Matera, A. (2020). Restrained eating and vegan, vegetarian and omnivore ietary intakes. *Nutrients*, 12 (2133), 1–16. https://doi.org/10.3390/nu12072133

Buttny, R., & Kinefuchi, E. (2020). Vegans' problem stories: negotiating vegan identity in dealing with omnivores. *Discourse & Society*, 31(6), 565–583. https://doi.org/10.1177/0957926520939689

Cherry, E. (2015). I was a teenage vegan: motivation and maintenance of lifestyle movements. *Sociological Inquiry*, 85(1), 55–74.

Cherry, E. (2006). Veganism as a cultural movement: a relational approach. *Social Movement Studies*, 5(2), 155–170.

Chlebowski, R. T., Mortimer, J. E., Crandall, C. J. et al. (2018). Persistent vasomotor symptoms and breast cancer in the Women's Health Initiative. *Menopause*, 26(6), 578–587. https://doi.org/10.1097/GME.0000000000001283

Cochrane, A., & Cojocaru, M. D. (2022). Veganism as political solidarity: beyond 'ethical veganism.' *Social Philoso*phy, 54(1), 59–76. https://doi.org/10.1111/josp.12460

Cole, M., & Morgan, K. (2011). Vegahobia: derogatory discourses of veganism and the reproduction of speciesism in UK national newspapers. *The British Journal of Sociology*, 62(1), 134–53. https://doi.org/10.1111/j.1468-4446.2010.01348.x

Costa, I., Gill, P. R., & Morda, R. et al. (2019). "More than a diet": a qualitative investigation of young vegan women's relationship to food. *Appetite*, 143, 104418. https://doi.org/10.1016/j.appet.2019.104418

Crafa, D., & Nagel, S. K. (2020). Traces of culture: the feedback loop between behavior, brain, and disorder. *Transcultural Psychiatry*, 57(3), 387–407. https://doi.org/10.1177/1363461519879515

Davis, L. J., Love, T. P., & Fares, P. (2019). Collective social identity: synthesizing identity theory and social identity theory using digital data. *Social Psychology Quarterly*, 82(3), 254–273. https://doi.org/10.1177/0190272519851025.

Dobersek, U., Wy, G., Adkins, J. et al. (2020). Meat and mental health: a systematic review of meat abstention and depression, anxiety, and related phenomena. *Critical Reviews in Food Science and Nutrition*, 61(4), 622–635. https://doi.org/10.1080/10408398.2020.1741505

Graça, J., Calheiros, M. M., & Oliveira, A. (2016). Situating moral disengagement: motivated reasoning in meat consumption and substitution. *Personality and Individuals Differences*, 90, 353–364. https://doi.org/10.1016/j.paid.2015.11.042

Graça, J., Calheiros, M. M., & Oliveira, A. (2015). Attached to meat? (Un) Willingness and intentions to adopt a more plant-based diet. *Appetite*, 95, 113–125. https://doi.org/10.1016/j.appet.2015.06.024

Greenebaum, J. (2012b). Veganism, identity and the quest for authenticity. *Food, Culture & Society*, 15(1), 129–144. https://doi.org/10.2752/175174412X131905 10222101

de Groeve, B., Bleys, B., & Hudders, L. (2022). Ideological resistance to veg*n advocacy: an identity-based motivational account. *Frontier Psychology*, 13, 996250. https://doi.org/10.3389/fpsyg.2022.996250

de Groeve, B., & Rosenfeld, D. L. (2022). Morally admirable or moralistically deplorable? A theoretical framework for understanding character judgments of vegan advocates. *Appetite*, 168, 105693. https://doi.org/10.1016/j.appet.2021.105693

Ellemers, N. (2017). *Morality and the regulation of social behavior: groups as moral anchors.* London & New York: Routledge.
Ellemers, N., Van Rijswijk, W., & Roefs, M. et al. (1997). Bias in intergroup perceptions: balancing group identity with social reality. *Personality and Social Psychology Bulletin*, 23(2), 186–198. https://doi.org/10.1177/0146167297232007
Feng, Y., Chen, H., & Kong, Q. (2020) An expert with whom I can identify: the role of narratives in influencers marketing. *International Journal of Advertising*, 40(7), 972–993. https://doi.org/10.1080/02650487.2020.1824751
Fessler, D. M. T., Arguello, A. P., Mekdara, M. J. et al. (2003). Disgust sensitivity and meat consumption: a test of an emotivist account of moral vegetarianism. *Appetite*, 14(2), 31–41. https://doi.org/10.1016/S0195-6663(03)00037-0
Giraud, E. H. (2021). *Veganism: politics, practice, and theory.* London: Bloomsbury Academic.
Greenebaum, J. (2012b). Veganism, identity and the quest for authenticity. *Food, Culture & Society*, 15(1), 129–144. https://doi.org/10.2752/175174412X13190510222101
Greenaway, K. H., Cruwys, T., Haslam, S. A. et al. (2016). Social identities promote well-being because they satisfy global psychological needs. *European Journal of Social Psychology*, 46(3), 294–307. https://doi.org/10.1002/ejsp.2169
Hamilton, M. (2006). Eating death: vegetarians, meat and violence. *Food, Culture & Society*, 9(2), 155–177. https://doi.org/10.2752/155280106778606053
Haslam, S. A., & Ellemers, N. (2011). Social identity theory. In P. A. Van Lange, A. W. Kruganski & E. T. Higgins (Eds.), *Handbook of theories of social psychology:* volume 2 (pp. 379–398). Sage Publications. https://doi.org/10.4135/9781446249222.n45
Intezar, H. (2020). Speaking pictures, silent voices: female athletes and the negotiation of selfhood. *Integrative Psychological Behaviour Science.* 55, 89–111. https://doi.org/10.1007/s12124-020-09577-6
Ioannidou, M., Lesk, V., Stewart- Knox, B. et al. (2023). Feeling morally troubled about meat, dairy, egg, and fish consumption: dissonance reduction strategies among different dietary groups. *Appetite*, 190, 107024. https://doi.org/10.1016/j.appet.2023.107024
Joy, M. (2020). *The vegan matrix: understanding and discussing privilege among vegans to build a more inclusive and empowered movement.* Brooklyn: Lantern Publishing.
Joy, M. (2011). *Why love dogs, eat pigs, and wear cows: an introduction to carnism.* San Francisco, CA: Conari Press.
Judge, M., Fernando, J., & Begeny, C. (2022). Dietary behaviour as a form of collective action: a social identity model of vegan activism. *Appetite*, 168, 105730. https://doi.org/10.1016/j.appet.2021.105730
Kapoor, A., Baig, M., Tunio, S. A. et al. (2017). Neuropsychiatric and neurological problems among vitamin B12 Deficient young vegetarians. *Neurosciences*, 22(3), 228–232. https://doi.org/10.17712/nsj.2017.3.20160445
Katz, D. L. (2019). Plant-based diets for reversing disease and saving the planet: past, present, and future. *Advances in Nutrition*, 10(4), S304–S307. https://doi.org/10.1093/advances/nmy124
Kirsten-Effi, H., Seib-Pfeifer, L. E., Lüth, C. A. et al. (2020). Validation and application of a German version of the dietarian identity questionnaire: revealing differences between omnivores, vegetarians, and vegans. *Food Quality & Preferences*, 86, 103988. https://doi.org/10.1016/j.foodqual.2020.103988
Lara, A. (2021). *Decentring subjectivity in everyday eating and drinking: digesting reality.* London & New York: Routledge.

Li, X., Cao, H. J., Xie, S. Y. et al. (2019). Adhering to a vegetarian diet may create a greater risk of depressive symptoms in the elderly male Chinese population. *Journal of Affective Disorders*, 243, 182–187. https://doi.org/10.1016/j.jad.2018.09.033

MacInnis, C. C., & Hodson, G. (2021). Tensions within and between vegans and vegetarians: meat-free motivations matter. *Appetite*, 164, 105246. https://doi.org/10.1016/j.appet.2021.105246

Markowski, K. L., & Roxburgh, S. (2019). 'If I became a vegan, my family and friends would hate me:' anticipating vegan stigma as a barrier to plant-based diets. *Appetite*, 135, 1–9. https://doi.org/10.1016/j.appet.2018.12.040

Melina, V., Craig, W., & Levin, S. (2016). Position of the academy of nutrition and dietetics: vegetarian diets. *Journal of the Academy of Nutrition and Dietetics*, 116(12), 1970–1980. https://doi.org/10.1016/j.jand.2016.09.025

Minson, J. A., & Monin, B. (2012). Do-gooder derogation: disparaging morally motivated minorities to defuse anticipated reproach. *Social Psychological & Personality Science*, 3(2), 200–207. https://. doi.org/10.1177/1948550611415695

Mlicki, P. P., & Ellemers, N. (1996). Being different or being better? National stereotypes and identifications of Polish and Dutch students. *European Journal of Social Psychology*, 26(1), 97–114. https://doi.org/10.1002/(SICI)1099-0992(199601)26:1<97::AID-EJSP739>3.0.CO;2-F

Morson, G. S., & Emerson, C. (1990). *Mikhail Bakhtin: creation of a prosaics*. Stanford, CA: Stanford University Press.

Napoli, J., & Ouschan, R. (2020). Vegan stories: revealing archetypes and their moral foundations. *Qualitative Market Research*, 23(1), 145–169. https://doi.org/10.1108/QMR-06-2018-0064

Neuman, N. (2020). Social conventions and boundary work in an online Q&A: the example of vegetarianism and veganism. *Sociological Research Online*, 25(4), 609–625. https://doi.org/10.1177/1360780419898201

Nielsen, G. (2002). *The norms of answerability, social theory between Bakhtin and Habermas*. New York: State University of New York Press.

Niva, M., Vainio, A., & Jallinoja, P. (2019). The unselfish vegan. In C. De Backer, M. L. Fisher, J. Dare and L. Costello (Eds.), *To eat or not to eat meat. How vegetarian dietary choices influence our social lives* (pp. 91–101). London: Rowman & Littlefield Publishers.

Phua, J., Jin, V. S., & Kim, J. (2020). The role of celebrity endorsers' and consumers' vegan identity in marketing communications about veganism. *Journal of Marketing Communications*, 26, 813–835. https://doi.org/10.1080/13527266.2019.1590854

Randall, T. (2018). Heganism. *Between The Species*, 22(1). Retrieved from https://digitalcommons.calpoly.edu/bts/vol22/iss1/6

Reed, W. L. (2014). Romantic literature in light of Bakhtin. London: Bloomsbury.

Ruby, M. B. (2012). Vegetarianism. A blossoming field of study, *Appetite*, 58, 141–150. https://doi.org/10.1016/j.appet.2011.09.019

Salehi, G., Diaz, E. M., & Redondo, R. (2020). Consumers switching to vegan, vegetarian, and plant-based (veg*an) diets: a systematic review. Conference contribution. https://doi.org/10.6084/m9.figshare.12522758.v1

Schouten, A. P., Janssen, L., & Verspaget, M. (2020). Celebrity vs. influencer endorsements in advertising: the role of identification, credibility, and product-endorser fit. *International Journal of Advertising*, 39(2), 258–281. https://doi.org/10.1080/02650487.2019.1634898

Scott, E. (2020). Healthism and veganism: discursive constructions of food and health in an online vegan community. In D. Lupton & Z. Fieldman (Eds.) *Digital food cultures* (pp. 68–81). New York: Routledge. https://doi.org/10.4324/9780429402135-7

Sebastiani, G., Barbero, A. H., Borrás-Novell, C. et al. (2019). The effects of vegetarian and vegan diet during pregnancy on the health of mothers and offspring. *Nutrients*, 11(3), 557. https://doi.org/10.3390/nu11030557

Sedmak, A., & Svetina, M. (2023). Components of adolescents' attraction with YouTubers. *Current Psychology*, 42, 6167–6197. https://doi.org/10.1007/s12144-023-04784-x

Shotwell, A. (2016). *Against purity: living ethically in compromised times*. Minneapolis: University of Minnesota Press.

Simons, J., Vierboom, C., Klink-Lehmann, J. et al. (2021) Vegetarianism/ veganism: a way to feel good. *Sustainability*, 13(7), 3618. https://doi.org/10.3390/su13073618

Sneijder, P., & Hedwig, F. M. (2005). 'Health should not have to be a problem': talking health and accountability in an internet forum on veganism. *Journal of Health Psychology*, 9(4), 599–616. https://doi.org/10.1177/1359105304044046

Stuart, A., Thomas, E., & Donaghue, N. et al. (2013). 'We may be pirates, but we are not protesters': identity in the Sea Shepherd Conservation Society. *Political Psychology*, 34(5), 753–777. https://doi.org/10.1111/pops.12016

Tajfel, H., & Turner, J. C. (1979). An integrative theory of intergroup conflict. In W. G. Austin & S. Worchel (Eds.) *The social psychology of intergroup relations* (pp. 33–47). Monterey: Brooks: Cole Publications.

Turner, R. (2019). Veganism: ethics in everyday life. *American Journal of Cultural Sociology*, 7(511), 54–78. https://doi.org/10.1057/s41290-017-0052-8

Turner, J. C., Hogg, M. A., Oakes, P. J. et al. (1987). *Rediscovering the social group: A self-categorization theory*. Oxford/New York: Blackwell.

Twine, R. (2014). Vegan killjoys at the table – contesting happiness and negotiating relationships with food practices. *Societies*, 4(4), 623–639. https://doi.org/10.3390/soc4040623

Ulusoy, E. (2015). I think, therefore I am vegan. In C. Shultz, R. Benton, & O. Kravets (Eds.), *Proceedings of the 40th Annual Macromarketing Conference* (pp. 420–424). Chicago, IL: Macromarketing Society.

van Driel, L., & Dumitrica, D. (2020). Selling brands while staying "Authentic": the professionalization of Instagram influencers. *Convergence*, 27(1), 66–84. https://doi.org/10.1177/1354856520902136

Vestergren, S., Drury, J., & Chiriac, E. H. (2019). How participation in collective action changes relationships, behaviors, and beliefs: an interview study of the role of inter- and intragroup process. *Journal of Social & Political Psychology*, 7(1), 76–99. https://doi.org/10.5964/jspp.v7i1.903

Vieira, L. N. (2020). Machine translation in the news: a framing analysis of the written press. *Translation Spaces*, 9(1), 98–122. Advance online publication. https://doi.org/10.1075/ts.00023.nun

Vögele, C., & Gibson, E. L. (2010). Mood, emotions, and eating disorders. In W. S. Agras (Ed.), *The Oxford handbook of eating disorders* (pp. 180–205). Oxford: Oxford University Press.

Williams, E., Vardavoulia, A., Larry, P. et al. (2023). Experiences of initiating and maintaining a vegan diet among young adults: a qualitative study. *Appetite*, 180(2), 106357. https://doi.org/10.1016/j.appet.2022.106357

5

HOW IT ALL ENDED, AND HOW IS IT GOING?

And now that I discovered that ex-vegan sobriety …

(Orlando)

In Chapter 3, we discussed the *Speech Genres* for *Becoming* vegan, while Chapter 4 explored the interviewees's second *Threshold-moment* of *Being* vegan, as well as the complexities within the dialogical relationship between the *I-for-myself*, the *Vegan-other-for-me*, and the *Non-vegan-other-for-me*. More specifically, it examined the *intra*-subjective and *inter*-subjective tensions encountered by the *I-for-myself* with the emergence of a vegan identity. Although, notably, a number of the participants maintained that they did not develop a vegan identity, they were still confronted with a sense of *Self* turbulence, nonetheless.

The subject of why individuals find it difficult to sustain a *Being* vegan is not necessarily a popular area of discussion. The scholarship that does broach the topic often links it to political ideology (Hodson and Earle, 2018). Hodson and Earle (2018) propose that vegans and former-vegans with conservative political stances are more likely to *Become* vegan for self-beneficial reasons, displaying less concern toward animal rights, the environment, or feeding the poor. Consequently, they are more likely to 'lapse' back into Carnism and experience minimal *intra*-subjective tension. Grünhage and Reuter's (2021) work is supplements this view by arguing for a 'substantive association between political orientation and self-restriction in eating,' which is linked with one's 'moral makeup' (Grünhage and Reuter, 2021: 18). For example, those with left-wing political orientations tend to exhibit higher levels of moral self-restraint in relation to meat consumption, while those with right-wing political orientations are less likely to practise moral self-restraint concerning meat consumption and food in general.

DOI: 10.4324/9781003384526-5

I acknowledge that, for many, diets can be highly political, especially those that advocate for the elimination of meat and animal products. My intention in this chapter, however, is to momentarily shift the spotlight from socio-politics to politics of the *Self*, which is an overlooked area in relation to those who have 'lapsed' from Veganism. Towards the end of the previous chapter, we traced *intra*-subjective struggles within the participants's *Utterances*, stemming from difficulties in maintaining *Being* vegan. For a holistic overview of their journey, here, we will focus on the build-up towards and after the interviewees's final *Threshold* decision to stop *Being* vegan, and the implications on their sense of *Self* through the process.

The two *Primary Speech Genres* emerging from the participants's final *Threshold-moment* were '*Post-vegan Sobriety*' and *Rediscovering a Double-voiced Utterance*. The former consisted of the *Secondary Speech Genres* of *Disconnecting* and *Reconnecting*, while the latter was comprised of *Guilt* and what the interviewees referred to as '*Fake News*' (Table 5.1).

The Primary Speech Genre of 'Ex-vegan Sobriety'

TABLE 5.1 *Soundbites for the Primary Speech Genre of Ex-vegan Sobriety*

Primary Genre	*Secondary Genre*	*Quotes*
'Ex-vegan Sobriety'	Disconnecting	*... so when the pandemic started, I used that as an excuse to stop seeing them [vegan-other-for-me] and I haven't tell them (Orlando).*
		I do have one vegan friend and I haven't told her, but mainly because we're not super close anymore either (Puck).
	Reconnecting	*So it was just things like, like I'd bake some bread one day, and I kind of filmed myself putting an egg wash on this loaf [laughs]. And then erm..., yeah, and then one day I just thought, you know what, I'm just going to have to just put it all out there (Bianca).*
		Definitely, definitely, I don't think I could do it if I didn't have such supportive friends, honestly. Also just like plain cheese pizza, they were like, yes, get it [laughs]. It's funny for them because it's such a normal thing to just eat a cheese pizza, but for me like crying over my cheese pizza, how good it is, they think it's so funny, so they've been really supportive and they've been really helpful (Puck).
		When all of this lockdown started I used Facebook to start again our friendship (Orlando).

The Secondary Speech Genre of Disconnecting

Our analysis in previous chapters has highlighted the significance of temporal space in relation to *Self* and identity formation. This, in itself, is not relatively revolutionary. Indeed, social scientists have long professed the influential role of temporal proximity in forging a political group identity (Santos and Buzinde, 2007) and a social identity (Pratt and Hanson, 1994), with power as a key component in the process. As we mentioned in Chapter 4, however, in addition to joining local vegan activist groups, a number of interviewees also frequented online spaces and virtual communities for *Self*-affirmation and, in some cases, a collective identity. Recent studies have proposed that national and global lockdowns offered a significant opportunity for individuals to enact desired dietary changes. On the one hand, some individuals chose to make changes for health and/or ethical purposes (Marty, de Lauzon-Guillain and Labesse, 2021), while on the other hand, some gravitated towards an increase in their consumption of comfort foods (Bennett, Young and Butler, 2021).

Williams, Vardavoulia, Lally et al. (2023), therefore, propose that lockdowns may have initiated the gravitation towards a vegan diet for many people, while also functioning as an obstructed for those already practising Veganism. The conversations undertaken for this study coincided with the Global Covid-19 lockdowns, and the interviews with the participants indicated that the lockdowns not only functioned as a catalyst for several of the interviewees to disconnect themselves from the *vegan-other-for-me* in both their real life and virtual life, but also offered a *time-space* for re-assessing their 'vegan self' at an ontological level. You will note that I have hyphenated *time-space* rather than referring to the terms separately as time and space. The reason for this is that Bakhtin's work on the temporal and spatial parameters of time, referred to as the *Chronotope*, argues for a complex interdependent relationship between time and space. The *Chronotope*, similar to other Bakhtinian concepts, is abstract in nature. To animate his idea, Bakhtin draws on Einstein's theory of relativity. Essentially, the Bakhtinian *Chronotope* serves as a means of measuring how, in a particular age, *Genre* or text, *real* historical time and space – as well as fictional time and space – are interdependent. More importantly, for us here, the *Chronotope* is a medium for not only 'understanding experience' but also a 'specific form-shaping ideology' for understanding individual and collective 'events and actions' (Morson and Emerson, 1990: 250). The *I-for-myself's* experience of time, Bakhtin continues, is a 'given' phenomenon of 'immediate reality' (Bakhtin, 1984: 85). As Markova and Novàes (2020) note, for Bakhtin, 'human life must be primarily considered through the concept of temporality,' through which the *Self* and the *Self-Other* relationship emerge (Markova and Novàes, 2020: 118).

Sideward Glance

In Chapter 2 we overviewed the interdisciplinary nature of Bakhtin's work, particularly the Dialogical tune in psychology. Notably, although Bakhtin significantly broadens his perspective on the Chronotope in The Dialogic Imagination, the concept of the Chronotope was initially designed as a contribution to genre theory within the novel (Bakhtin, 1981). Unsurprisingly, then, the concept of Chronotope has also been employed within psychology for disclosing more nuanced aspects of embodiment and lived experiences (see Cresswell and Sullivan, 2018).

Guided by the *Speech Genres* and *Utterances* emerging from the conversations with the interviewees, I would argue that *Being* vegan can also be understood as existing within a collective *Chronotropic time-space*; regardless of whether the *Chronotropic time-space* consisted of concrete temporality in the form of a local vegan community or in the form of a more abstract online vegan communities. As we discuss in the next section, for Orlando, the global lockdowns functioned as a *time-space* that extracted him from his vegan *Chronotropic time-space*, particularly as he felt that his '*transition to a non-vegan will have been longer if Covid hadn't happened maybe my grandma will still be here.*'

> I decided that I will be non-vegan again was when my grandma died. But I was feeling bad, okay? (Orlando)

While for Portia, who predominantly engaged with online vegan communities leading up to and during lockdown, she made the decision to stop engaging with online vegan spaces:

> So I actually quit social media towards the beginning of this year, naturally … I thought you know what, I don't need social media right now and it was just prior to everything happening at the moment so it was timed quite well, to be honest.

Arguably, the presence of a collective vegan *Chronotropic time-space* is reinforced by the differentiation in the experience of those who chose *not* to become a part of a vegan community, online or otherwise. If you are chapter-hopping, I would suggest reading the *Maintaining a Double-Voiced Speech Genre* section in Chapter 4, if you have not already done so.

Chronotopes, then, can be understood as being embodied, as they are 'constitutive of human experience,' such as the corporeal situation of one's body in a particulate *time-space* (Cresswell and Sullivan, 2018: 126). In the previous chapter, we also discussed how, from a dialogical perspective, embodiment can be viewed as a complex matrix between language – for example, *Utterances* and *Speech Genres* – and emotionality (the emotions a word evokes in us) in a given *time-space*. One's participation in a community, in this context, let us say a collective *Chronotropic time-space*, illustrates how language is embodied. Therefore, 'language communities … address speech genres in this sense that treats language as embodied' (Cresswell and Baerveldt, 2011: 477). Particularly, the turmoil and struggle experienced by the *I-for-myself* arise when there is a juxtaposition between how one *ought* to feel (expected embodied experience) and how one actually feels (lived embodied experience). In the following few paragraphs, we will explore the interviewees' *Speech Genres*, which reveal a drive towards 'being faithful' or 'faithfulness' to oneself (Cresswell and Baerveldt, 2011). Throughout our analysis, we have been highlighting the reciprocal nature of the *Dialogical Self*, and how the *I-for-myself* cannot occur and endure in a vacuum; it is in need of an *Other*. It is important, however, that we do not reduce the *Dialogical Self* to one that is put forward from a social constructionist perspective (Gergen and Thatchenkery, 2004; Gergen, 1991). For Bakhtin (1990), the *Self* is not puppeteered by social constructions. Rather, *experiential action* is fundamental, and what came through strongly was the participants's *embodied* experience.

Before we move forward, however, I would like to unpick the term 'faithful' or 'faithfulness' in a little more detail, and whom is one being faithful.

> emotional-volitional tone of a once-occurant actual consciousness conveyed more aptly with the word faithfulness (being true to).
>
> (Bakhtin, 1990: 38)

The above quote encapsulates what Bakhtin meant by being faithful to another. One is faithful to another in terms of sympathising and understanding the 'emotional-volitional' within their *Speech Genres*. In other words, comprehending the tone, style, and intonation within the *Other's Utterances*, sympathising how life is experienced from within this particular community and collective *Chronotropic time-space*. If you have not already done so, at this point, I would encourage you to read Chapter 4, where the *I-for-myself* of the interviewees enters into a dialogical relationship with that of the *Vegan-other-for-me*. The interviewees aligned their faithfulness to their vegan community while they are within this collective *Chronotropic time-space*, sympathising with the community's experiences and emulating the same response. From a Bakhtinian, perspective, however, because of their *Double-voiced* consciousness, the *I-for-myself* can co-exist with multiple-faithfullnesses (Bakhitn, 1984, 1990).

This is because, in a dialogical interaction, one can always remain 'answerably active' with a 'loophole' (Bakhtin, 1993: 36).

Sideward Glance

As a reminder, in the world of Dialogism, Answerability, or 'answerably active' refers to existing in a social space where rhetorical interaction is an ongoing event, and carries multiple values and meanings simultaneously. It is heteroglossia, and Being is not a concrete given.

However, the analysis in Chapter 4 revealed that the interviewees did not share this experience. To the extent that their *Speech Genres* merged with that of the vegan community, their consciousness and multivocality also merged into *Single-voiced Speech Genres*, therefore, experiencing a *Finalised* sense of *Self* and identity formation. As mentioned earlier, this chapter is about the interviewees re-capturing their *Unfinalisability*. At this *Threshold-moment* of crisis, the interviewees had the opportunity to continue *Being* vegan, or move beyond the *Denial* and acknowledge their embodied experiences.

From a dialogical perspective, the *Self* is a member of, and can be faithful to, multiple-language communities (Bakhtin, 1990). Previously, we noted that some of the participants's *Utterances* were indicative of experiencing isolation in their physical *time-space* once they *Became* vegan, and the development of a sense of collectiveness in the online *time-space*. For several, the beginning of global lockdown offered a *time-space* where they felt they could not only *disconnect* from the *Vegan-other-for-me*, but also *reconnect* with the *non-vegan-other-for-me* and re-acclimate their sense of *Selfhood*: '*I wanted*, and *what I wanted to do*' (*Portia*). The noteworthy point here is not necessarily the dichotomy experienced by the interviewees, but rather that it offered their *I-for-myself* a return to a *Polyphonic time-space*.

> I wasn't with people as much [during lockdown] it helped me kind of think about *what I wanted*, and *what I wanted to do*, so it happened during the pandemic where I was like, you know what, *I don't know why I'm still doing this*, I don't feel good, I feel guilty, and I ate meat again (Portia).

Current scholarship extensively explores discourses surrounding 'backlash,' 'isolation,' 'trolling' and socio-ideological negativity towards Veganism and those practising Veganism (Wright, 2015). Additionally, research has examined the backlash from *within* the vegan community towards practitioners and activists who draw parallels between animal slaughter and slavery or the Holocaust (Zoledziowski, 2021), which was a sentiment shared by Cordelia:

> … I never liked the loaded language that vegans use, my own opinion but there was a lot of cows get raped, if you excuse me using those kind of terms and murder and comparing it to the holocaust which never agreed with me at all, I didn't think it was very nice comparisons, it almost devalues the actual event of what they're comparing it to because yes, what animals go through in factory farming is awful but I don't think you can compare that to the human experience of these things that they're comparing to, so those never…

We have also explored *intra*-group tension within Veganism, where vegans determine what it *means* to be vegan and whether one is 'vegan enough' if they chose to consume animal products such as honey and indeed whether one should continue to be vegan during pregnancy. There is, however, limited scholarship concerning *intra*-group tensions and the backlash experienced by those who, for whatever reason, cannot maintain *Being* vegan long term, and can be classified as 'former-vegans.' As Portia explained about her experience:

> … I think veganism doesn't acknowledge that some people can't eat a diet with lots of beans, … I've heard of vegans who are soy free but I don't know how they do it, there's just, yeah, there's, it felt very, like I felt like the vegans, it's almost as if they were, like people who say they're bad towards non-vegans, I think they were worse towards other vegans. So I felt like I was always trying to fit in with the other vegans, on social media, so sorry I'm off topic, but…

There has also been a rise in mass-market publications, such as magazine articles and blogs by former-vegan influencers, which relay their experiences of receiving backlash from their followers and the negative impact this has had on their wellbeing (Bellefonds, 2020). Recent news articles have also noted that *intra*-group tensions and *intra*-subjective tensions are highest for those who *leave* Veganism (Bellefonds, 2020). This is because 'fallen' vegans are perceived as affront to the politics embedded within Veganism, and symbolic of undermining the health benefits achievable through the vegan diet (Berry, 2019). Former-vegan influencer known as 'Rawvana,' for example, received continuous negativity as users's tags questioned her integrity as a person for no longer *Being* vegan: '*Lie*vana,' '*Fake*vana,' 'deceitful,' 'disgusting,' 'sickening,' and 'scamming' (Berry, 2019). In an interview with *Women's Health,* 'Rawvana' recalled that she was 'shock[ed] and felt confused and ashamed at the response' of her followers (Bellefonds, 2020). Similarly, Alyse Parker, another former-vegan influencer) also admits that her 'mental state for the next six months after I told my followers I was quitting veganism was the worst it had been since I was a teenager' (Bellefonds, 2020). Similarly, Alexander Jamieson, informed *Women's Health* that after her announcement:

> A lot of vegans secretly reached out saying they has health problem but felt like they couldn't tell their loved ones who were vegan. I joke that I became a vegan confessional booth.
>
> (Bellefonds, 2020)

I refer to popular vloggers, influencers, and health magazines tentatively and with caution, as there is always the possibility of such material being perceived by many, both within and outside of academia, as not yielding any particularly insightful commentary on the early stages of transitioning to *Becoming* vegan, *Being* vegan, and transitioning out of Veganism. The experiences of several of the interviewees, however, do resonate with the experience of former-vegan influencers. They were also aware of *intra*-group negativity but also of the collective social identity discussed in the previous chapter: '*if they would have become my friends, I feel like it would have been harder to make that decision for myself to leave veganism*'.

> I think that if I would have gotten involved with other vegan people, and even especially if they would have become my friends, I feel like it would have been harder to make that decision for myself to leave veganism, because there's a lot of like shaming and there's a lot of guilt that comes from the vegan community when you leave (Puck).

The *Speech Genres* of the interviewees who did choose to become a part of a vegan community or friendship group also reflected that they were anticipatory of experiencing similar negative rhetoric themselves once they made the decision to stop *Being* vegan.

> And that did me a lot of good [disconnecting from social media] so I didn't have any backlash of loads of people finding out I wasn't vegan anymore or having to feel like I needed to put it out there or going through unfollowing all these people (Cordelia).
>
> Oh yeah, I definitely don't [keep in contact with vegan friends], yeah, they have [stopped communicating with Portia], we've drifted apart, pandemic definitely drifted everybody apart, but that helped [laughs] (Portia).
>
> I never officially told anybody because I was so afraid. I think a lot of vegans are kind of afraid, or ex-vegans are afraid to come back to eating that way because they don't know how people are going to respond (Bianca).

From a dialogical perspective, the participants' anticipatory response itself, is an interesting one as it implies what Bakhtin refers to as a '*sideward glance*,' or rather, the lack of a *Sideward Glace* (Bakhtin, 1984: 195). The *Sideward Glance* is part of what Bakhtin calls the 'hidden polemic,' an *Active Double-voiced discourse*. In a hidden polemic dialogical interaction, the speaker's discourse (in this case, our interviewees) is directed at its referential object (in this case, the *Vegan-other-for-me*). What makes this interaction *Double-voiced* is that the speaker (our interviewees), as Bakhtin calls it, 'cringe[s]' in the presence of a listener's (*Vegan-other-for-me*) words, and they take a *Sideward Glance*, which anticipates a possible hostile reply. The speaker (*I-for-myself*) responds to this anticipated answer by striking '*a polemical blow… at the other's discourse on the same theme*' (the *Vegan other-for-me*), thus, ensuring that the interaction is *dialogic* and the *I-for-myself* retains a *Double-voiced Speech Genre* (Bakhtin, 1984: 195). The participants *Utterances* quoted above, however, extricated themselves from delivering a Bakhtinian 'polemical blow' to the other, as they chose to disconnect from the internet, or attending their vegan community meetings. Hence, not disclosing their decision to no longer *Being* vegan. Gertrude's experience with her mentor was particularly insightful,

> … I feel incredibly guilty with [mentor] because I became really good friends with her, but then I changed my diet and I haven't told her, but I feel like I would consider her a friend, I don't really want to lose her as a friend, I feel like we've really developed a relationship, but and I know it, I know telling her would end our friendship, completely.

Gertrude explained that her mentor had been vegan for three decades and maintained the stance of 'vegan or die,' which she respected immensely, and did not '*want to have that confrontation.*' Similarly, Leigha (see Chapter 4), also actively chose not to enter a '*confrontation*' with the *Vegan-other-for-me*. We have argued that, within certain collective vegan communities, the *I-for-myself* becomes *Finalised* ('*she's a vegan or die kind of person'*) and is no longer in the process of *Becoming*, therefore, losing its *Answerability* towards the *Other* (Bakhtin, 1990). We will return to this in Chapter 6. For now, it is important to highlight that participants did not only anticipate a negative response from the *Vegan-other-for-me*, but also from the *Non-vegan-other-for-me*.

> I haven't told my family, I'm not super close to my family anymore, I do feel like they would be like, ha-ha, I told you so, and I'm like I lasted six years, like leave me alone (Puck).

> he's actually vegan more for the reason of like the environment, he, his view on a lot of veganism like he, he's really open, he still believes that you know, there's a reason why animals are put on earth and it's for people to consume them, not just so they can range freely, he still believes that and he's really open to me not being vegan anymore (Kate).

On the one hand, Kate's partner, who continued *Being* vegan after she stopped, was supportive of her decision. On the other hand, Puck anticipated an unfavourable reaction from the *Non-vegan-other-for-me*. Notably, Kate's partner's motivation—environmental Veganism—differs from his previous animal ethics-driven reasons for Being vegan. In comparison to Kate, who struggled considerably with the notion of re-consuming meat, her partner adopted a more flexible approach: '*he's thinking about maybe one day he'll start eating eggs and fish again but as of now he has not changed it.*' This somewhat resonates with the *Speech Genres* identified in Chapters 3 and 4. Those who *Become* vegan for animal ethics, for instance, or shift towards animal ethics while *Being* vegan, experience a higher degree of *intra*-subjective tension in terms of self-perception and identity.

The Secondary Speech Genre of Reconnecting

At this point, I am sure you are familiar with the concept of *Unfinalisability* and its status as the cornerstone of the Bakhtinian *Dialogical Self*, where the *I-for-myself* can never become static. In order to remain irreducible and *Becoming*, the *I-for-myself* must continue to enter dialogical relationships with the *Other*.

> The self cannot, therefore, become an answerable, self-active or self-determinate agent in the world *without the aesthetic activity of the other.*
>
> (Bakhtin, 1993: 188, *emphasis added*)

Once participants disconnected from the *Vegan-other-for-me* for self-determination, they began reconnecting with the *None-vegan-other-for me.*

> I took a picture of my meal, which was rib eye steak with some, you know, like peas and chips and everything. And that's when I got like loads of messages off people *[laughs]*. But they weren't like, you know, horrible messages, they were all so supportive, people just asking, you know, "Are you still vegan?", and I'd just, I'd say like, "No, not any more". And everyone was just like, *"Oh, thank God"*, or like, *"Yay"* (Bianca).
>
> My friends have been very supportive … But like my two or three best friends, they were like, *"This could be really good for you,"* and they were just very encouraging, I have been sending them photos of my food, they were like, *"Oh, that looks so good,"* and they've had a lot of fun like experiencing things with me, like I had a candy bar for the first time in six years, that was so good (Puck).

The majority of participants experienced an element of embarrassment as they '*came to terms with things*,' particularly their behaviour and attitude towards the *None-vegan-other-for-me* while *Being* vegan: *Erm… and, yeah, I used to post some really embarrassing things on Facebook about like the wool industry, which is not true in the slightest* (Bianca). The *Speech Genres* within the *Utterances* above emphasises the argument we made in Chapter 4, that, from a Bakhtinian dialectic perspective, ethical responsibility is imperative when it comes to the dual dynamic of discursive *inter*-subjectivity. As, in a dialogical relationship, the *Utterances* of the *Other* are an essential aspect of *intra*-subjectivity. Puck's and Bianca's *Utterances: 'This could be really good for you'*; *'Yay'*; *'fun'*; *'supportive,'* contain what classical psychology may refer to as positive reinforcement. Of course, this was not limited to Puck and Bianca. Above, we highlighted Kate's dynamics with her boyfriend who remained vegan at the time these interviews were conducted: *'he's really open to me not being vegan anymore.'* The positive and constructive presence of the *Other* was also evident for Orlando and Cordelia:

> Yes. They support me, um, well they, my mum told me that she wanted me to be, well the best I could, so she helped me transition to a non-vegan lifestyle again. Because at first I felt really guilty of eating animal products again and I was questioning myself if I was doing the right thing, if I go vegan again or something (Orlando).

> A few friends that I speak with more regularly, so the one who was vegan and is now ex-vegan, she's one of my closest friends so I told her straightaway [about *Being* vegan] (Cordelia).

Our dialogical relationships with the *Other*, therefore, should be *constructive*, as it is the dynamic of the *Becoming* of *Selfhood*, of identity, and indeed culture itself. In this sense, dialogical interactions are not only the locomotive of individual *Becoming*, but also society's socio-ideological *becoming* (see Chapter 6). Orlando's *Utterances*, and those of other participants discussed in this section, *'Because at first I felt really guilty of eating animal products again … so that way I could feel like less guilty,'* are illustrative of an *ethical Other*. I would like to take a moment and explain what Bakhtin (1993) means here by the ethical *Other*, as the concept—or the concept in action—is rather illuminating when we consider certain *Utterances* in relation to the *None-vegan-other-for-me*. In its simplest form, an ethical *Other* can be understood as an empathetic *Other* who, when in dialogue with an *I*, considers their historical living, or, in psychological terms, their lived experiences. Therefore, an empathetic *Other*'s act cannot be 'universal' and generic towards the *I*. The *Utterances* below exemplify the importance of an ethical *Other* during the participants's final *Threshold-moment*:

> so I talked to my mum and *she started buying me* [ethically sources animal products] *so that way I could feel like less guilty* (Orlando).

> Another really close friend, I told her and *she went, oh that's really good news*, like *I'm happy that you've got an answer kind of thing. A couple of other friends were like, oh I'm glad, just happy that I had an answer* (Cordilia).

> *Oh my God, my mum spent like a week* just being like have milk, have cheese. I think we had, I think we had like sausages, and it was just the best thing ever and *I was just, yeah. It was just like no, you're not doing this anymore and I was like...* Like because it's Christmas, like we have like turkey and things like that and it was just, you know, trying to get back to normal, I guess (Goneril).

> And, yeah, and when I told her that I wasn't any more, she was a little bit surprised. And, but I don't think she was upset ... So I think it'll happen at some point, but, yeah she wasn't, yeah, it was a good response, actually, from everyone (Bianca).

I would also like to draw attention to the following words within Cordelia's *Utterances*: *I'm happy that you've got an answer ... happy that I had an answer*.' In Chapter 3, we made the argument that, during their first *Threshold moment*, a number of participants occupied a *time-space* of ambiguity, a fundamental requirement for *intra*-subjectivity and *inter*-subjectivity, where the *I-for-myself* is seeking the *Other* in the process of *Becoming*. The implication that Cordelia, and other interviewees, now have an '*answer*' at their third *Threshold-moment* consolidates their experience and our onto-epistemological approach. It is not through binding the *I-for-myself* to the *Voice* and values of particular dialectical community that displays 'faithfulness,' but rather a gesture of *understanding* the value and dialectics of a particular community, while remaining faithful to oneself by maintaining *Double-voiced Speech Genres* within our *Utterances*.

Sideward Glance

Bakhtin's concept of the ethical Other is a component of what he refers to as Aesthetic Activity. Bakhtin argues, the Other must establish the consciousness of the I (and vice versa) through an act of empathy. We will develop this in more detail in the final chapter.

Rediscovering a *Double-Voiced Utterance*

At this point, I am sure that you are familiar with the significance of remaining '*answerably active*,' and the *Unfinalized* openness of the *Self-Other* dialogical relationship, which is at the epicentre of *Answerability*. The aim of this final section is to explore the *Polyphony*, or the recapturing of a *Double-voiced* consciousness, within the participants's *Utterances* once they stopped *Being* vegan. Once again, the following quotes may be lengthy, but they are crucial for capturing the participants' phenomenology and authentic *Voices*. In the following passages, I have italicised the particularly significant *Utterances*, as I wish to retain their verve, which I feel would have been lost by shortening them.

> *My perspective has changed drastically.* I remember being a vegan I was like one of the like militant vegans and I was just like you know, everybody has to be vegan because this is the only way that it'll be good for everybody, for the environment, for the animals, for our own health, *yeah, and now I look back and I'm just like I sometimes wonder if like I was really a part of like a cult because,* and I was doing it for *so long I just like, this just was just my belief, like my lifestyle, there's no way that I was not going to think that way, but luckily my perspective changed*, I put my health first and everything's just, it's just different and *I don't think that way anymore you know, and I'm still growing,* I'm 25 but I'm still like learning, I'm being more open to a lot of things now (Kate).

> Well I think another important thing maybe is that when, as I told you I wanted to lose weight when I started being vegan [see Chapter 3]. I think I developed an eating disorder, *so I think like that veganism was something to mask my eating disorder*, to eat less or *if something gave me food I will say "no thank you, I'm vegan"* but it was because I was afraid of eating food, you know? (Orlando).

Orlando's post-vegan experience differed from that of other participants in the sense that, on reflection, he felt that he had developed irregular eating patterns, going beyond the prohibition of animal products. Vegan scholarship, such as Wright (2015), however, has objected to the connection because, from their standpoint, it not only dilutes Veganism's original ethos—animal ethics—but also links it with pathological eating disorders. Broader literature around Veganism and patterns of restrictive eating is limited, particularly in terms of qualitative data exploring individual experiences. Some clinical studies, for instance, have shown that individuals following a vegan diet are at lower risk of developing pathological eating disorders (Heiss, Coffino, and Hormes, 2017). Alternatively, more recent studies have highlighted that those following a vegan diet exhibited a higher-level of pathological eating behaviours through cognitive restraint (McLean, Lavale, Kulkarni et al., 2022; McLean, Moeck, Sharp et al., 2021).

Debating the relationship between Veganism and pathological eating disorders, however, is not the scope of our discussion. Rather it is the phenomenology and meaning-making of Veganism itself, and individual experiences in terms of identity and self-perception. Ultimately, it is not a conversation concerning correlation and causations, but one of foregrounding the *Polyphony* within mainstream and academic vegan *Voices.* Why mention it, then? My simplest response to this would be that these *Utterances* emerged in the data. I felt it was essential for me to remain 'true' and convey what some interviewees felt best described their broader experiences with Veganism.

> And now that I discovered that ex-vegan sobriety I've seen a lot of people that have come or have past that, or that have an eating disorder and they mask it with veganism … Yes. Because they are, or at least in my local community they tend to separate foods into good and bad foods, and that's not good for something with an eating disorder (Orlando).

Orlando's experience, along with many others who engage with similar social media platforms, echoes the argument proposed by Arppe and Väänänen-stronger (2018), which suggests that in dietary movements, communities play a pivotal role in defining the boundaries of forbidden and permissible foods.

While reading the quoted above, I hope you have also begun to notice the shift in the *Speech Genres* within the interviewees's *Utterances* as they rediscovered their individuality and *Double-voicedness*. Their post-vegan *Speech Genres* are not monolithic (see Chapter 4) and do not illustrate the tendency to unify *Utterances* or enforce uniformity over plurality:

> I think I would say that I'm just like an individual and I don't have to follow, like there's no, like even though I felt like I was like trying to follow veganism, like there was somebody watching me all the time, there is nobody watching me and I can eat whatever I want, and who cares what people think (Portia).

Kate conveyed that once she stopped *Being* vegan her '*perspective changed drastically*,' a sentiment echoed by Bianca, who explained that '*when you're vegan you don't see what's happening, [and] it's only after that you notice what you've done to yourself*.' When discussing his position on the role of words in his system of thought, Bakhtin argues that every *Utterance* is half given and half created (Bakhtin, 1986, 1984, 1981). Essentially, when the *I-for-myself* enters into a dialogical communication with the *Other*, the *I* uses language and symbol inherited from a given language community (i.e., Veganism). However, during this interaction there is a process of appropriation by which the word (i.e., Veganism) acquires a personal and subjective texture. As Cordelia reflected:

> So, you know, I feel from a vegan's perspective, yeah, I've done exactly the worst thing possible. But for me, I feel very content in knowing that I'm a lot more connected to nature, humanity, life as whole through my diet, I'm more aware (Cordelia).

TABLE 5.2 *Soundbites* for the *Primary Speech Genre of Rediscovering a Double-Voiced Utterance*

Primary Genre	*Secondary Genre*	*Quotes*
Rediscovering a Double-Voiced Utterance	Confession	*But, yeah, now I feel a ton of regret for ever making him go vegan erm... because, you know, like if you ever look back at like old pictures like before you're vegan, and then the change that you see is so dramatic. And I remember, I have a photo of him where, before he was vegan he was like so young and vibrant and so much colour in his skin, and then like photos from not even a few months ago, and the colours all gone, you know, he's like pale, dull, it's just such a dramatic change (Bianca).*
		Also one of the major turning points of me to stop being vegan was as I told you when the pandemic started, well my grandma died of Covid. ...I felt guilty of all the times I refused to eat whatever she made for lunch for me and that I was vegan I will say no. So I felt really guilty of all that, that now I won't be able to eat her food again. So that also helped me to be, to stop being (Orlando).
	'Fake News'	*It doesn't acknowledge individuality at all, not everyone can eat the same thing, and be okay (Portia).*
		Oh for sure, I don't think there is such a thing as a health vegan. I don't think that's a category, because it's not healthy, really (Gertrude).

The third *Threshold-moment* not only implies the re-establishment of individual appropriation within the participants's *Utterances* but also a sense of *Self* and identity re-construction (*Unfinalisability*), which was, arguably, absent during their second *Threshold-moment* (Table 5.2).

Secondary Speech Genre of Confession

After the re-emergence of their *Double-voiced Speech Genres*, *Confession* became a reoccurring *Secondary Speech Genre* within a number of individual *Utterances*. It was not guilt around the re-consumption of meat that was the initial issue.

Rather, it was guilt concerning becoming the *Vegan-other-for-me* to their *Non-vegan-other-for-me* family and friends during their second *Threshold moment* (see Chapter 4). For example, Bianca's position of becoming a *Vegan-other-for-me,* for her partner, was not intentional. Nonetheless, she was '*excited*' and '*ecstatic*' about having '*a vegan boyfriend.*' She continued to explain '*But I never really tried to force him into it or anything, but I would always like cook the meals. And he was always happy to eat vegan food, anyway.*' Regarding her mother going vegan, however, Bianca remained insistent:

> But with my mum, so I actually made her go vegan, which is something that is my biggest regret ... And erm... yeah, and I knew that she was kind of suffering a little bit on the vegan diet, because she was having a lot of joint pain, she was like having trouble sort of speaking her mind, getting her words out. And she's like, she's not that old, she's in her 60s.

Similar to Bianca, Cordelia conveyed feeling guilty for becoming her partner's *Vegan-other-for-me*. Particularly as '*he found the transition more difficult than* [Cordelia], *even though he'd been vegan less time*':

> So I think he was officially vegan for 7 months but that... That was more of an issue for me than me transitioning [out of being vegan]. I felt so guilty and awful that I'd encouraged him there was never any pressure there ... but I just couldn't help feeling awful because he suffered the health negatives a lot quicker than I did ... I feel so awful, I just can't help but feel bad about [him] because I feel like I've done this to him and like he's dropped weight, he had hair loss, he's got really chronic fatigue, he still does suffer, like he'll fall asleep quite easily, his libido completely crashed and then his diet prior wasn't good, which I don't think helped, he had a really ... I did that to him, I just felt horrendous, so horrendous.

Thus far, we have considered the relationship between the *I* (*I-for-myself*) and the *Other* (*Other-for-me*). Another facet of Bakhtin's notion of *Unfinalisability* is the relationship the *I* has with itself, in terms of self-development. In a chapter entitled *Author and Hero in Aesthetic Activity*, Bakhtin (1990) writes about the *I-for-myself's* reflexivity on their own life, akin to what he refers to as *Confession*, where one seeks redemption. When one makes a *Confession*, Bakhtin continues (1990), they do so with the *Other's* response in mind. Therefore, an *Utterance* that encapsulates the *Speech Genre* of *Confession* not only takes the form of a soliloquy but is also *Double-voiced*. There is an element of *Confession* in the *Utterances* of Binca, Cordelia, Orlando, and Portia. As they spoke about their regrets, language such as, '*bless her, she's very, I think, influenced by other people, so she likes to kind of follow a crowd,*' and, '*there was never any pressure there,*' can potentially be read as anticipatory responses from the *Other*. During a *Confession Secondary Speech Genre*, the *I-for-myself* takes account of one's own act (functioning as a *vegan-other-for me*), and in confessing, by uttering it out aloud, the *I-for-myself* is acknowledging and taking accountability for one's own acts. This is noticeable as the participants refer to themselves direct and continuously.

Earlier, we touched on the topic of language communities and, from a Bakhtinian perspective (1986), how the *I-for-myself* can be a member of several language communities, with the prefixing of a *Double-voiced* consciousness. We also, however, discussed the tendency of vegan communities, to which the interviewees belonged, to carry a *Finalised Single-voiced* consciousness. We have discussed this extensively in previous chapters. Nonetheless, Portia's experience, quoted below, exemplifies unitary *Single-voicedness* and the emergence of a *Double-voiced* consciousness when embodied experiences do not align with expectations:

> I also think that maybe around six months in like *I wasn't really being honest with myself, that I missed eating meat*, because on social media you see all these people who are like, I don't eat meat, I'm totally fine without it, I have never craved it ever ...

Recent social psychological research (Kirstena-effi, Seib-Pfrifera, Lütha et al., 2020; Reddy and van Damb, 2020) has explored a deeper understanding of the contextual aspects of identity in relation to food. Reddy and van Damb (2020) note that, as individuals, we centralise food in social events ('*really wanting to go out with my friends to eat wings, and I couldn't do any of that*'), cultural celebrations, family settings ('*but I actually found myself wanting to eat my mom's lasagne, or a homemade dish*'), and perceive it as a persistent part of traditional beliefs; especially when it comes to traditions concerning culture and ethnicity (D'Sylva and Beagan, 2011).

> *I think every day my grandma asked me*, you know, why can't you just eat eggs, you know, eggs are like, you're not hurting anybody, it's just an unfertilised egg, and I think every single day I had to talk to her that I just couldn't, it was my way of life that I'd chose for myself. *And I have a lot of guilt actually because I think like my grandparents really liked cooking and it's like their way of showing love*, so I feel really bad currently because I couldn't eat their food when I was there last, so yeah.

Portia's reflection on her cultural heritage, while *Being* Vegan, highlights the tension between two different language communities, as does Orlando's. They relayed the sense of guilt they experienced for rejecting their respective cultural communities.

Secondary Speech Genre of 'Fake News'

The final *Secondary Speech Genre* we will discuss in this chapter is that of '*Fake News*,' which is in sharp contrast with the *Speech Genres* discussed in the previous chapter, where a sense of *Collective Identity* led to a unified *Voice*. For a more consistent understanding of the participants's experiences, if you have not already done so, I would highly encourage that you to stop and read Chapter 4 before continuing. The sense of *Collective Identity* and the unification of *Voice* was no longer apparent when I enquired about their final thoughts regarding Veganism as a whole and their experience with Veganism. I have quoted four participants below, if you would like a comprehensive overview to this question, please read the *Pen Portraits* presented in Chapter 2.

> I feel... I think just one of the things of veganism is the facts that *they give out which aren't based on fact* ... yes they're fed soy crops [animals] but it's not the soy itself, it's soy cakes ... so I guess, I wish vegans would look into it further and not just look at the whole fact that they get presented... *I just realised that things aren't black and white*, and that it's not veganism and non-veganism, like there's a middle area, and yeah (Cordelia).

> Erm... but, yeah, like *I do think that veganism as a whole does make you more ethically conscious*. So there is a good side to veganism, I think, but I definitely don't think it's, *I don't think it's as ethical as eating sustainably sourced animal products, because I think a lot of vegans forget or they don't want to acknowledge that the amount of killing that has to happen for the crops, crops to grow, you know, like birds, insects, rodents*, erm... yeah, I think it kind of goes over their head or they don't want to believe that's what happens, when it's a lot more sustainable and ethical to eat meat (Bianca).

> *You need to investigate yourself, not only on paper but investigate* in, research about it in forums or as I now know in Reddit maybe how people felt in that diet. And if you're having problems look them up and see how they are related and that maybe a lot of people have gone that way (Orlando).

> I didn't do a lot of research at all, because I was young, *I didn't think that like it was going to actually impact my life*. And yeah, that's basically the internet made me vegan [laughs] (Puck).

It is not necessarily the *content* of the quotes that I wish to highlight, as debating the pros and cons of Veganism has not been the intention of our analyses. Rather, what I would like to showcase here is the *direction* of the *Utterances* and the number of *Voices* that can be heard within them. For example, I hope you are able to identify the nuance and contrast between the participants's *Speech Genres* during their second and third *Threshold-moments*. In comparison, the *Utterances* of the third *Threshold-moment* imply *inter*-subjective tensions (between the *I-for-myself*, the *Non-vegan-other-for-me*, and the *Vegan-other-for-me*), whereas the *Speech Genres* of the second *Threshold-moment* implied *intra*-subjective tensions (tensions within the *I-for-myself*). Portia's statement: '*I wish vegans would look into it further and not just look at the whole fact that they get presented*,' and Bianca's final thought that '*there is a good side to veganism, I think, but I definitely don't think it's, I don't think it's as ethical as eating sustainably*,' allow us to identify the emergence of their *Double-voice*.

I would also like to highlight that none of the interviewees perceived Veganism itself as a negative influence. They did, however, question the Western rhetorical discourses around the concept, especially some pockets of vegan communities which, for them, promoted a static ideological stance towards Veganism. Indeed, for Puck, *Being* vegan '*taught [them] a lot about compassion*,' and to be more mindful '*when consuming animal products*.' However, they also continued to express that Veganism '*could be classified as a religion … which is kind of scary*.' The overall arching *Speech Genre* within the participants's *Utterances*, when it came to wanting to *Become* vegan, was the advocacy for independent research—research that moved beyond the 'Fake news' of influencers, of vegan literature, and of '*vegan medical experts*,' encountered online, and emphasised the need to seek advice about independent individual experiences.

Chapter Summary

The discussion and analysis in this chapter have highlighted the *inter*-subjective tensions participants experienced at their third *Threshold-moment*. From a social psychological perspective, we not only explored the shifts in participants's social and group identities but also their re-discovery of their sense of *Self* and the multivocality of their *Voice*. For example, we have noted the changes in their embodied *Self*; a persistent feeling of guilt at the beginning, not only for re-consuming animal products, but also for acting as a *Vegan-other-for-me* for *Others*; the re-connection with the Non-vegan-other-for-me; and the dis-connecting from particular social networks, both physically and online. We also observed the interviewees's shift in understanding concepts such as Veganism and Sustainability, which showcases the dialogical conceptions of *meaning* and meaning-making: that concepts are fundamentally multi-voiced. That is, they live in the plurality of multiple *Voices* and not in the singularity of a static ideological 'fact.' In Chapter 1, we outlined the multiple contested definitions of 'Veganism,' primarily divided into two camps: Veganism as a practice-based-ism, and Veganism as a broader ideology-based-ism. We also posed the question of whether individual experiences are undervalued within such definitions, namely, the position of the practitioner. The three analysis chapters, including this one, have endeavoured to illustrate how, through the lens of a Bakhtinian onto-epistemology, a word like Veganism is always pre-saturated with the heterogeneity of meanings and values deposited in it by previous cultures, and that such meaning come into being through the *Utterances* of individuals. Therefore, situating the *practitioners*'s lived experiences and meaning-making *within* the word.

What I hope these analysis chapters have also prompted us to consider is whether perceiving or advocating for Veganism to be defined as either a 'one or the other.' In other words, a practice-based-ism or as a ideology-based-ism might be over simplistic. In Chapters 3 and 4, for instance, we followed how, for some of the interviewees, a practice-based-ism, — the decision not to consume animal products due to motivations such as health, the environment, animal ethics, or a combination — became a broader ideology-based-ism during their second *Threshold-moment*, albeit to varying degrees. This shift occurred particularly when considering the impact of *Being* vegan had on their self-perception and identity. *Being* vegan (ideologically) or eating vegan (practise based), therefore, synthesises to produce a vegan-self through eating practises and habits. Laakso, Niva, Eranti et al. (2022) explored the impact of social media rhetoric on Veganism, and how it facilitates the re-configuration of individual eating habits. Similarly, Lara (2021) discussed the institutional politics behind consuming habits in general, as well as Veganism. She argues that an 'institutional vegan ideology' homogenises, which erodes individuality while simultaneously promoting a false sense of individuality (Lara, 2021: 59). How do we then find equilibrium between the ethos of Veganism and the individual *Spirit* (Bakhtin, 1993, 1990)?

> I think I would say that I'm just like an individual and I don't have to follow, like there's no, like even though I felt *like I was like trying to follow veganism, like there was somebody watching me all the time, there is nobody watching me and I can eat whatever I want*, and who cares what people think.

I, of course, do not profess to have an answer to this, nor was it ever my desire to provide one; it would be terribly unBakhtinian of me. Above, I have quoted one of the *Utterances* that struck me most during my conversation with Portia, specifically, her recollection of the experience where she felt as though '*there was somebody watching* [her] *all the time,*' which echoes experiences with religious ideologies. In the following chapter, I will discuss the concepts of *Ideology* and *Aesthetics*, and the shaping of individual experiences within them.

References

Arppe, T., Mäkelä, J., & Väänänen, V. (2011). Living food diet and veganism: individual vs collective boundaries of the forbidden. *Anthropology of Food*, 50(2), 275–297. https://doi.org/10.1177/0539018410396618

Bakhtin, M. (1993). *Toward a philosophy of the act*. Austin: University of Texas Press.

Bakhtin, M. (1990). *Art and answerability: early philosophical essays*. Austin: University of Texas Press.

Bakhtin, M. (1984). *Problems of Dostoevsky's poetics*. Minneapolis: University of Minnesota Press.

Bellefonds, C. D. (2020). The vegans who quit: these women face major backlash from their followers – and are ready to talk about it. *Women's Health*. https://www.womenshealthmag.com/food/a32211871/veganinfluencers-who-quit/.

Bennett, G., Young, E., Butler, I., et al. (2021). The impact of lockdown during the covid-19 outbreak on dietary habits in various population groups: a scoping review. *Frontiers in Nutrition*, 8, Article 626432. https://doi.org/10.3389/fnut.2021.626432

Berry, S. (2019). Why those abandoning veganism experience 'violent' backlash. *Lifestyle, Health & Wellness*. https://www.smh.com.au/lifestyle/health-and-wellness/why-those-abandoning-veganism-experience-violent-backlash-20190909-p52pgo.html

Cresswell, J., & Sullivan, P. (2018). Bakhtin's chronotope, connotations, and discursive psychology: towards a richer interpretation of experience. *Qualitative Research in Psychology*, 17(1), 121–142. https://doi.org/10.1080/14780887.2018.1548674

Cresswell, J., & Baerveldt, C. (2011). Bakhtin's realism and embodiment: towards a revision of the dialogical self. *Culture & Psychology*, 17(2), 263–277. https://doi.org/10.1177/1354067X11398308

D'Sylva, A., & Beagan, B. L. (2011). "Food is culture, but it's also power": the role of food in ethnic and gender identity construction among goan Canadian women. *Journal of Gender Studies*, 20(3), 279–289. https://doi.org/10.1080/09589236.2011.593326

Faunalytics. (2016). Study of current and former vegetarians and vegans: secondary study. https://faunalytics.org/wp-content/uploads/2016/02/Faunalytics-Study-of-Current-and-Former-Vegetarians-and-Vegans-%E2%80%93-Secondary-Findings-.pdf

Gergen, K., & Thatchenkery, T. (2004). Organization science as social construction: postmodern potential. *Journal of Applied Behavioral Science*, 40(2), 228–249. https://doi.org/10.1177/0021886396324002

Gergen, K. (1991). *The saturated self: dilemmas of identity in contemporary life*. New York: Basic.

Grünhage, T., & Reuter, M. (2021). What makes diets political? Moral foundations and the left-wing-vegan connection. *Social Justice Research*, 34, 18–52. https://doi.org/10.1007/s11211-020-00361-w

Heiss, S., Cofno, J. A., & Hormes, J. M. (2017) Eating and health behaviors in vegans compared to omnivores: dispelling common myths. *Appetite*, 118, 129–135. https://doi.org/10.1016/j.appet.2017.08.001

Hodson, G., & Earle, H. (2018). Conservatism predicts lapses from vegetarian/vegan diets to mean consumption (through lower social justice concerns and social support.' *Appetite*, 120, 78–81. https://doi.org/10.1016/j.appet.2017.08.027

Kirsten-Effi, H., Seib-Pfeifer, L. E., Lüth, C. A. et al. (2020). Validation and application of a German version of the dietarian identity questionnaire: revealing differences between omnivores, vegetarians, and vegans. *Food Quality & Preferences*, 86, 103988. https://doi.org/10.1016/j.foodqual.2020.103988

Laakso, S., Niva, M., Eranti, V. et al. (2022). Reconfiguring everyday eating: vegan challenge discussions in social media, food. *Culture & Society*, 25(2), 268–289. https://doi.org/10.1080/15528014.2021.1882796

Lara, A. (2021). *Decentring subjectivity in everyday eating and drinking: digesting reality*. London & New York: Routledge.

Lockwood, A. (2019). Do 84% of vegans and vegetarians really go back to meat? https://plantbasednews.org/opinion/do-84-vegans-and-vegetarians-give-up-diets/

Markovà, I., & Novaes, A. (2020). Chronotopes. *Culture & Psychology*, 26(1), 117–138. https://doi.org/10.1177/1354067X19888189

Marty, L., de Lauzon-Guillain, B., Labesse, D., et al. (2021). Food choice motives and the nutritional quality of diet during the Covid-19 lockdown in France. *Appetite*, 157, Article 105005. https://doi.org/10.1016/j.appet.2020.105005

McLean, C. P., Lavale, A., Kulkarni, J. et al. (2022). Psychometric properties and factor structure of the eating disorder examination-questionnaire in omnivores, vegetarians, and vegans. *Appetite*, 43, 374–384. https://doi.org/10.1016/j.bodyim.2022.10.006

McLean, C. P., Moeck, E. K., Sharp, G. et al. (2021). Characteristics and clinical implications of the relationship between veganism and pathological eating behaviours. *Eating and Weight Disorders - Studies on Anorexia, Bulimia and Obesity*, 27, 1881–1886 https://doi.org/10.1007/s40519-021-01330-1

Sanford, M., & Lorimer, J. (2022). Veganuary and the vegan sausage (t)rolls: conflict and commercial engagement in online climate-diet discourse. *Humanities and Social Sciences Communications*, 9(255), 1–13. https://doi.org/10.1057/s41599-022-01464-2

Smith, B. S. (2017). This is the percent of vegetarians and vegans that go back to meat. https://www.thehealthy.com/food/vegetarians-vegans-go-back-meat/

Reddy, G., & van Dam, R. M. (2020). Food, culture, and identity in multicultural societies: insights from Singapore. *Appetite*, 149, 104633. https://doi.org/10.1016/j.appet.2020.104633

Williams, E., Vardavoulia, A., Larry, P., et al. (2023). Experiences of initiating and maintaining a vegan diet among young adults: a qualitative study. *Appetite*, 180(2), 106357. https://doi.org/10.1016/j.appet.2022.106357

Wright, L. (2015). *The vegan studies project: food animals, and gender in the age of terror*. Athens: University of Georgia Press.

Zoledziowski, A. (2021). Vegan influencers keep comparing meat-eating to the holocaust and slavery. *Vice News*. https://www.vice.com/en/article/wx8b9m/vegan-influencers-james-aspey-fullyrawkristina-comparing-meat-holocaust-slavery

6

MOVING FORWARD(?)

> *I feel like if you're an ethical vegan, more so than doing it for health reasons, the only person that's ever going to change your mind is you. I had every intention of doing it forever.*
>
> (Cordelia)

We discussed the stealth emergence of Veganism as what Horkheimer and Adorno (2002) refer to as a 'culture industry:'

> Culture today is infecting everything with sameness. Film, radio, and magazines form a system. Each branch of culture is unanimous within itself and all are unanimous together. Even the aesthetic manifestations of political opposites proclaim the same inflexible rhythm.

For many academics and activists, the diffusion of Vegan ethea throughout society, specifically popular culture, represents a superficial democratisation that distracts from the original purpose of Veganism. For instance, there has been a shift from concerns about animal welfare, ethics, and liberation, or from Vegan activism to popular plant-based capitalism. Additionally, Veganism has also become enmeshed with studies of oppression and intersectionality (Kheel, 2004), such as Ecofeminism (Carol and Gruen, 2022; Vèron and White, 2021; Gaard, 2011), Critical race studies (Deckha, 2012; Harper, 2010), and Gender theory (Oliver, 2023; van der Horst, Sällylä and Michielsen, 2023). With the current diversity of interpretations and definitions, Dutkiewicz and Dickstein's (2021) argument for defining Veganism as a practices-based phenomenon and detaching it from ideology based-isms is not uncalled for. Although such

DOI: 10.4324/9781003384526-6

initiatives are understandable from a theoretical perspective, towards the end of our analysis chapters, based on the experiences of our interviewees, I posed the question whether such a disentanglement is possible on an experiential level. I do not profess to have offered a solution to this conundrum. Indeed, we may have increased Sisyphus's toil even further. In *Towards a Philosophy of Act*, Bakhtin (1993) notes that,

> It is pointless to speak of some sort of special theoretical ought [Veganism]; insofar as I am thinking, I must think veridically; veridicality or being-true is the ought of thinking. (Bakhtin, 1993: 4)

What Bakhtin (1993) is referring to here is *reciprocal dependence*, which we discussed in Chapter 1. *reciprocal dependence* suggests that if, for 'being-true,' Veganism needs to exist as a practices-based phenomenon, then it *cannot exist* without Veganism as an ideology based-isms. In this chapter, I would like to return to the point of how we define and understand *Ideology* and ideological concepts in a post-modern world. Is it sufficient for us to extend our understanding to its plural, 'ideologies,' which conjures an image of multiple *static*, systematic organisations functioning as tectonic plates for societal social structures, or do we need to revolutionise our meaning-making approach even further? More importantly, what is the role of the individual within the definition-making process.

Conceptualising *Ideology*

I would like to begin this section with a caveat. The academic authorship on *Ideology* is rich and extensive, and by no means do I make the claim of doing that complexity justice in this chapter. I will, however, make brief reference to pivotal figures in theorising *Ideology*, before moving on to explain it from a Bakhtinian standpoint. Historically, social theorists, such as Marx have applied '*Ideology*' as a framework to describe the dominant ideas and values within a given society. More specifically, these ideas and values not only produce hegemonic discourses of knowledge but also perpetuate asymmetrical power relations between the Classes. From this interpretation, understanding a given ideological concept is, first, arche above and beyond the grasp of an individual because of its *Finalised* and totalised —or, as Bakhtin phrases it, 'to sign within a closed system already accepted and authorized' (Bakhtin, 1986: 58). Second, its social structural connections imply that it is politically driven. As Emerson (1983) notes, Western usage of *Ideology* 'suggests something inflexible and propagandistic, something politically unfree' (Emerson, 1983: 247).

For Bakhtin and his contemporaries, however, *Ideology* simply represented a socially determined 'idea system,' and was understood in a less prejudicial and political manner (Bakhtin, 1986). In the 1981 edition of *The Dialogic*

Imagination Holquist (as the editor) and Emerson (as the translator) also note that, in a Bakhtinian sense, because *meanings* within ideologies are socially formed, ideologies also encapsulate 'semiotic values': 'semiotic in the sense that it involves the concrete exchange of signs in society and history' (Bakhtin, 1981: 429). In our case, this would be the *Ideology* of Veganism.

Sideward Glance

In its simplest form, 'semiotics' is the study of signs, their significance, and how individuals within a certain society make-sense of the meaning of said signs. From a dialogical perspective one would also consider how individuals also give meaning to signs in their respective societies. For a more comprehensive discussion on semiotics in psychology see De Luca Picione (2020).

Essentially, a given *Ideology*, an active perspective of thought, is *a part of* a *collection* of ideologies within a cultural system. Notably, an *Ideology* is *not* The System. Our analysis chapters, however, were indicative of the monolithic nature of our interviewees's encounter with Veganism, to the extent that, for them, it became The System. In the Introductory chapter we discussed the nature of language and the *living discourse*.

I found my interviews with Gertrude and Regan particularly thought-provoking as, compared to other participants, neither considered Veganism to be a particularly healthy diet, and sporadically transitioned in and out of *Being* vegan. Their motivations were also solely moralistic. The effect this had on their self-perception, however, was strikingly divergent. For the former, it was an experience of restlessness and turmoil, while for the latter, it was one largely of ease and acceptance. My intention is to discuss Gertrude's and Regan's experiences from a very specific viewpoint: their respective interpretation and understanding of vegan *Ideology*. More specifically, their experience with an *ideological* perspective itself, and its impact on their *Spirit* (*I-for-myself*). Below, I present two very distinctive experiences with Veganism, which I argue, are rooted in the interviewees's meaning-making and interaction with Veganism and *Vegan Ideology*, embedded within—specifically in terms of their self-perception and internalisation of that language.

At this point, I think it is important to outline two distinctive rhetorical frameworks within which a Vegan *Ideology* can be understood in relation to the individual. On the one hand, Bakhtin (1981) discusses 'individual subjectivism,' where language is interpreted as systemic byproduct of the individual psyche and creativity. On the other hand, Bakhtin (1981) also critically considers 'abstract objectivism,' where the individual occupies a position of passivity within linguistic structures. Simply put, we are not wordsmiths, as the latter position suggests; rather, language occupies a 'truth' beyond our grasp. It holds a meaning independent of the speaker and the interpreter. In terms of the history of language and meaning, for this project, there are two noteworthy points. First, for Ferdinand de Saussure, the word, such as 'Veganism' is locked within a *finite* cognitive construct. Second, for Bakhtin, the production of a meaning behind a word is, potentially, *infinite*, as it is embedded within social structures. The production of a meaning(s) behind a word is, therefore, is reciprocal.

Centripetal *and* Centrifugal *Forces in Language and* Aesthetic Activity

Bakhtin (1993) maintains that the *Self* cannot exist and cannot self-determine or attain consciousness *without the aesthetic activity of the other* (Bakhtin, 1993: 188, *emphasis added*). In his essay, *Author and Hero in Aesthetic Activity*, Bakhtin (1990) outlines the principles of *Aesthetic Activity*, which emphasises the relationship between the *I* and the *Other* in dialogue, and notes that 'it is our [dialogical] relationship that determines an object and its structure' —in other words, the lived experience of the *Spirit*. Indeed, in our previous analysis chapters, we have applied the *Aesthetic Activity* as a conceptual framework while discussing the contraposed dynamics between the *I-for-myself*, *I-for-other*, and *Other-for me*. In this Chapter, the *Other* is representative of ideological stances within this process; hence, I have taken creative liberty here and used the term *Ideological Aesthetic Activity*.

Sideward Glance

For those who may be interested, Bakhtin's (1981) most comprehensive contemplation and definition of Aesthetic Activity appears in his essay, Author and Hero in Aesthetic Activity. In this essay, Bakhtin is concerning with the relationship between the Author (Other) and the Hero (I), and the phenomenological 'acts' out of which Being is composed. For us, these 'acts' of phenomenological experience have been the: I-for-myself, I-for-other, and Other-for-me. Aesthetic Activity, then, is the act of the Other supporting the I into actualisation.

In the context of identity and *Selfhood*, ideological positions are fundamental, as subscribing to one, or the other, has a different impact on an individual. Bakhtin (1981: 07) notes that *Utterances*, and intonation within said *Utterances*, between the *I* and the *Other*, convey 'two embattled tendencies' of *Centripetal* and *Centrifugal* in the process of *Aesthetic Activity*. Moreover, 'Every concrete utterance of a speaking subject serves as a point where centrifugal as well as centripetal forces [are] brought to bear' (Bakhtin, 1981: 274). While a *Centripetal* ideological stance encapsulates tendencies of unification, standardisation, and a *Finalisation* of *Selfhood* and individual experiences. *Centrifugal Utterances* within ideological positions represent the presence of heteroglossia, stratification and *de*centralisation, and an *Unfinalisability* of the *Self.* I think it is important to mention that, according to Bakhtin, *Utterances* with *Centripetal* unifying forces are not necessarily negative. Indeed, they exist for the 'maximum of mutual understanding' within language. *Centripetal* forces, however, must operate 'in the midst of' of *heterology* (Bakhtin, 1981: 270). If you have being following the analysis chapters, I hope you would agree that, during the interviewees's vegan journey, the fine balance between *Centripetal* and *Centrifugal* forces, to which Bakhtin refers, became unsynchronised. For the interest of illustrating an argument, the two ideological stances presented here are dichotomous in nature and can be interpreted as either *Centripetal* (monolithic) or *Centrifugal* (heterologic).

Centripetal Ideological *Aesthetic Activity* and Lived Experiences

I acknowledge that my conversations with both interviewees revealed similar *Speech Genres* to those of other participants, with some degrees of—for example, concerns about the environment and animal ethics. What I found striking, however, was their self-positioning within Veganism. On the one hand, from our interaction, it appears that Gertrude's introduction to Veganism in her early 20s can be characterised as a monolithic ideological stance towards Veganism. Gertrude's *Utterances* suggested that she viewed Veganism as a dogmatic set of beliefs and practises. Interestingly, while she disagreed with the 'combative' environment, and how the 'message' of Veganism was being conveyed, she simultaneously internalised its core ideological values.

> ... so I joined [a vegan] Reddit because I'm not really technological, and but I thought I'll join Reddit and I'll get support that way and that before I got the [animal organisation] welfare mentor, and unfortunately *Reddit was not the best experience for me, there are some very, very militant people on there*, and I found it quite depressing, like *how do you expect to change people's views and make them change their habits when you're already saying like death to non-vegans, to blood mouths,* and you know, like I mean it was very combative, combative, and if you're not 100% with us you're against us.

For instance, in addition to the *Speech Genres* we observed in previous chapters, the excerpt above illustrates *Centripetal Ideological Aesthetic Activity*, where phrases such as '*death to non-vegans*' and '*blood mouths*' encourage an *Utterance* of uniformity and a shared, or static, meaning of Veganism. Gertrude explained that, although she had been vegan for only a short time, it was for 'totally ethical' reasons, and her encounter with a *Centripetal Ideological Aesthetic Activity* seems to have influenced Gertrude's *I-for-myself* (*Spirit*):

> I don't think there is such a thing as a health vegan. I don't think that's a category, because it's not healthy, really … I feel that my desire, I feel like my, I honestly feel like my health is not as important as these animals suffering.

She not only disagreed with the health *Speech Genres* surrounding Veganism but also decentralised herself in relation to what Gertrude perceived as 'animal suffering.' Ironically, the unifying tendency of *Centripetal Ideological Aesthetic Activity* is unsettling for the self-identity of those who fail to cohere to its circumscribed values. This unsettledness in itself, is not detrimental for Bakhtinian *Aesthetic Activity.* Indeed, such tensions are pivotal for maintaining the forward momentum of a dialogical interaction and *Unfinalisability.* Said tensions, however, should not be framed within a wider *static* ideological structure.

> No, I did not join [an animal ethics organisation], but I do get emails from them, and petitions every day, and in general I don't do it because *it kind of affects my mood, when I read about all this stuff, so I kind of bypass it now*. And I think it's a very kind of *a callous way to look at it, but I'm being self-protective, like I can only handle so much and right now* … I'm a member of the Arizona Humane Society, I worked with them for more than half my life, since I was 18 I've fostered for them and worked with them …

Ideological Aesthetic Activity leads to modes of thought, and when analysed dialogically, *Centripetal Ideological Aesthetic Activi*ty reveals the juxtaposing tensions experienced by individuals within a *Finalised Ideology.* As Gertrude continued to explain: '*So there's a lot of conflict internally for me.*' Within a *Centripetal Ideological* understanding, as a concept, 'Veganism' is bestowed with the characteristic of natural sublimity—an organic, self-contained, and self-sufficient word with intrinsic value: *Finalised.* The excerpt above is not only illustrative of this but also suggests that this form of ideological composition of Veganism is detached from Gertrude's mean-making process. Particularly, *Utterances* such as '*that whole, you know, morality and right and wrong, black and white thing*' and '*but how can I say I love animals if I'm eating animals.*' Under a *Centripetal* and *Centrifugal* paradigm, one could argue that Gertrude's *Utterances* suggest an outward force away from a unifying vegan ideological stance. Such interpretations could be plausible if her *Utterances* evoked a diversity of discourse. This, however, is not the case. The dichotomy within Gertrude's *Utterances*, for example, reveals a clear opposition or tension between her living experience and an 'ideal form of Veganism,' hence, generating a *Centripetal* modality.

For instance, despite 'suffer[ing]' with anaemia for most of her adult life, after further engagement with vegan literature and vegan social media (see Chapter 3), Gertrude made the decision to '*go cold turkey*' and *Become* vegan, relying on supplements. Nonetheless, after continuous health struggles, she began to incorporate red meat back into her diet. She described her current diet as what contemporary scholarship may refers to as 'flexitarian' or flexitarianism (Raphaely and Marinova, 2014). Previous research has also referred to individuals such as Gertrude and the other interviewees in this project as 'conscientious omnivores' (Rothgerber, 2014). Studies have found that 'conscientious omnivores' report higher levels of 'violations' in their diets, and a lower degree of guilt is associated with said 'violations.' The use of the term 'violation' itself to describe dietary choices in this context is rather interesting. Towards the end of her book, Giraud (2021) poses a poignant question: would 'post-vegan' practises and notions such as flexitarianism, which coerces Veganism into green capitalism, render animal ethical Veganism a 'marginal concern' (Giraud, 2021: 146–152)? From an animal-rights and/or socio-economic perspective, Giraud raises a thought-provoking conundrum. Similarly, theoretically, inconsistency between one's moral attitudes and behaviour has been coined the meat paradox (Loughnan and Davies, 2020; Loughnan, Haslam, and Bastian, 2014, 2010). Scholarship in this area has posited that individuals who consume meat feel conflicted or discomforted about their meat consumption, particularly when the harm inflicted on animals is brought to the foreground (Rothgerber, 2020, Loughnan, Haslam and Bastian, 2014, 2010; Plous, 2003).

Festinger (1957) proposed that individuals who experience conflict between their moralistic attitudes and practises, simultaneously holding two inconsistent values, undergo cognitive dissonance. Classical psychology would argue that to dissipate the negative tensions within oneself, individuals create and implement strategies to change either their behaviour or their values (Festinger and Carlsmith, 1959; Festinger, 1957; Brehm, 1956). Perhaps Gertrude's lived experience and her *Centripetal* ideological understanding offer some insight into Giraud's (2021) reflexive question and this particular area of scholarship. What I would like to focus on here are the 'grey areas' that a dialogical approach discloses.

> I'd say two out of three meals a day I'm eating vegan, and one meal a day I'm eating something with animal products, for which *I felt incredibly hypocritical* (Gertrude).

For a dialogical analysis perspective, we can gain nuanced insight into the 'meat paradox' phenomenon, as well as the inner tension and hostility Gertrude expresses towards herself, along with the multiple forms of guilt experienced by other interviewees. As Bakhtin phrases it, 'two worlds confront each other, two worlds that have absolutely no communication with each other and are mutually impervious: the world of culture and the world of life' (Bakhtin, 1990: 2). Here, we will replace 'culture' with a *Centripetal* understanding of *Ideology* as a concept, which in turn, renders the discourse surrounding Veganism susceptible to 'ideological monologism' (Bakhtin, 1981: 88).

As mentioned earlier, Gertrude had been assigned a mentor whom she could approach with questions concerning *Being* vegan.

> I was researching where can I get ethically raised eggs in my neighbourhood … I don't think there's anything wrong with people raising eggs, chickens in their backyard that are healthy and happy and they lay eggs as a by-product and you buy those eggs, and then when I wrote to my mentor, I said, you know, I'm considering doing this and she said, *"I'm a vegan, I don't eat eggs and you shouldn't either," period. "I'm a vegan, I don't eat honey, and all honey is evil, period."*

Gertrude's mentor's *Utterance* exemplify unifying and centralising *Centripetal* forces of 'verbal-ideological life' (Bakhtin, 1981: 273). Such experiences, however, were not limited to Gertrude. After transitioning away from Veganism, Portia, for example, had similarly 'tricky' centripetal encounters with individuals practising Veganism.

> … I've found out I live near a very old school friend and I kept wanting to reach out to her, eventually I did, found out she was vegan but *prior to finding out that she was vegan I'd already explained I'd been ill recently and things like that and I mentioned it was due to my diet* and I'd said oh, I was vegan too and stuff *and she kind of brushed it off with the whole, oh it's not for everyone kind of thing …*

Portia's recounting of her embodied lived experience, however, was met with a unified ideological view. She reiterated that she chose not to discuss her experience of *Being* vegan any further: *'I didn't want to push my views on her and you know.'* Cordelia went on to explain other encounters with individuals who were in their *Being* vegan *Threshold-moment.*

> … And today, I got speaking to someone and he was like, oh yeah, I'm a vegan, blah-blah-blah-blah-blah, just blasé in conversation and I said oh, I was vegan for 2 years and not anymore and briefly mentioned something, whilst I was telling him a voice note he sent to me that he was like, 'oh you know, I do miss fish, I think if I could go out and catch a fish now I would eat it.'

After receiving the voice note, Cordelia attempted to inject *Double-voicedness* into the *Aesthetic Activity* forming process of someone practising Veganism, hence, attempting to transcend their experience from *Centripetal* forces, Cordelia said: *I said okay, well maybe you know, intuition and you feeling that, perhaps that's a sign that maybe you should have something like that, would you be comfortable doing that.* It is important to highlight that Cordelia reiterated she did not wish to '*tell someone what to do*,' but did have the desire to share her journey: '*I'd say, would you like to listen to my experience of veganism because I had every intention of doing it forever.*' For a Bakhtin (1990) standpoint, Cordelia is positioning herself as an *Other* when she meets a vegan *I*, presenting them with a bigger picture, or 'excess of seeing,' which they cannot foresee in their current moment (Bakhtin, 1981: 22).

Sideward Glance

Bakhtin also refers to the 'excess of seeing' as Outsideness. For many Bakhtinian scholars, his concept of Outsideness functions as a continual conduit thought the Bakhtinian cannon, as it ties together this works on Ethics, Aesthetics, the *Dialogical Self*, and inter-subjectivity.

She also conceded, however, that she did not expect the vegan individual to reciprocate, as she remembered her own attitudes while *Being* vegan.

> I knew all the quips like the back of my hand, so if they were like, oh yeah, I think it's better for the environment and cow farts do this much CO2 or whatever and I'd go, well you know, it's not even the farts, it's the burps or whatever and ya-da-ya-da-ya-da, you know, I could relate to them, I'd hope that perhaps I could give them… *[Sighs]* It is a tricky one.

Centripetal Ideology, then, not only centralise *Utterances* and thoughts, bringing them back to a unifying ideological position on animal ethics, but also foreground *Aesthetic* challenges as a consequence of this. Gertrude, for example, reflected on an alternative future, where she could have continued *Being* vegan, and embodied a different lived experience:

> But in my mind I think you know, if at some point in the distant future I am living by myself, I would probably go back to that [*Being* vegan] simply because it, my morality, but my morality tells me it's not okay to hurt these animals for my pleasure.

Gertrude's compromising with her *Centripetal* ideological stance was not a comfortable process for her sense of *Self*: '*I realise that I have this conflict and I can't easily resolve it, so I have to compromise, I have to make adjustments.*' Unifying language, within itself, is not problematic for Bakhtin. However, unifying language, where the *Word* no longer occupies a space 'on the boundary between its own context and *another, alien, context*,' and is hence *void* of *any* dialogical dynamic, is problematic (Bakhtin, 1981: 284, *emphasis added*). This is what Bakhtin refers to as a 'poetic' genre, where there is 'a unitary and singular Ptolemaic world outside of which nothing else exists and nothing else is needed.' In this space, there is no compromise in the meaning of a *Word* (Bakhtin, 1981: 285). Consequently, perhaps this is why, during our conversations, Gertrude's *Utterances* disclosed the highest degree of dialogical tension. As discussed in previous chapters, self-perception and identity formation is a matter of negotiation in a communicative *Act* between the *I* and *Other*. For example, as individuals, we organise components of the world that we —such as vegan Ideology— within our *own* consciousness and create our own identity in relation to said elements. Moreover, when we interact with social objects or Words, such as Veganism, we should be 'entering-the-communion' or 'entering a unity' with said *Word*/object (Bakhtin, 1990: 42). Thus, we construct a *personal* understanding. When attempting to understand a given *Word*/object, *negotiating* is key for positioning oneself within the situation (Paré, 2007). However, not having the space to negotiate her lived and embodied experiences manifested in *intra*-subjectivity as well as *inter*-subjectivity:

> ... so then I was feeling like I was against my own family, I was turned against my own family, you know, I felt like they were doing bad things, I feel like everyone around me was doing bad things and it was not healthy for me to feel that way, you know?

The validation of an individual's sense of *Self* and existence, Bakhtin continues, does not manifest through 'concrete' social practice and dictates. Indeed, what is 'answerable (the *I-for-myself*) should 'not dissolve in what is specialized (politics)' (Bakhtin, 1990: 42). If such conditions do occur, as was the case for Gertrude—'*she [her mentor] doesn't really care about that part of it [individual circumstances], you know, for her it's first morality, morality comes first, your internal morality comes before your relationships*'—we experience an unsustainable what we experience is an unsustainable '*technical or instrumental action.*' This understanding of a vegan *Ideology* is, as Bakhtin would phrase it, non-reciprocally dependent. As our analysis of Gertrude's experience suggests, to a certain degree, this imposed a sense of *Finitisability* within her lived and embodied experience. The *Centripetal* forces within her *Utterances* disclose an element of 'non-being' of the *I-for-myself*, where her sense of *Self* is determined and/or predetermined through her *Centripetal* ideological understanding of Veganism.

If you have made it this far into the chapter, or indeed the book, you may be asking, 'where do we go from here then?' To borrow Yeat's phraseology, 'to the other side of the half-penny,' of course. In the next section, we explore the *Centrifugal* ideological perspectives that allow force within *Utterances* and language allow for pockets of individual space(s) and *Answerability*, in turn altering individual experiences with value systems, such as Veganism.

Centrifugal Ideological *Aesthetic Activity* and Lived Experiences

In its simplest sense, *Centrifugal* texture within *Utterances* lends them permeability; hence, they are *Utterances* that promote *Polyphony* and diversity within the meaning-making of concepts such as Veganism (Bakhtin, 1981). Static ideological values of Veganism, or what Bakhtin refers to as the *Ought*, therefore, become decentralised as they interact with individual lived and embodied experiences. This does not propose, however, that there is a given dichotomy between *Centrifugal* ideological social structures and the individual, nor does it predicate that ideologies are founded *exclusively* within individual experiences and activities. A Bakhtinian approach advocates for a reciprocal dynamic between the individual and society, whereby one actively creates the social structure within which their ideology occurs. A given *Ideology*, therefore, is not a unifying *Centripetal* force but rather, it is one of diversifying and co-creation: *Centrifugal*. The ideological values within Veganism, therefore, become *reciprocally dependent* on the individual and their experience. Particularly, there is the creation of a *time-space* that allows them to remain *Unfinalised* and their *I-for-myself* to remain *Answerable*.

In her paper on Bakhtin, language, and its internalisation process, Emerson (1983) discusses how all semiotic 'sign systems,' consisting of words and image, are ideological, and all ideologies contain semiotic value. It is important to clarify that, within the Bakhtinian canon, 'semiotics' does not only refer to images and emblems; language, or the word, is also considered semiotic. Moreover, a given *Ideology*, is understood as being rooted in four social factors, rather than being perceived as organic and natural (Vološinov, 1976). Below, as I outline the four prerequisites identified by the Bakhtin Circle, I will draw on interview excerpts from my conversation with Regan and argue that her *Centrifugal* ideological understanding of Veganism manifested in a more muted inner struggle as she transitioned into and out of *Being* vegan.

As was the case with Gertrude, Regan's experience aligned with the first prerequisite identified by Bakhtin (1990): 'Each ideological product is meaningful not in the soul but in the objectively accessible ideological material,' or a *priori* (Emerson, 1983: 247). Essentially, an ideological understanding of an object (Veganism) exists external to the individual. Some of you may pause, here, as this prerequisite could seem oxymoronic or counter-productive from an intellectual argument perspective. Indeed, the previous section has, almost, deplored the impact of unifying *Centripetal* forces within *Utterances.* However, we also acknowledged previously that, for Bakhtin (1990), centralising forces within language and the Word, are not unfavourable. Rather they are necessary for the phenomenology of language is the guarantee of a 'certain maximum of mutual understanding' (Bakhtin, 1981: 270). A social group or social understanding is, therefore, a central aspect of *Ideology* formation and understanding of said *Ideology.*

> ... so it was kind of a thing [Veganism] I was always aware of in terms of lifestyle choices, I guess, yeah. I guess, you're aware of it [veganism], you like, never like, I guess, seek it out unless you want to know more about it. Erm..., yeah, and then, because we would talk about like morals and ethics and, you know, conservation and those sorts of things in school.

Regan's *Utterances* confirm that she had '*had like two stints of veganism,*' and during the second '*stint,*' she was '*a lot less like pragmatic*' about it and much '*more staunch in [her] beliefs,*' for instance, supporting the advocacy of '*meat is murder-type stuff.*'

> Yeah. So I guess I've always, I had a friend in high school who was vegetarian and I decided to be vegetarian for a year and then after that I decided to be vegan, because I just thought it was a bit more, because, you know, she was also vegetarian for the animals.

Regan's interaction is not only indicative of the *I-for-myself* and *I-for-other* relationship we discussed in Chapters 3 to 5, but it also illustrative of the second social factor in the process of *Ideology* formation: the requirement of an 'inter-individual territory' (Vološinov, 1973: 11). Essentially, a co-determinate space where the *Self* and *Other* enter a dialogue, through which an *Ideology* beings to form, shape, and acquire meaning. Regan also relayed the influence of *social units* and a *social space* in her transition from vegetarianism to Veganism—for instance, being introduced to vegan literature and documentaries, animal ethics, and developing a collective and social vegan identity.

> .... and I thought about, you know, and at that time [an animal ethics organisation] was really big in those sorts of things and I was just sort of aware of it, and then I decided to be vegan. This would have been when I was 17.

What distinguished Regan's experience from that of other interviewees, particularly Gertrude's, was the maintenance of her self-narrative, or the *I-for-myself,* throughout her experience of *Being* vegan. Much like Gertrude, Regan's reasons for *Being* vegan were morally driven, and to a certain degree, she did consider herself as an activist. Nevertheless, although it made her *'feel a bit guilty at first,'* during her first phase of *Being* vegan, Regan made a conscious decision to stop practising Veganism, and returned to vegetarianism while she was at university. When prompted, she recalled that *Being* vegan was not sustainable for *her* health due to the resources available: *'I would eat like salads and like chips, and that's not really a diet, it's more just like something that's really unsustainable … but it just wasn't sustainable.'*

This is reflective of the Bakhtinian requisite that the space, and the *Ideology* that assembles within it, is not entrusted with a 'natural' status or viewed as a concrete truth. This is because, 'every act of understanding [an ideology] involves an act of translation and a negotiation of values' (Emerson, 1983: 248). In contrast to Gertrude (*'I was alienated from my own'*), the *Speech Genre* within Regan's *Utterances* is *Centrifugal.* Although she felt guilt for consuming animal products, she also maintained that it *'felt like it was the right decision [*for herself*], so…'* Additionally, whereas Gertrude expressed a deep drive to *Become* vegan again, when asked whether she would *Become* vegan again, Regan expressed doubt: *'At this rate, no, it's already been like my second attempt, so, no.'*

The *Centrifugal* and diversifying intonation within Regan's *Utterance* leads us to the third Bakhtin requisite of *Ideology* formation: that all ideologies must be understood *inter-systematically.* This means that each social unit within society possesses certain characterises, such as class, religion, geographical location, which enriche them with a distinct dialect. This, in turn, means that each social unit manifests its *own* value and lived experience of a given *Ideology.* The importance of acknowledging the interrelation and *inter-systematic* understanding of ideologies within a Bakhtinian lens is paramount.

> I know telling her would end our friendship, completely.… but she doesn't really care about that part of it, you know, it's really to her is first morality, morality comes first, your internal morality comes before your relationships …
>
> her situation is vastly different from mine, she never had children, her husband is a vegan, they live with a, they have their own garden, their own fresh produce, and I think it's a lot easier to make that decision when you're only impacting yourself (Gertrude).

The excerpt above not only illustrates that, within a *Centripetal* understanding of vegan *Ideology*, the element of interaction between different social units was absent, but also that vegan *Ideology* is conveyed through an 'organic stylistics' genre, where there is no other form of existence, other than *Being* vegan (Bakhtin, 1984: 88): *'I mean she's been vegan for 30 something years, she's a vegan or die kind of person.'* In additional, familial circumstances and economical differences can also be considered as a systematic difference and were present in two of the interviewees's *Utterances*, which they felt were not widely acknowledged or recognised within discourses surrounding Veganism

> I would say yes, so another reason that I stopped being vegan was money, it's incredibly expensive to maintain that diet, and to maintain that diet in a way that is healthy, I think people can do it if you have the resources which in my case was money (Puck).
>
> I couldn't buy, I don't know, vegan shampoo or vegan soap or something like that because I didn't have enough money to buy vegan versions of those, but when it comes to food and clothing, yes, it was vegan (Orlando).

The final factor put forward by Bakhtin is for individuals and society to critically reconceptualise the definition of the *Word* itself. Words—let us use Veganism as an example—are discourses. Hence, they cannot be given meaning, nor can their meaning be detached from the *Voice* that utters them. For the sustainability of the *Word* (Veganism) and the practitioner (*Being* vegan), we must recognise and acknowledge all usage and contexts encapsulated within the *Word*. If we decline to do so, potentially, the *Word* could mean nothing at all, placing us on the path to revisit *Sisyphus* and Dutkiewicz and Dickstein's (2021) proposal for limiting the definition of Veganism to a 'minimal one.'

From an academic perspective, I understand the worth and effectiveness of their proposition. However, viewing this from a *Dialogical* psychology perspective, and the experience of the interviewees in this project, gives me pause for thought. In practice a minimal approach to a cultural phenomenon such as Veganism not only seems reductive but, in relation to individual experience with said phenomena, potentially disruptive. Indeed, Regan, who I have argued held a *Centrifugal* vegan *Ideology*, merged Veganism with her own socially and experientially marked dialects. Unsurprisingly, she expressed her concerns about holding a singular monolithic understanding:

> I think that a lot of vegans these days are tending to be very like black and white in terms of their thinking, and that's not the way to go about it. Just like with any diet, it's all about, you know, making the right choices most of the time, I guess, and it's mostly about being as pragmatic as you can, like doing as least damage as you can, like doing as little harm as you can, but obviously that's within the scale of you harming yourself, obviously, don't do it that way, like that's when you should always stop and, you know, people go into like the nitty gritty of like the whole mussels thing and like is that okay, or they'll go into like the whole idea of what about honey, is honey okay to eat and how about like the very fine, minute details, but then miss the point completely.

Dialogical psychologists have also maintained that meaning of signs, such as *Words*, are always about change (Marková, 2003a), and the same applies to the individual: 'mystery and change *is* our psychological milieu' (Ferreira, Salgado, and Cunha, 2006: 11, *emphasis added*).

Conclusion: (Un)Final Reflections

From multiple disciplinary perspectives, academics have observed how differential boundaries are etched around vegan Ideology and Carnist Ideology in order to understand sustainability and animal agriculture (Yeh, 2014; Pachucki, Pendergrass, and Lamont, 2007; Lamont, 2002). What I hope our discussion(s) within this monograph has offered is that, while we strive, and rightly so, for advocating practises and policies of sustainability, it is also essential for us to factor in the practitioner's experience, language, and *time-space*, within the process of meaning-making.

Sideward Glance

The concept of Relativism has been used and applied in a broad manner of ways. Relativism, as I will use in my discussion, can be understood as the philosophical position that, a given truth for one individual, or a particular social group, may not necessarily be true for another individual and social group. That is, understanding the truth(s) adjust and are context dependent. The proposition of a truth, for example, is relative to the values, attitudes, and psychological aspects of the individual and/or their social setting(s).

Does a *Dialogical* approach, then, imply a *Relativist* paradigm to socio-ideological movements? My response to that would be no, and in order to explain my answer, I would like to discuss *Dialogical Ideology* a little further. Reflecting on our discussion in Chapter 2, if you will, imagine this as similar to Bakhtin's perception of truth as *pravda* and its relation to *istina*. Bakhtin also proposes, however, that this premise should not be confused with *Relativism*. Indeed, the intrinsic relativism within the view of each individual, where they perceive a different 'shade' of truth (*pravda*) is prevailed by the fact that each individual's captured 'shade' (*pravda*) adheres to the same universal truth *istina*.

> There is no relativism here whatsoever: the truth [*pravda*] of Being-as-event contains within itself totally the whole extra-temporal absoluteness of theoretical truth [*istina*]. (Bakhtin, 1993: 71)

An ideological perspective, such as Veganism, then, is composed of a super-structure (*istina*) and sub-structures. While the former (super-structure) encompasses the *official* ideological form, arguably animal ethics and the vetoing of *Speciesism*, the latter (sub-structure) transcends beyond ethical boundaries to incorporate inequalities and oppression in general, becoming the *unofficial* ideological form (*pravda*). The sub-structure's unofficiality, however, does not necessarily temper or distil one's embodied and emotive experience with the *Ideology*. We could easily continue our investigations into *Dialogical Ideology* but, for now, I am going to leave it at that.

Finally, at this point, you may also ask, *'what does language and Ideology have to do with individual psyche, Selfhood, and identity?'* A Bakhtinian response to this would be that language has a powerful influence over *Ideology* and *ideological* construction, which, in turn, shape our thoughts; through which we once again begin to re-construct ideological meanings, hence, coming full circle. The insensitivity to ideological meanings or *Words*, such as Veganism, Bakhtin suggests, is the ultimate danger behind the fascination with only seeking the arbitrary nature of signs and language. Taking this into consideration, perhaps, to avoid self-fragmentation and identity tensions, as experienced by several of the participants interviewed for this project, *Ideology* and social phenomenon such as Veganism need to be understood *inter*-subjectively and *intra*-subjectively.

References

Bakhtin, M. (1993). *Toward a philosophy of the act*. Austin: University of Texas Press.

Bakhtin, M. (1990). *Art and answerability: early philosophical essays*. Austin: University of Texas Press.

Bakhtin, M. (1981). *The dialogic imagination: four essays*. Austin: University of Texas Press.

Brehm, J. W. (1956). Postdecision changes in the desirability of alternatives. *The Journal of Abnormal and Social Psychology*, 52(3), 384. https://doi.org/10.1037/h0041006

Bento, T., Cuncha, C., & Salgado, J. (2006). Ambiguity and the dialogical self: in search for a dialogical psychology. *Studies in Psychology*, 27(1), 19–32. https://doi.org/10.1174/021093906776173216

Carol, J. A., & Gruen, L. (Eds.). (2022). *Ecofeminism: feminist intersections with other animals and the earth*. New York: Bloomsbury Academic.

Emerson, C. E. (1983). The outer word and inner speech: Bakhtin, Vygotsky, and the internalization of language. *Critical Inquiry*, 10(2), 245–264. https://doi.org/10.1086/448245

Festinger, L. (1957). *A theory of cognitive dissonance*. Stanford, CA: Stanford University Press.

Festinger, L., & Carlsmith, J. M. (1959). Cognitive consequences of forced compliance. *The Journal of Abnormal and Social Psychology*, 58(2), 203. https://doi.org/10.1037/h0041593

Gaard, G. (2011). Ecofeminism revisited: rejecting essentialism and re-placing species in a material feminist environmentalism. *Feminist Formations*, 23(2), 26–53. https://doi.org/10.1353/ff.2011.0017

Harper, A. B. (2010). Race as a 'Feeble Matter' in veganism: interrogating whiteness, geopolitical privilege, and consumption philosophy of 'Cruelty-Free' products. *Journal for Critical Animal Studies*, 8(3), 5–27.

Horkheimer, M., & Adorno, T. W. (2002). The culture industry: enlightenment as mass deception. In S. N. Noerr (Ed.), *Dialectic of enlightenment: philosophical fragments* (pp. 94–136). Stanford, CA: Stanford University Press.

Kheel, M. (2004). Vegetarianism and ecofeminism: toppling patriarchy with a fork. In S. F. Sapontzis (Ed.), *Food for thought: the debate overeating meat* (pp. 327–341). New York: Prometheus Books.

Lamont, M., & Molnár, V. (2002). The study of boundaries in the social sciences. *Annual Review of Sociology*, 28(1), 167–195.

Loughnan, S., & Davies, T. (2020). The meat paradox. In K. Dhont and G. Hodson (Eds.), *Why people love and exploit animals: bridging insights from academia and advocacy* (pp. 177–187). Abingdon: Routledge.

Loughnan, S., Bastian, B., & Haslam, N. (2014). The psychology of eating animals. *Current Direction in Psychological Science*, 23(2), 1–5. https://doi.org/10.1177/0963721414525781

Loughnan, S., Haslam, N., & Bastian, B. (2010). The role of meat consumption in the denial of moral status and mind to meat animals. *Appetite*, 55, 156–159. https://doi.org/10.1016/j.appet.2010.05.043

Markovà, I. (2003). *Diagonality and social representations*. Cambridge: Cambridge University Press.

Oliver, C. (2023). Mock meat, masculinity, and redemption narratives: vegan men's negotiations and performances of gender and eating. *Social Movement Studies*, 22(1), 62–79. https://doi.org/10.1080/14742837.2021.1989293

Pachucki, M. A., Pendergrass, S., & Lamont, M. (2007). Boundary processes: recent theoretical developments and new contributions. *Poetics*, 35(6), 331–351.

Plous, S. (2003). Is there such a thing as prejudice towards animals? In S. Plous (Ed.), *Understanding prejudice and discrimination* (pp. 509–528). New York, NY: McGraw-Hill.

Rothgerber, H. (2015). Can you have your meat and eat it too? Conscientious omnivores, vegetarians, and adherence to diet. *Appetite*, 84, 196–203. https://doi.org/10.1016/j.appet.2014.10.012

van der Horst, H., Sällylä, A., & Michielsen, Y. (2023). Game changers for meat and masculinity? Male athletes' perspective on mixed and plant-based diets. *Appetite*, 187, 106525, 1–11. https://doi.org/10.1016/j.appet.2023.106585

Veron, O., & White, R. (2021). Anarchism, feminism and veganism: a convergence of struggles. In S. Springer, J. Mateer, M. Locret-Collet, & M. Acker (Eds.), *Undoing human supremacy: anarchist political ecology in the face of anthroparchy* (pp. 68–89). London: Rowman & Littlefield.

Volosinov, V. N. (1976). *Freudianism: a Marxist critique*. New York: Academic Press.

Yeh, H. Y. (2014). Voice with every bite: dietary identity and vegetarians. "The-Second-Best" boundary work. *Food, Culture, and Society*, 17(4), 591–613. https://doi.org/10.2752/175174414X13948130848502

GLOSSARY

Answerability
Answerability refers to the condition of the *I-for-myself* remaining unfinalised within a dialogical interaction. In other words, the *I-for-myself* retains a *Double-voice* within its *Utterances*. As the consciousness and Voice of the *I-for-myself* does not merge with that of the *Other*, it remains *Answerable*.

Dialogue
For Bakhtin, communication takes place between the *I* and Others within a dialogue. However, for an exchange to be truly dialogical, it requires the presence of two separate *voices* and noncoinciding consciousnesses. A dialogical communication assumes no last word, hence, no finality.

Dialogical Self
The *Dialogical Self* can be understood as a theoretical framework, which not only contextualises and explains the position of the individual within society, but also the formation of one's consciousness with a polyphonic society. The *Dialogical Self* consists of three components: *the I-for-myself, I-for-other, and Other-for-me.*

Double-Voiced
Double-voiced Utterances are the cornerstone of a dialogical interaction, as the words the sounding of a second *Voice*, with an alternative value, is an essential part of the heteroglossia. Here, the *Self* utilise 'someone else's discourse for [their] own purpose by inserting a new semantic intention' into an utterance, 'which already has, and which retains' values of its own' (Bakhtin, 1984: 189).

Finalisable

The finalisability of the *Self*, or the *I-for-myself*, takes place in a monolithic, *Single-Voiced*, socio-linguistic environment. Where the Self no longer remains *answerable* to the *Other* as the chain of dialogical interaction has been broken. As Bakhtin notes, 'In the process of dialogic communication, the object [Self] is transformed into the subject (the *Other's I*)' (Bakhtin, 1986:145).

Identity Theory and Social Identity Theory

Generally, there are two disciplinary approaches to identity research. On the one hand we have *Identity Theory*, which is associated with the discipline of sociology. On the other hand, we have *Social Identity Theory*, which is generally associated with the discipline of Psychology. *Identity Theory* tends to explicate how individuals organise their identity meanings and perform them in social situations. In contrast, *Social Identity Theory* focuses on identity processes through inter- and intra-group dynamics.

Intersubjectivity

This monograph has taken a Bakhtinian approach to *intersubjectivity*, which represents the *Self* and *Other* relationship: 'my projection of myself into him [the Other] must be followed by a return into myself, … only from this place can the material derived from my projecting myself into the other be rendered meaningful' (Bakhtin, 1990: 26). In essence, the *Self* gains a sense of existence through a dialogical relationship with the *Other* and vice, hence, our experiences become *intersubjective*. Importantly, this reciprocal relationship is not *asymmetrical*.

Intra-subjectivity

In this project *intra-subjective* or *intra-subjective* tensions refer to the internal quibbles within the Self. Quibbles and dialogical tensions stemming from a, potentially, asymmetrical relationship between the *Self* and *Other*.

Polyphony

Polyphony can be defined as a societal state of existence. Consisting of smaller *dialogues* and *dialogical* relationships. More specifically, it refers to a social state of communication where independent and unmerged *Voices* and consciousnesses co-exist.

Primary Speech Genre

Primary genres legislate words, phrases, and expressions that are acceptable in everyday life; in a sense they are the amoebic forms of genre.

Priori

Attempting to define Priori from a Bakhtinian perspective is a complex process, and has been discussed at length in Chapter 2. A *Priori* as an *Istina* truth is the existence of a fact or concept at a universal level. A *Prior* truth as a *Pravda* is the approach Bakhtin proposes for the Social Sciences. In the case of a *Priori* as a *Pravda* is a truth 'for someone,' as they experience the *Istina* truth and bestow it with their own lived experience.

Secondary Speech Genre

Genres, from a Bakhtinian perspective, are understood not only as a broad and flexible set of *stylistic literary traditions* but also as a provider of *social context*; *Speech Genres*, which have been used as analytical tools in this monograph, provide a specific way of visualising a given part of reality, and are located within *Utterances*. Bakhtin also notes that genres in one area of life may be imported into another. Bakhtin continues by making the distinction between *Primary Speech Genres* and *Secondary Speech Genres.*

Secondary Genre

Secondary genres arise in 'complex and comparatively highly developed and organised cultural communication' (Bakhtin, 1986: 62). Moreover, in the 'process of their formation . . . [secondary genres] absorb and digest various primary genres', which, in turn, are 'altered and assume a special character when they enter into complex ones' (Bakhtin, 1986: 62).

Single-Voiced

Single-voiced Utterances can be found within a monolithic discourse in society, which also leads to *Single-voices* merged consciousness (no polyphony). The reason for this is that, in this content, the individual, or individual experience, has been *finalised* as there is not a dialogic relationship between the *Self* and *Other.*

Unfinalisable

The antithesis to '*Finalisable*.' *Unfinalisable* refers to the dialogical relationship between the *Self* and Other, which consists of *Double-voiced Utterances*, therefore, consists of multiple consciousnesses. As a result, the *Self* remains *Answerable* (*Answerability*) to the *Other*. In such a heterogonic socio-linguistic space, living and lived experiences are an ongoing event and *Voices* are polyphonic.

Utterance

Utterances can be considered as the building blocks of Bakhtin's work on language, as they are distinct chunks of language-in-use; an utterance can be both spoken and written. They have no determined length and can be as short as a single word or as long as a novel and may also be embedded within other utterances (*Double-voiced*). *Utterances* can also be considered as an umbrella term to describe anything that is said within a dialogue. Moreover, an utterance is marked by what Bakhtin terms *Addressivity* and *Answerability*. An *Utterance*, for instance, is always addressed *to someone* and anticipates a *response* from the *Other*, who anticipates an answer.

Voice

In its simplest form, *Voice* can be understood as an ideological position held by an individual and is embedded with an *Utterance*; they also carry social customs and values. A *Voice* can be *Single-voiced* or *Double-voiced*, and *Voice(s)* within a dialogical relationship test dominant social ideologies.

INDEX

Note: **Bold** page numbers refer to tables.

For Product Safety Concerns and Information please contact our EU representative GPSR@taylorandfrancis.com
Taylor & Francis Verlag GmbH, Kaufingerstraße 24, 80331 München, Germany

www.ingramcontent.com/pod-product-compliance
Ingram Content Group UK Ltd.
Pitfield, Milton Keynes, MK11 3LW, UK
UKHW020001200926
475702UK00015B/2421

* 9 7 8 1 0 3 2 4 7 0 7 9 5 *